83772

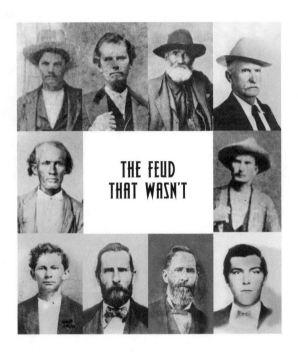

THE FEUD
THAT WASN'T

Number Fifteen:
Sam Rayburn Series on Rural Life
Sponsored by Texas A&M University–Commerce
M. Hunter Hayes, *General Editor*

THE FEUD THAT WASN'T

The Taylor Ring,
Bill Sutton,
John Wesley Hardin, and
Violence in Texas

JAMES M. SMALLWOOD

TEXAS A&M UNIVERSITY PRESS
College Station

Copyright © 2008 by James M. Smallwood
Manufactured in the United States of America
All rights reserved
First edition
This paper meets the requirements of ANSI/NISO Z39.48–1992 (Permanence of
Paper). Binding materials have been chosen for durability.

Library of Congress Cataloging-in-Publication Data
Smallwood, James.
The feud that wasn't : the Taylor Ring, Bill Sutton, John Wesley Hardin,
and violence in Texas / James M. Smallwood. — 1st ed.
p. cm. — (Sam Rayburn series on rural life ; no. 15)
Includes bibliographical references and index.
ISBN-13: 978-1-60344-017-2 (cloth : alk. paper)
ISBN-10: 1-60344-017-8 (cloth : alk. paper)
1. Taylor, Creed, d. 1906. 2. Taylor, Creed, d. 1906—Friends and associates. 3. Hardin,
John Wesley, 1853–1895. 4. Sutton, William, d. 1874. 5. Outlaws—Texas—Biography.
6. Peace officers—Texas—Biography. 7. Violence—Texas—History—19th century.
8. Crime—Texas—History—19th century. 9. Reconstruction (U.S. history, 1865–
1877)—Texas. 10. Texas—History—1846–1950. I. Title.
F391.T22S63 2008
976.4'06—dc22
2007033913

CONTENTS

ILLUSTRATIONS

SERIES EDITOR'S FOREWORD

With *The Feud That Wasn't: The Taylor Ring, Bill Sutton, John Wesley Hardin, and Violence in Texas,* James Smallwood has set himself the arduous task of correcting a legacy of myths and conjecture that reach well into the twentieth century. As Smallwood observes in his introduction, "myth, legend, and lore sometimes displace history in the mind of the reading public, many of whom believe that *myth is history.*" Whereas Thomas Carlyle once reduced history to a "distillation of rumour" during a flight of rhetorical expression, Smallwood scrupulously separates facts from assumptions, gossip, and propaganda in order to provide his readers with a detailed account of this important period in Texas history and American history, and he does so in a vivid narrative that blends accuracy and style without sacrificing either as it confronts the views and supposed facts that have been handed down for generations. This, of course, comes as little surprise to readers acquainted with Smallwood's scholarship.

The sixth volume in The Sam Rayburn Series on Rural Life, *Murder and Mayhem: The War of Reconstruction Texas* (2003), provides a well-documented corrective to previous examinations of what become known as the "Lee-Peacock Feud." In that volume, Smallwood and his co-authors, Barry A. Crouch and Larry Peacock, not only effectively capture the era and this continuation of violence at the end of the Civil War into the Corners' region of Grayson, Fannin, Hunt and Collin counties, but they also present their evidence in a compelling fashion. Although *The Feud That Wasn't: The Taylor Ring, Bill Sutton, John Wesley Hardin, and Violence in Texas* remains much more than a companion to *Murder and Mayhem,* readers familiar with that earlier volume will certainly be rewarded with a book that complements its predecessor and likewise challenges persisting beliefs that have assumed the guise of fact. Even readers unfamiliar with Smallwood's work will quickly recognize in this present volume that they have as their guide an authority able to untangle the thick knots of lawlessness and distorted facts surrounding his subjects.

In rejecting the prevailing concept of a "feud" between William "Bill" Taylor and the "Taylor ring"—a descriptor of Smallwood's coinage that conveys an accurate image of this "loose organization" of nearly 200 men who "spread chaos and lawlessness into at least forty-five Texas counties" during its quarter-century rampage marked by plunder and murder since its founding by the brothers Creed and Pitkin Taylor in the 1850s—Smallwood avoids reducing this moment of history to simply the violent consequence of a familial predicament. Indeed, as Smallwood points out, the Taylor-Sutton troubles had implications for control of the Lone Star State.

Established on the Texas A&M University–Commerce campus in 1997 under the auspices of Texas A&M University Press, the Sam Rayburn Series on Rural Life has sought to illuminate the diverse nature of the culture and history of East Texas and the surrounding region. *The Feud That Wasn't: The Taylor Ring, Bill Sutton, John Wesley Hardin, and Violence in Texas* is a welcome addition to the series.

M. Hunter Hayes
General Editor

ACKNOWLEDGMENTS

I incurred many debts in researching and writing this volume. I am pleased to say that when doing the research, I met and made more new friends than I can count. First, I would like to thank Sheron Barnes and Elizabeth Corte of the Regional History Center of the Victoria College/University of Houston Library. Both grand young ladies, they cheerfully helped me when I was gathering material located in the archives of the Regional History Center. Ms. Corte handled my day-to-day problems, and Ms. Barnes, Director of the Center, solved my larger ones. Dr. Joe Dahlstrom, director of the library, supported my efforts when I was indexing the Barry A. Crouch Collection, now located in the Regional History Center. Victoria's newsman, columnist, and raconteur extraordinaire Henry Wolff Jr. shared his research on "Taylor-Sutton" with me, as did his wife, Linda. Henry and Linda also helped to find and to process illustrations for this volume. Donaly Brice (of El Paso fame) of the Texas State Library provided inspiration as well as practical assistance while I was working at the state library. Harold Weiss Jr. also provided inspiration even if he belonged to a political party that is not my own (I will win him over some day).

The longtime administrator and professor at Victoria College, Charles Spurlin, and his wonderful wife, Pat, assisted by researching in the American History Center of the University of Texas Libraries. Perhaps more important, Pat Spurlin fed me free food for lunch almost every day I was working through the Crouch Collection. She also packed dinner for me to feast on at suppertime. The enchiladas were most outstanding as was the tuna fish. But, then, everything that Pat cooked was super, too, once I told her that liver and onions were definitely out. If not for Pat, I might have starved to death.

Chuck Spurlin and Bob Allen—a one-time navy photographer who retired from the military and who later took a new job with Victoria College—also made tremendous efforts to help me track down illustrations for the volume. My good friend Chuck, a fellow of the Texas State Historical Association, also read and critiqued parts of the manuscript. His advice and general support kept me going when I needed a periodic boost. I just wish he was not so tall; I get tired of looking up at him. It hurts my neck.

I am indebted to Chuck Parsons, a quite capable historian who has written scores of articles and books in the last forty years or so. Chuck read portions of the original manuscript and offered timely advice relative to both content and writing style. He saved me from a number of sloppy errors. Further, he has written a number of articles and book chapters on the Taylor-Sutton tangle, and his research and his publications helped me tremendously.

I also have a debt to Professor Edward Byerley and all the Victoria College staff who produce *South Texas Studies* annually. In 2005, Dr. Byerley published a "spin-off" from my Sutton-Taylor work in which I did my best to dispel the notion that the Sutton-Taylor affair was a feud, as some people have previously labeled the topic. Rather, the troubles amounted to a law enforcement problem, amounted to lawmen going after felons. See "Sutton-Taylor: A Feud?" in *South Texas Studies* (Victoria: Victoria College Press, 2005), 1–27.

My young friend Kenneth Howell, a graduate of Texas A&M University with a Ph.D. in history, who is now teaching at Prairie View A&M, has always improved my morale when I am working on a project, and my work on this volume is no exception. Kenneth is so enthusiastic about the study of history that every time I talk with him, some of that enthusiasm rubs off on me. In addition, he read my introduction to this volume and helped me clarify some of my ideas and interpretations.

I owe a special debt to my late friend Barry A. Crouch. A Reconstruction scholar with a national reputation, Professor Crouch left all of his voluminous research to the Regional History Center in Victoria. My good friends Donaly Brice, Chuck Spurlin, and Bill Stein, who is a living legend in Colorado County, made two road trips to the state of Colorado to pick up the Crouch research. The material was so vast that they packed a van all the way to its ceiling and still there was more material, hence the need for the second trip. Over the years both Barry and I made sundry trips to the National Archives and Library of Congress, and most of the sources in the Barry Crouch Collection are primary materials drawn from those depositories. The Crouch Papers fill seventy-plus library cartons and were very valuable to me as I pursued the research. While I had most of the same source notes as Barry, I missed some material, and Barry's work filled that void.

Texas A&M University at Commerce Professor James A. "Bo" Grimshaw Jr., the former general editor of the Sam Rayburn Series on Rural Life in Texas (he is now retired) was supportive as always, as was our mutual friend, Dr. James Conrad, the library archivist at A&M at Commerce. The Sam Rayburn Series is most valuable in giving historians studying Texas an outlet for their work. My thanks go to all the administrators and donors who have set up the Series and have allowed it to flourish, their number including

M. Hunter Hayes, the new series editor who graciously agreed to write the foreword for this volume.

My thanks also go to all the editorial staff at the Texas A&M University Press in College Station; most of the editors assisted me in one way or another as the project moved along. In particular I credit Editor-in-Chief Mary Lenn Dixon. She never gave up on this project, and I hope that I have justified her faith in me.

While I thus had ample assistance in building this volume, any errors are mine alone.

INTRODUCTION

MONDAY, May 26, 1874, was a great day for the residents of Comanche County, Texas, and for many folks from the adjacent areas who came to Comanche town to enjoy a day filled with distractions to take their minds off their problems. All awakened to greet a warm, sunny day, one ideal for watching and wagering on the horse races and eating the food and drinking the liquor and having an entertaining time. The town's merchants rolled out the red carpet to all the visitors who would leave much money behind when they left. Indeed, the atmosphere was that of a county fair, a festival, a carnival. Even children were caught up in all the excitement. They chased each other all around town without even wondering why.[1]

Monday was also the twenty-first birthday of the young psychotic murderer John Wesley Hardin, who, rumor had it, had already killed at least twenty men. He celebrated by drinking most of the day away when not riding his horse Rondo to several victories in the races. In all, the wayward youngster won $3,000, fifteen saddle horses, fifty beeves, and a wagon. His winnings were all the more pleasurable because many of his raiders were in town to celebrate with him and to protect him from the authorities if necessary. Jim Taylor, a nephew of the redoubtable revolutionary hero-turned-cattle-rustler Creed Taylor, was there, as were the Anderson brothers, Ham and John; the Dixons, Bud and Tom; and Alex Barekman. John Wesley's brother Jo was in the crowd, as was their father James Gibson Hardin, both of whom had aided and abetted many of John Wesley's crimes. They were often his accessories both before and after the fact. Jo was an attorney who postured as a staunch upholder of the law but who, in fact, was a corrupt man who engaged in real estate swindles and who was much involved with the cattle-rustling, horse-stealing Taylor crime ring led by John Wesley and Jim Taylor. Jo was most adept at dummying up false bills of sale for stolen cattle. Wesley's father was a Mason, a teacher, and a Methodist preacher, a supposed man of God who postured as an upright citizen but who always helped his sons even if their crimes were as serious as cold-blooded murder.[2]

After John Wesley became involved with the Taylors, area lawmen began referring to the Taylor ring as the "Taylor-Hardin Gang" or the "Hardin-Taylor Gang." More than semantics, the addition of the young killer's name demonstrated how important he had become to the ring even though he did not join the Taylors until 1871. Of the bunch with him that day in Comanche, Jim Taylor was probably the most important—and dangerous. Although still a young man, he had been, since 1865, a major leader of the Taylor band, whose members spread terror and murder in their wake.

After the competitions of the day in Comanche, Hardin, Taylor, and Bud Dixon, among others of the ring, wandered from saloon to saloon throwing around twenty-dollar gold pieces as if they were only small bits of shiny but worthless metal. By the time they reached Jim Wright's saloon on the public square, Hardin and his friends were drunk and determined to get even more

John Wesley Hardin (1853–1895) joined the Taylor Ring prior to his twenty-first birthday and immediately became a major leader and an enforcer for the ring.
Courtesy Sharon Barnes, Director, Regional History Center at the Victoria College/ University of Houston at Victoria Library

so. Soon, John Wesley was staggering around Wright's place, becoming more boisterous and quarrelsome with each drink, something his friends expected. He had always been a mean drunk who seemed to cause mayhem and murder wherever he went.[3]

Hardin was a known felon, and someone alerted Comanche County Sheriff John Carnes that trouble would likely develop if Hardin kept drinking, as it always did when he was in his cups. The sheriff knew the vicious gunman well and tolerated him. Carnes had good reason to do so. He was a corrupt lawman who had earlier cooperated with and made money from the youngster's cattle-rustling operations in Comanche and Brown counties. The sheriff's self-interest told him that he must protect Hardin if possible, lest some gang member expose his role in the Taylor ring. Still, Carnes had to posture as a responsible county officer who championed law and order. Not wishing to confront Hardin directly, he sent Deputy Frank Wilson to the saloon where the deputy did exactly what Carnes ordered him to do. Wilson asked Hardin and his party to leave town before serious trouble found them. Apparently, after the sheriff's surrogate talked with him, the young hotspur decided to take the advice, but his friends decided that in his drunken condition, he would have trouble staying astride a horse. So, his younger brother Jeff went to find a buggy that he intended to pull around to the porch of the saloon.[4]

The young killer might have taken Wilson's advice, but after the lawman left, one of Hardin's men told him that Brown County Deputy Sheriff Charles "Charlie" Webb was walking toward the saloon. Like many other visitors, Webb was in town to see the races and perhaps wager. An ex-Texas Ranger, he also used the occasion to visit his sweetheart, whom observers said was one of the finest young ladies in the Lone Star State. After the competitions, Webb walked to the town square to meet a friend with whom he was to have dinner. He stepped up to the porch of Wright's saloon to wait for his friend.[5]

Hardin, Taylor, and Dixon knew Webb as a pesky lawman who had earlier interfered with the Hardin-Taylor band's cattle-rustling operations in Brown and Comanche counties, and it seemed a perfect time to challenge him, for he was alone and not expecting a fight. Indeed, the killers could not believe their luck. When Webb stepped on the porch, Hardin, Taylor, and Dixon (and possibly an unidentified fourth man) confronted him there. John Wesley purposefully tried to start an argument with the Brown County lawman. Webb declined to participate, carefully avoiding any talk that might anger the young desperado. The odds were against Webb, and he wanted to get out of town alive. But as Hardin was talking, the deputy noticed that Taylor and Dixon were moving, trying to flank him to broaden his shooting field, a development that gave the brigands an even bigger advantage. Quick to realize his peril, Webb started backing away, but the three felons followed him into the street.[6]

They began cursing Webb and then reached for their guns. Their target quickly did the same, but he was no match for all three. Moreover, he had a new revolver and was not accustomed to its "hair trigger." The gun fired prematurely as he was swinging it up, causing its bullet to hit Hardin in the left side rather than his chest. By then, all three desperadoes had fired at Webb. One bullet shattered his gun arm, a development that prevented him from returning fire accurately. Other slugs tore into the deputy's face, neck, left arm, and abdomen. As he collapsed upon one knee with blood gushing from his wounds, the lawman got off a second shot, but the slug went wild and buried itself in the ground. His days were finished. The single shot to the face, probably delivered by Hardin, had actually been enough to kill him. Although the lawman had fired his weapon and had tried to defend himself, witnesses at the scene considered his death to be a murder, a grand jury later agreeing by handing down indictments. The killing made statewide news. A faraway Dallas newspaper, for example, covered the story and attributed the killing to "a band of cattle thieves" who had been "operating" in Comanche and Brown counties.[7]

Although the desperadoes won the gunfight, the incident was the beginning of the end for John Wesley Hardin and the Taylor ring. Many members of the Taylor bunch were already dead. Others soon would be. For Hardin, the killing of Charlie Webb was the ticket that eventually sent him to the Texas Penitentiary in Huntsville, but the events that led up to that dreadful Monday in Comanche had a long history that began years before.

About that day in Comanche: According to some historians, Hardin had become embroiled in what has been known as the "Sutton-Taylor Feud." Billed as a great feud by many writers, the Sutton-Taylor affair was anything but, for the word "feud" suggests that two individuals had personal grudges to settle or that two families had differences wherein there was no real right or wrong. Black and white faded to nebulous gray: There were only personality clashes. One violent act followed another as two individuals or two families retaliated any time attacks came, which, in turn, led to another violent act followed by another retaliation until no one was left standing to fight. Such was not the case with the Sutton-Taylor imbroglio. Indeed, William "Bill" Sutton was the only member of his family to challenge the Taylors, and he represented the law, being a DeWitt County Deputy Sheriff whose job it was to ferret out criminals and bring them to justice. That meant bringing in the members of the Taylor ring, if possible.

Somewhat similar to the "Lee-Peacock Feud" in East-Northeast Texas, the Taylor-Sutton troubles in South Texas became part of a post-Civil War death struggle between loyal Unionists and former and neo-Confederates, a struggle where the stakes were high. The fight's outcome—coupled with the outcomes of similar episodes occurring throughout the settled portion of Texas—would determine just who would control the Lone Star State. Would it be the Unionists or the Rebels and their sympathizers? Would the Reconstruction process in Texas succeed or fail? As scholars such as Eric Foner *(America's Reconstruction),* George Rable *(But There Was No Peace),* and Richard Zuczek *(State of Rebellion)* have suggested, in much of the South, Reconstruction actually amounted to a Second Civil War, one waged in a new guise until white ex-Confederate Democrats had vanquished their enemies (white Unionists, freedpeople, and Yankee soldiers, teachers, and administrators). In other words, the South lost the first Civil War but won the second.

In South Texas, the "Taylor party" was known as the "Southern party" or the "Rebel element" because they wrapped themselves in the Confederate flag, postured as heroic defenders of old Dixie, and voiced support for the "Lost Cause" while demonizing the state's Unionist authorities as Yankee-controlled scalawags, as Southern traitors who were determined to help the Yankee carpetbaggers rape the South. In fact, there were few carpetbaggers in Texas, and the "scalawags" were Nationalists who were loyal to the federal government. Most were consistent. They were Unionists before, during, and after the war. Die-hard, violent ex-Confederates apparently did not understand that they were the real traitors, for they had used force when they sought to overthrow the United States Constitution. As well, the Taylor party stood for white supremacy, a view that demanded the total subordination of the new freedpeople and South Texas Hispanics, something that most white Southerners of the day understood and supported. Actually, such posturing by the Taylors provided a cover for crimes while also winning the hearts of many peaceful folks who identified with old Dixie and who were willing to cooperate with and protect those who appeared "wronged" by the Unionist authorities, those who appeared defiant, those who refused to submit, those who talked of that "Lost Cause." But talk was all the Taylors had. Not a single member of Creed Taylor's immediate family fought for the Confederacy during the war.

In South Texas the Unionist–ex-Confederate struggle was made more complex by the activities of the Taylor crime ring and other cattle and horse thieves. Men in the Taylor band cared little for the law, and for a time, people in such gangs and Klan-like terrorist groups had an informal relationship with Democrats (and some conservative Republicans) who were willing to tolerate high levels of violence all across Texas so long as such turmoil suited their political purposes of defeating the Reconstruction process and making certain that the Republican reformers of the era would fail. The same pattern occurred all across the interior of settled Texas. Various outlaw gangs and terrorist groups became paramilitary arms of the Democratic party. In essence, the party used such violent men, but, in turn, such men used the party whose members "looked the other way" when crimes were committed that served the party's interests. In the East-Northeast part of the state, for example, violence escalated beginning in 1865 and did not decline until the Democratic redeemers returned to power in 1872–73. The same was true for other parts of the state. Once back in power, the Democratic redeemers reversed course and began cracking down on violence, for it was no longer in their interests.

The significance of the Taylor problem in South Texas is best measured by considering the larger region where violence was epidemic and life was cheap, costing only a little lead. During Reconstruction, all of settled Texas seemed almost completely out of control and awash in blood. For example, the state led the nation in homicides for two years in a row and finished well ahead of the runner-up, Louisiana. The worst of the chaos was not in major cities and towns such as Austin and Galveston that were usually well garrisoned but, rather, in the countryside, in the rural areas, in places like DeWitt, Wilson, and Karnes counties, the heart of Taylor Country. Outlaws, ex-Rebel guerrilla raiders, Confederate deserters, terrorist groups like the Ku Klux Klan, common cattle rustlers and horse thieves—Texas had them all, the result being the escalation of violence and the failure of Reconstruction. All of the chaos destabilized the entire settled portion of the Lone Star State and guaranteed a victory for the former Confederates. In the doing, Texas, like the rest of the South, entered the dark ages where regression rather than progression was the rule. The South became America's number one problem economically, socially, and politically. Coupled with the ruin that was the Civil War, the failure of Reconstruction fostered it all. Part of the larger picture, the troubles in Taylor Country and the troubled career of John Wesley Hardin deserve a reexamination.

With much illicit money to be made, the Taylor ring's leaders could afford to hire the proverbial "gunslingers" to serve as protectors of and participants in the illegal operations that usually centered on cattle and horse theft. At times, Creed Taylor, the founder and the first leader of the ring, had as many as one hundred or more hired guns. When Hardin joined the Taylors, his first task was to help take a herd, most of the beeves stolen, up the Chisholm Trail to Abilene, Kansas. An average trail hand earned about $20 to $30 a month. The Taylors paid John Wesley $150 per month.

The staggering difference is explicable. They paid him to be an enforcer, to kill when necessary.

John Wesley Hardin's murderous career thus factored into the Sutton-Taylor troubles. Even when he was but a child, Hardin's family educated him to hate Yankees and to embrace the Southern cause. As an adult, he admitted that he was born and was raised as a Rebel. He claimed that Unionist rule in Texas led him into his horrid life of crime and that he was really a blameless victim of his times. As a young teenager not even old enough to shave, his Southern beliefs supposedly caused his first murder, that of a freedman who incurred his wrath. But, the trouble occurred when ex-Confederates were still in control of the state before the advent of Republican rule. Later, Hardin postured as a sincere follower of the Rebel cause, but in reality he only used his Southern stance to justify crimes that could not be otherwise justified. As well, Creed and Pitkin Taylor founded their criminal operation in the 1850s, well before Reconstruction and at a time when both Hardin and Sutton were but children. That said, during Reconstruction the Taylor party and John Wesley simply took advantage of the era's troubled politics, its troubled economy, and the social crisis that occurred because a majority of whites refused to accept black equality. They used such chaos as their excuse to commit heinous crimes. John Wesley and the Taylors traveled parallel paths that eventually intersected, paths that led to the murder and mayhem in South-Southeast Texas that culminated in the assassination of Deputy Webb, a decisive act that led to the downfall of both Hardin and the Taylor gang.

The epicenter of the Sutton-Taylor troubles that Hardin joined in 1871 was DeWitt County, but the struggle spilled into other adjacent or nearby counties that included Gonzales, Lavaca, Victoria, Goliad, Karnes, Wilson, Bastrop, and San Patricio. Other counties sometimes affected by the fight included Brown, Comanche, Lampasas, Kimble, Mason, and Gillespie, along with Refugio and Calhoun. Early on, even distant Panola County was disrupted because of the actions of some of the Taylors. As for Hardin, he raised hell all across East-Northeast Texas before he joined the Taylor ring in South Texas. At different times, Hardin could be found committing depredations in such counties as Hunt, Grayson, Montague, Fannin, Cooke, Collin, Dallas, Hill, Navarro, Freestone, Limestone, Comanche, Hamilton, Houston, Trinity, Polk, Mason, Gillespie, and other areas as well.

Sometimes written about with reverence as a Southern hero, Hardin was anything but. He was a psychotic sociopath who became a multiple slayer. But in the past, many people buried the truth and glorified him, his actions, and his ego. One glittering example was the release of the 1950s movie

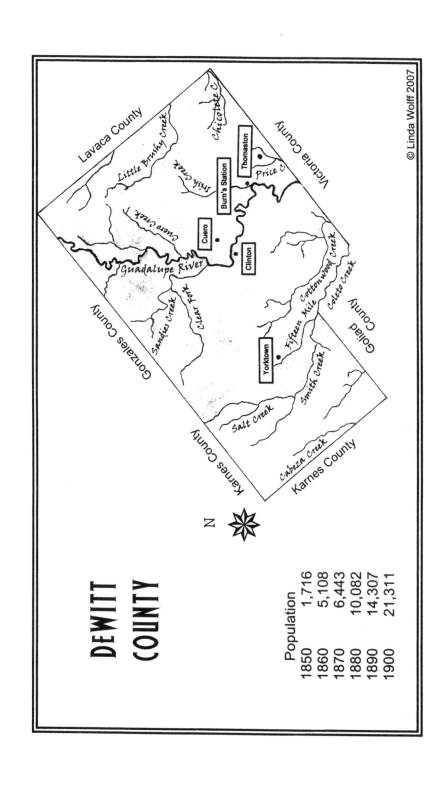

DeWITT COUNTY

Lavaca County

Gonzales County

Karnes County

Goliad County

Victoria County

Chicolete C

Little Brushy Creek

Irish Creek

Thomaston

Burn's Station

Price C

Cuero Creek

Cuero

Clinton

Clear Fork

Sandies Creek

Guadalupe River

Cotton wood Creek

Coleto Creek

Fifteen Mile

Yorktown

Smith Creek

Salt Creek

Cabeza Creek

N

Population

1850	1,716
1860	5,108
1870	6,443
1880	10,082
1890	14,307
1900	21,311

The Lawless Breed. The film starred Rock Hudson, at the time one of Hollywood's most sought-after leading men, a box office star. Just his name on the marquee virtually guaranteed that the movie would have a huge impact and voluminous ticket sales. And just what did the ticket buyers, many of them children, get? The film depicted Hardin as a victim rather than as the cold-blooded murderer he actually was. He was supposedly victimized by those cruel scalawags and carpetbaggers, those Southern traitors and those Yankee interlopers who meddled with what was all right and good about old Dixie. Although the Taylor ring was not glorified in the film, many historians and the general public put the Taylors in the same category that supposedly caused Hardin to go bad; that is, they were but Southern loyalists fighting evil Yankee rule while stealing only a few cows and horses and killing only a few people, all of whom, of course, deserved killing. But, in truth, such people had few sincere beliefs and continued to use the "Lost Cause" to cover their crimes.

In using the term "Taylor ring," I differ from those who came before me, for no one has used the phrase when discussing what has been referred to as the "Sutton-Taylor Feud." I have not used the conceptual framework of "feud" because what I found was far more startling. The Freedmen's Bureau records and the record of the Fifth Military District in the National Archives, coupled with other primary materials in the Texas State Library and secondary sources, reveal the names of men in the ring and the counties where the ring operated and/or where its members committed atrocities. The numbers are staggering. Altogether, 197 men (identified by name) were, permanently or temporarily from the 1850s to circa 1880, in the Taylor criminal ring that operated in forty-five different counties. Their names are listed in the appendix.

However, I should explain my terms. In using the words "ring," "gang," or "band," I do not mean to imply that all men were in the criminal conspiracy at the same time in all the same places. When one hears the word "gang," one is tempted to think of groups like the "James Gang" or the "Younger Gang." One is tempted to think of a small group of well-organized and forever loyal compatriots whose membership was ever constant unless authorities killed or captured sundry members and broke up the cabal. Such a description of a "gang" does not apply to the Taylor ring. Rather, it was a loose organization of men who had kindred interests and who sometimes rode with the Taylors and acted in concert with them but who sometimes acted independently while continuing to have the same goal: plunder. Clearly, the ring members were part of the rabble, out for quick money but using the "Lost Cause" as a justification. The Democrats made good use of their violence. The chaos they spawned helped the "Redeemers" defeat the white Unionists, the Yankee occupiers, and the freedpeople. In the twenty-five years—in that full quarter of a century—men in the ring came and went in situations that were loose and fluid. As well, the floating gang was not equally active in all forty-five counties, for some places saw far more action than others.

The historiography focusing on the Sutton-Taylor troubles is varied. Robert Sutton Jr. and Chuck Parsons have penned the definitive works on the "feud," the former contributing a short book, the latter adding several lengthy articles and book chapters.[8] Both authors focused on DeWitt County, an area that saw almost constant turmoil because of the Taylor ring's activities. One contemporary of the "feud," Lewis Delony, contributed a short book that covered a few aspects of the Taylor-Sutton tangle. Others have contributed short books or article-length studies, but they are suspect because all have obvious biases. As well, no one has examined the Taylor band's total area of operations and the totality of their deeds.

Except for the works by Sutton, Parsons, and Delony, traditional studies followed the William A. Dunning School in explaining Reconstruction. Holding sway from about the 1890s to the 1960s, the Dunning School stressed the goodness of the Confederate South, which was undone by evil Yankees, Southern scalawags, and the ignorant ex-slaves. Decent whites fought the evil rule and ultimately prevailed. Proponents of Dunning embraced outlaws and terrorist Klan groups, made excuses for their crimes, and threw all the blame on Yankees, scalawags, and so on.[9]

Writing from the late 1960s to the present, many academic historians, revisionist in nature, have discredited the old Dunning School. Yet, many laymen continue to accept Dunning mythology. Unfortunately, myth, legend, and lore sometimes displace history in the mind of the reading public, many of whom apparently believe that *myth is history.*[10] This volume will at least continue the debate on Reconstruction that has raged since the 1890s, the debate seeming to have no end as long as myth stands on equal footing with history.

Founding the Taylors'
South Texas Crime Ring

THE scion of the Taylor family was Josiah Taylor who in 1813 was one of the leaders of the ill-fated Gutierrez-Magee filibuster. He fought at the disastrous Battles of Medina and La Bahia before intrepid Spanish soldiers forced the expedition to withdraw. In the campaign Josiah received a total of seven gunshot wounds but lived to make his escape. After Stephen F. Austin opened the land of the Tejas to American settlement, Josiah returned to Texas in 1824, bringing with him his wife Hepzibeth who would become the matriarch of a large family. The couple first settled below Liberty on the Trinity River. After a year, they moved to "Taylor's Bayou" and stayed for four years. Then they made a final journey and put down permanent roots in Green DeWitt's grant. There they received a league of land in today's DeWitt County along the Guadalupe River, not far from today's Cuero. Together, they became pioneer farmers and ranchers. Hepzibeth gave Josiah six sons: William, Creed, Josiah Jr., Rufus, Pitkin, and James. Although Josiah Sr. died young in 1830, his progeny flourished.[1]

Josiah's most famous son was Tennessee-born Creed (1820–1906). Growing up in a farming and ranching family, he attended school in Gonzales until the outbreak of the Texas Revolution. According to some sources, as a teenager he fought in various clashes, including the Battles of Gonzales and Mission Concepcion. Taking orders from Ben Milam, he participated in the storming of San Antonio. After the disaster at the Alamo, he took his family to safety before joining General Sam Houston's forces at San Jacinto, arriving there in time to participate in the epic battle, as did his younger brother Josiah Jr. Later, he fought Indians on the frontier, including the Comanches at the Battle of Plum Creek in 1840. Becoming a ranger in 1841, he served under Jack Coffee Hays, seeing action in such battles as those at Bandera Pass

Josiah Taylor (1781–1830), patriarch of the Taylor clan, was a Virginian who first came to Texas in 1812 with the abortive Gutierrez-Magee Expedition. He returned in 1824, bringing his family along. The Taylors eventually settled in what became DeWitt County.
Courtesy Sharon Barnes, Director, Regional History Center at the Victoria College/University of Houston at Victoria Library

and Salado Creek. In the latter fray, he suffered a serious wound, but he was fated to survive. During the Mexican War (1846–48) he fought at Palo Alto and Buena Vista and in other fights as well.[2]

While Creed Taylor had an impressive resume, at least one researcher, L. W. Kemp, believed that the hero may have embellished his service record. Writing in 1936, Kemp studied the official records of the General Land Office and other material in the archives of the Texas State Library. What the researcher found was startling. For example, Creed claimed that he participated in the Battle of San Antonio, November 8, 1835. However, according to the Texas Comptroller's Military Service Records, Col. Edward Burleson and Capt. R. M. Coleman signed his discharge on September 28, 1835. Creed claimed to have fought in the Battle of San Jacinto, but his name is absent from the official roll of those who participated in that epic struggle. As well, the Comptroller's records for 1836 reflected that Creed served in the army for one just month and twelve days, from July 4 to August 16. The battle occurred on March 13, 1836, several months before Creed reenlisted.[3] So, then, it may well be that the hero embellished his record. If so, it goes to the heart of his character; perhaps his word cannot be trusted by historians examining his family's problems with peace officers in Taylor Country.

After the Texas Revolution, Creed started a family. He returned to DeWitt County, married Nancy Matilda Goodbread, and sired two sons and a daughter. After Nancy's death, he migrated first to Kimble County and then to Wilson County where he settled on Ecleto Creek and began raising cattle and horses. Later, he established another spread in Karnes County, also along the Ecleto. He married Lavina Spencer and had several more children. Two of his sons from his first marriage—John Hays (always called "Hays") born in 1836 and Phillip G. (always called "Doughboy," sometimes spelled "Doboy") born in 1837—were destined to lead the Taylor ring. Under Creed's supervision, they enlarged the Taylor crime ring by hiring more gunmen.[4]

However, it was Creed and his brother Pitkin who founded the ring. They apparently began causing concern to authorities in South Texas during the 1850s. The clan developed extensive and lucrative cattle operations scattered over several counties, including Kimble, Karnes, Gonzales, Wilson, and DeWitt. Other ranchers in each area where cattle turned up stolen blamed the Taylors, calling the men of the family a pack of horse thieves and cattle rustlers. To deal with them, some leaders organized vigilance committees. In DeWitt County, the place where problems seemed the most severe, the officers of the county committee included the one-time Texas Ranger Joe Tumlinson, the one-time Sheriff John Littleton, and James "Jim" Cox. To counter the committee, Creed Taylor pulled together a force of about eighty men, most of them hired gunslingers. That effectively created a stalemate that lasted through the Civil War and allowed the Taylors to continue their operations, some legal, some not.[5]

That secession and war created animosities in the South Texas region was demonstrated sundry times. In Karnes County, for example, an elderly man named Riddle, who owned a mill, was a staunch Unionist, so much so that he refused to grind corn for the Confederacy's supporters, including women whose husbands were away at war. The Taylors claimed to be Confederate to the core. One of the clan's icons, Pitkin, backed up his claims with deeds. He retaliated against Riddle by leading a pro-Confederate group that found and lynched the old man, who died in terror while begging for his life. Despite being thorough with their lip service glorifying the Confederacy, there is no record that any of the Taylor bunch served in the military during the conflict. How the younger generation of the family managed to escape conscription is unknown. During the war some military men suspected the Taylors of profiteering by raiding areas of South Texas and blaming their deeds on Mexican desperadoes, Indians, and Confederate deserters. Certainly, the area was home to all manner of lawlessness, including murder, robbery, cattle rustling, and horse stealing, and the Taylors had a hand in destabilizing the entire area.[6] Lawlessness triumphed over law.

The emerging Cattle Kingdom muddled the tense feelings between ex-Confederates, including the Taylor clan, and Unionists in the region. Millions of longhorns were running wild in South Texas. During the days of the Spanish Empire, Hispanics established huge cattle ranches in the region. But with Mexican independence in the early 1820s, the Spaniards withdrew. Subsequently, Mexican authority extended only weakly into South Texas, a borderland across the Rio Grande and hundreds of miles from Mexico City. The ranches fell into disrepair. The cattle ran wild. They were most fruitful and multiplied to untold numbers, totaling perhaps as many as five million head by circa 1865. According to one observer, cattle were so numerous in South Texas as to be never out of the sight of a cross-country traveler. Before the Civil War, Texans had a difficult time finding markets for the cattle, but some made money by driving herds to regional centers. As well, using the coastal waters and various watercrafts, cattle men could get small herds to New Orleans.

By 1865, an eastern railroad reached the railhead of Sedalia in western Missouri. Cattlemen then inaugurated the "long drives," catching, branding, and herding Texas longhorns to Sedalia from whence beeves could reach all the Northern and Southern markets. Although the Sedalia Trail ran through thick forests and passed over the Ozark Plateau, Texans still made money when they reached the railhead. As the railroad extended westward, new railheads, new cow towns, sprang up. The Chisholm Trail became a major thoroughfare that led from South Texas to Abilene, Kansas.[7]

Eventually, as the railroads built farther westward, cattlemen made the long drives through entirely open country, making the trips more profitable and much easier on both man and beast. And as the Cattle Kingdom grew, stockmen became rich—or at least had that opportunity if they had good luck. Possibilities for fortune led to abuses. Although the region's counties required registering brands and had brand inspectors, organized crime grew. Cattle rustling in South Texas became legion, and over-branding or "brand-blotting" became widely practiced. The days of the open range in South Texas compounded the problems, for cattle might wander and graze miles from home. Registered brands supposedly showed ownership, but brigands frequently added another brand that meshed with the original. Alternately, some thieves did not bother to "blot" or over-brand. They simply quickly gathered their stolen herds and pushed them up the trail rapidly, thus escaping both the rightful owners and the law. Rustlers victimized stockmen to such a degree that some of those ranchers abandoned the cattle business, or nearly so. For example, Brown County rancher David Baugh once ran a herd of about five hundred, but by 1874, he only ran about one hundred, his losses due to cattle thieves. The problem? Various sources held that members of the Taylor crime ring were the worst rustlers in all of Central and South Texas.[8]

One source believed that the Taylors viewed cattle rustling as just another business, just another opportunity to make money. Rustling became an easy get-rich-quick scheme, and the Taylor band seized the opportunity. Violence always followed when lawmen or soldiers tried to bring the gang to heel.[9]

As the Reconstruction drama played itself out, the extended Taylor family, still headed by patriarchs Creed and Pitkin, continued to lead the former Confederates who refused to accept the judgment of the late war. They postured as Southern loyalists to win the support of ex-Confederates. As one historian said, the Taylors represented the "Rebel element." As his brother Pitkin gradually retreated into the background, Creed became the principal leader of the ring. Even after his sons and nephews were old enough to take over operations, Creed remained the driving force who planned the action of the ring and developed strategy to ensure the continuing dominance of the Taylor clan. Called "naturally reckless and daring," Creed's sons Hays and Doughboy came to the attention of military authorities within six months after General Robert E. Lee surrendered at Appomattox.[10]

Yet, law officers first went after their cousin William P. "Buck" Taylor—one of Pitkin's sons and the nephew of Creed—who was born on November 1, 1837. By the fall of 1865, lawmen of Victoria County were looking for the twenty-seven-year-old Buck. He had recruited a small band of raiders, including Bob F. Civas. They assaulted and battered the teacher and some of the students of the county's new school for the freedpeople and their children. There appeared to be no specific reason for the attack; rather, Buck hated the idea of educating freedpeople, considering them scum, fit only for being the servants of whites. Blacks had always been Aristotle's mudsill for Southern civilization. Buck was determined that they remain so. Later, in July of 1867, many whites in DeWitt County followed Buck's example. Because of blind racial hatred, they attacked the teacher and students of Clinton's new school for the freedpeople. Buck may have led the group, for he continued to oppose any uplift for the black community. Like the Taylor clan, most white Texans intended that, at best, blacks would be tolerated as a source of cheap, menial labor but would remain a labor pool that possessed no legal or civic rights.[11]

As whites continued to subdue blacks, Buck and his band took to robbing travelers on the roads of Victoria and DeWitt counties whenever they outnumbered such wayfarers. Area lawmen, however, learned Buck's identity. That led civil officers and military commanders, whose forces started occupying Texas on June 19, 1865, to suspect him and the felons who followed him of multiple murders that occurred in DeWitt County near Yorktown. In September 1865, Capt. Henry J. Nolan was leading some members of the Eighteenth New York Cavalry on escort duty when two of the men on tired horses fell behind. Upon noticing that the two had fallen back, the captain sent a small detachment to find them. Some distance away, the squad found the dead bodies of their two comrades lying beside the road. Headquartered at Yorktown, the New Yorkers soon heard from former Rebels in the county who wrote anonymous letters to post headquarters threatening to attack their garrison and "wipe them out." The same ex-Confederates wrote or told area Unionists that they would die soon after the Northern troopers left. Knowing that he was suspect and that lawmen would soon be after him, Buck did what many a raider did during the Civil War and Reconstruction—that is, he committed devilry in one vicinity before running to hide in another while adopting an alias to confuse both the authorities and, later, historians.[12]

When law officers got on his trail, Buck slipped into distant Panola County where for a brief time he remained law-abiding. But he could not stay out of trouble. He soon joined a new wild bunch that numbered twenty-six raiders, four of whom had creatively taken the last name of "Smith." December 1865 found Buck and some of the renegades deviling a freedman named Littles. They forced their way into his home, where they assaulted, robbed, and shot him. The same month, a "party of desperadoes" got on the trail of four discharged United States soldiers who left San Antonio and who were moving northeast, taking a route to their homes. When they passed through Panola County, the raiders murdered all four in "cold blood," to hear a witness tell it. It may have been Buck's band who did the killings, for they were committing general mayhem in the county when the discharged soldiers rode through. Later, while riding with guerrillas William "Wild Bill" Bateman, Charles Hodge, and others, Buck robbed several more freedmen, including one black man who lived in Greenwood. At times, the gang slipped across the Louisiana border to commit yet more robberies, with ex-slaves being their usual targets. When Louisiana lawmen got on the gang's trail, Buck and the rest slipped back into Texas, with Panola County as their destination.[13]

The violent crimes of ex-Confederates like the Taylor clan occurred in most parts of settled Texas and destabilized the entire state. Some former Rebels attacked out of hatred toward blacks and/or for all Yankees. While he commanded the cavalry in the District of Texas, Colonel George Armstrong Custer commented several times on the violent conditions in the Lone Star State. Writing in January 1866, Custer held that "the original secessionists . . . are as much secessionists today in belief and sentiments as [they were] one year ago." He added that those former Rebels were as willing to oppose the Union government as they had been during the actual war. The colonel said that if they believed a revolt could be successful, the former Confederates and their sympathizers would be in "open armed hostility" to the government.[14]

Custer explained the position of Provisional Governor A. J. Hamilton. Referring to the massive violence occurring in Texas, Hamilton told him that if Congress did not act soon, he (Hamilton) would have to resign and leave the state because Unionists appeared to be in danger everywhere. Hamilton added that were it not for troops in Austin, he could not remain in office for even a single day, saying that his life "would not be worth a farthing." About the upcoming political convention of 1866, the provisional governor believed that there would be a dozen ex-Confederates delegates to every one Union man, especially because of voter intimidation. Those Rebel sympathizers would "vie to see who could express the most contempt . . . for the government."[15] Custer said that had he the power, such convention delegates would not meet "unless in a military prison."[16]

According to Custer, the Union was losing its battle in the countryside. Wherever military authorities stationed troops, most ex-Confederates and assorted common criminals seemed well behaved, but in areas where the troops were absent, Rebel hatred gave vent to all manner of crimes.[17] Later, as if to verify that Custer was correct, DeWitt County rowdies accosted and questioned a young traveler named Lamont simply because he had a northern accent. Then, hearing that he was from Boston, Massachusetts, the brigands threatened to kill him if he did not leave their county immediately. Thereafter, the youngster traveled by night and hid by day. He reported his travail to William Horton, a Freedmen's Bureau agent temporarily stationed in Hallettsville, Lavaca County. The Northerner told Horton that DeWitt County was in a "terrible condition."[18]

Custer said that hostility to the United States was "deep rooted and bitter." Loyalty was only a veneer ex-Confederates used in the hopes of regaining control of the state. He informed a political friend in Washington that a Unionist ran up the Stars and Stripes from a flagpole on his property. Ex-Rebel vigilantes visited him and explained that he must haul down that flag. When the man refused, the vigilantes murdered him. "There are many outrages like this," Custer maintained, and they occurred around the entire state. He held that the Civil War generation of Texans would never be loyal. He added that the government needed a "get tough" remedy: The Rebels needed to understand that "Treason *is* a Crime [Custer's emphasis]."[19]

Later, another trooper expanded on Custer's analysis of the problems with the former Confederates who refused to give up their fight. Writing much later in June 1869 from Greenville, Texas, Lt. William Hoffman crafted words to describe North and East Texas, but his words applied to South Texas and all of the Confederate South as well. The Southern Rebels, Hoffman said, had a hatred so deep for the freedpeople and for the white Unionists that it could never be overcome. Often, those former Confederates struck out hard at the freedmen and their white allies. Even worse, from Hoffman's point of view, the hatred would pass from one generation to the next: "The coming generation, children and children's children[,] are zealously reared to the one great tenet: implacable hatred for the [Union] government."[20] The subsequent history of Texas and the rest of the South suggests that the young lieutenant knew of what he spoke.

Meanwhile, other Taylors had been busy during the winter of 1865 and spring of 1866. A nephew of Creed Taylor, Martin Taylor—about twenty-two years old by 1865—murdered a Unionist in Victoria County. Local lawmen quickly assembled a posse and went after him. He eluded his pursuers even though they chased him for miles before losing his trail. Martin went into hiding, but a person who knew him gave the authorities a good description of him, information that would help lawmen identify him should they see him. He was a "little man" who sported a white beard. He had small, dark eyes, and his movements were very deliberate. Although Martin disappeared for a time, area peace officers still had headaches because Hays Taylor began to cause trouble. Acting as a trail boss (or trail "contractor"), he drove a herd of cattle, some of them stolen, from Wilson County to Indianola for shipment to New Orleans. After completing their task, he and some of his men went to the nearest saloon to celebrate their prosperity. Hays was at the bar drinking when two black soldiers bellied up. Offended that the freedmen were at the same bar as whites, Hays exchanged harsh words with the soldiers. He told them that they must "stand aside" because he would not be at the same bar with them.

One of the blacks took exception to Hays's remark. He told Taylor that he was as good as any white man and that he was not going to stand aside. After a few minutes, when the soldiers' attention focused on something else, Hays quickly pulled his revolver and shot the two troopers. He killed one and wounded the other, after which his cohorts drew guns and held all in the saloon at bay by threatening more destruction. Swearing that he would kill anyone who interfered with him, Hays began backing away until he reached the saloon door, whereupon he turned and broke into a run toward his horse. He bounced atop and rode out. His men quickly followed. Safely out of town, Hays and his men scattered just in case a posse came after them.[21]

Now alone, Hays headed for home, but he soon encountered a military squad of five, led by a black sergeant. After noting that the sergeant rode a fine mule that looked like one belonging to George Walton of Hallettsville that had been stolen, Hays spoke his mind to the squad, accusing its leader of theft. More insults followed, and Hays drew a gun and fatally shot the sergeant in the head while receiving a wound in the arm when the dying man returned fire. But Hays was free to go on his way, for the other troopers lost all heart when the firing began. They quickly wheeled their mounts away and rode for a safer environ. Hays robbed the dead man's pocket and claimed possession of the sergeant's weapons and his mule.[22]

Towing the mule behind his horse, Hays rode for Helena, the town not far from one of his father's operations. He found Creed in a local saloon. His wounded arm in a makeshift sling, Hays told his father about the incident with the troopers. After calling the sergeant and his men no-good "niggers," Creed told his son that the sergeant's mule was not the one belonging to their friend, for that animal had been found. Creed convinced Hays to take the mule to an isolated area, kill it, and bury it so that such evidence would never fall into the hands of the authorities. Not wanting to kill such a fine animal, Hays argued but finally accepted his father's advice and ridded himself of the incriminating beast. Afterward, Hays went on the dodge, moving around almost constantly, staying with first one relative or friend and then another. Only in that way could he escape charges for the murders that he committed. Some sources hold that a bit later, Creed and kinsman Joe Taylor helped Hays get to Monterrey, Mexico, to ensure that he would not fall into the hands of the law. There was a problem, however. Hays missed his family and friends, so he did not long remain south of the border; instead, he brazenly returned to the area where lawmen well knew his crimes.[23]

Meanwhile, the political season of 1866 began when the Constitutional Convention convened in February. The delegates' actions seemed to prove that such observers as Custer were correct in their analysis of Rebel-dominated Texas. In selecting a president of the convention, delegates voted three to one for wartime Confederate James Throckmorton. Learning of that development, Custer expressed disgust. He said Throckmorton and his close associate John Hancock were Rebels at heart, adding that they condemned the federal government at every opportunity. Even strongly garrisoned Travis County sent former secessionists to the convention. As for race relations, Custer talked with Hamilton who knew of at least fifty cases of whites murdering blacks. As late as 1866, Hamilton told Custer that "traffic [slavery] in human beings" still existed in Texas. Military and Freedmen's Bureau investigations proved that such was true. In some extreme cases, slavery existed in Texas as late as 1869. Both Hamilton and Custer averred that not a day passed when they were not informed of another murder motivated by racial hatred and/or politics. Yet, civil authorities were powerless to bring criminals to justice. They "openly defied" civil rule. They threatened to attack anyone who gave evidence of their crimes. Hamilton and Custer believed that many more occupation troops were needed to restore law and order and to protect white Unionists and the freedpeople. They wanted a permanent military garrison for almost all of the counties of settled Texas.[24]

William Alexander was another observer who reacted to the overwhelming violence in Texas. Writing to Judge Salmon Chase in July of 1866, Alexander held that Rebel Texans were still as defiant as they were when they voted to secede from the Union in 1861. In part, Alexander blamed Congress for not doing more to reform the South and in part blamed President Andrew Johnson for making "loyalty odious and treason respectable." "Criminal law," Alexander exclaimed, "is a dead letter in Texas." Vicious public sentiments were "superior to all law." The Union government in Washington needed to understand that "irresistible physical force" had to be used to let the ex-Rebels know they must obey the law. Referring to the recent convention cited by Hamilton, Alexander believed that "Hamilton had his chance and blew it." According to Alexander, when convention members refused to take an oath to support the Union government, Hamilton should have dispersed the delegates and sent them home rather than deal with their babbling opposition. Like Custer, Alexander believed that military rule was necessary to control the people with Confederate sentiments. Murders were an everyday occurrence, said Alexander, but "Rebel [news]papers" tried to suppress such news while all the time bawling about "universal amnesty" for former Confederates.[25]

Writing later, General Charles Griffin confirmed that both Custer and Alexander were correct. He told General Philip Sheridan that most Texans had "very bitter" feelings about their situation. Griffin added that unless the high command stationed troops in an area, the vicinity's majority embraced the "Lost Cause." Ex-Rebels controlled county governments and allowed lawlessness if freedpeople and white Union men were the victims. Griffin asked Sheridan to transfer some forces on the Indian and Mexican frontiers to the interior of the state because crime was so rampant.[26]

By the summer of 1866, authorities in South Texas were routinely referring to the "Taylor gang," for members of the crime ring remained busy. Officials had charged Buck Taylor and his cousin Martin with various violent crimes that included one count of murder and two of attempted murder. Others in the gang committed multiple killings. The shooters in those crimes were John and James Wright; Charles "Charlie" Taylor; Bill, Jim, and Tom Dodd; two men named Pruitt, George being the first name of one; Bill Green; Jesus Gonzales; John Edwards; and at least two other men. Together, on the Colorado River near LaGrange, they ambushed five recently discharged Yankee soldiers. They eliminated three at one time, shooting them to death using both Spencer carbines and sixguns. They accepted the surrender of two more, whom they bound before beating them to death. The murderers carried the bloody dead men to the river, cut open three of the bodies from groin to chest, removed some of their innards, and inserted rocks, hoping that the extra weight would sink them. Tiring of that work, the raiders buried the other two at the bottom of the river in the shallows and put big rocks on their bodies to hold them down. They were left with a dead mule. They pitched it into the water, too. Bystanders near Columbus recovered two of the bodies after they saw them floating down the Colorado River.[27]

Charlie Taylor continued to cause trouble. He lived in Karnes County where Creed had a ranching operation. Charlie was a distant cousin of the Creed and Pitkin Taylor clan, and he often rode with the other Taylor men. Causing mayhem during the early phase of Reconstruction, he was a young, restless hotspur who became resentful of white Unionists and ex-slaves, most of whom were striving for a better material life. He became a highwayman but also specialized in horse theft and cattle rustling. He added another murder to his resume when he shot a white man named Polk in March 1866. Polk apparently became a target because he spoke out in favor of the freedpeople and against the Taylor raiders, their number including Charlie. Although Karnes County Sheriff John W. Littleton personally took Polk into his home to care for him, the gunshot wound proved to be fatal. Polk died about three weeks later.[28]

In June some of the Taylor men were still on a killing spree. Tom and William Dodd, Charlie Taylor, and Jim Wright murdered another soldier. The desperadoes saw the man pass through Gonzales and went after him. They caught him as he was about to ford Peach Creek and opened up with their rifles. They fired rounds repeatedly until a final blast knocked the soldier off his horse. They gathered around to make sure he was dead. After dragging the corpse to the right side of the road, they robbed the pockets of the dead man. The soldier had been riding a fine, large, bay horse that the murderers took to the place of a cohort, the felon Ed Glover.[29]

Almost simultaneously, others in the gang, led by Hays Taylor, began causing trouble around Victoria, Hallettsville, and Clinton. Calling Hays and his men "a gang of unlawful young men" who had nothing at stake in adhering to the laws of civilized society, Capt. Garza Haraszthy of the Clinton post informed his superior that the gang was beating and robbing freedmen and terrorizing poor whites. The captain reported that in his first three months as commander of the post, he had received twenty-five complaints from freedmen about being abused by whites. He added that the plight of black and white Unionists would become worse if his superiors removed troops from the area. In a later report, Haraszthy gave information about raiders operating around Victoria and Hallettsville. Area farmers and planters who had signed labor contracts with blacks had worked them unmercifully but then drove them away once they harvested crops. Whites simply would not give their charges their share of the crops, thus violating the labor contracts. Some whites paid Hays Taylor and his raiders to run the blacks off and to threaten them with death if they complained to authorities.[30]

On August 21, 1866, Hays Taylor murdered Pvt. Samuel Hargus of the Seventh United States Cavalry. Once a slave, Hargus joined the Union army in November 1863 when he was but twenty-one. He stormed his way through the rest of the Civil War. Determined to carve out an army career, he was on detached duty, serving at Lavaca, Calhoun County, while working for the Quartermaster's Department. A superior ordered the private to take two horses and one mule to Indianola. Concurrently, Hays, Joseph Clarke, and others were driving a herd of stolen cattle from Wilson County to Indianola for shipment to New Orleans. Along with others in the ring, the Kelly brothers of Lavaca County—two of whom married into the Taylor family—helped Hays and Clarke steal the beeves and purloin a few horses, but they returned home once the cattle drive began. Once they delivered the herd, Hays and Clarke rode away to return from whence they had come. They crossed Hargus's path while he was en route to the town they had just left.

Hays and his cohort spotted Hargus, set up an ambush, and used their rifles to kill him before they robbed his pockets and took possession of the mule and horses, including the one the private had been riding. Unknown to the murderers, John McDaniels and Clayton Garner witnessed the slaying and provided good descriptions of the killers in affidavits to General Charles Griffin. They described Hays as about 20 years old, a small man with a dark complexion and dark hair and eyes. He also sported a dark moustache. The informants said Clarke was about seventeen years old, stood about five feet six inches, and had "light" hair and eyes. The army commander at Indianola gained intelligence that the two murderers lived on one of Creed's places near Sutherland Springs in Wilson County. General Griffin turned the information over to civil authorities in Calhoun County, but no legal action was forthcoming. The county sheriff would not go after Taylor and Clarke, and no grand jury indictment followed.

Because he could not get results in any other way, Griffin wrote Governor Throckmorton divulging the facts. The general told the governor that Hays was the "son of old Crede Taylor of notoriety and cousin of the reported desperado and murderer Buck Taylor." Griffin explained that after their crime, Hays and Clarke rode to Creed's ranch on the Ecleto and could be found in or around Creed's spread. Griffin asked Throckmorton to intervene, to see that justice would be done, and to convene a grand jury to hand down indictments for robbery and murder. Although the action came late, a Calhoun County grand jury eventually found true bills on the charges, but when lawmen sought the perpetrators, they had vanished. They murdered another freedman on August 31, an atrocity for which they were not charged. One source stated that the men were also stealing horses in the area.[31]

While Hays and Clarke were avoiding punishment, Buck Taylor committed more devilry in DeWitt County. In September, Buck, Martin, and several of their men ambushed a small squad of troopers, killing Captain Nolan and at least one enlisted man. Both belonged to the Eighteenth New York Cavalry Regiment. There appeared to be no provocation for the murders, although the Taylors did not need one, for they were attacking Union soldiers any time they had a chance. They had vanished when the authorities went looking for them.[32]

In November 1866, other members of the gang murdered a Tejano, apparently with little cause but robbery. Jim and John Wright, Alex Reed, Bill and Tom Dodd, and John Edwards all saw the Hispanic hiking along the Rio Frio, coming up the west side. Tom Dodd greeted the man and offered a ride. After the Tejano climbed up behind him, all the men rode to Alex Reed's place and went into a pasture. There, the brigands shot the Hispanic to pieces. After robbing the man, who had practically nothing, they left the corpse where it fell.[33]

In late 1866 Buck, who had once again returned to DeWitt County, somewhat brazenly attended a dance even though military and civilian authorities had a good description of him. As fate would have it, a black sergeant, coming out of the post at Victoria and acting on a tip from an informant, arrived and spent time studying the crowd, looking for the felon. But Buck was watching the sergeant, and just as the trooper recognized him and started to arrest him, Taylor quickly drew a gun and shot the black man dead. Firing more than one shot, he also wounded an innocent bystander. In the resulting confusion of the panicked crowd, Buck made good his escape. After the sergeant's death, Freedmen's Bureau Agent Capt. Edmond Miller, who served in Victoria, reported to his superiors about the problems that Buck and other Taylors were causing and asked for a squad of cavalry to bring the brigands to justice. The leaders of the undermanned military could not honor Miller's request because of manpower shortages, so Buck Taylor remained on the loose. He returned to Panola County, where he took delight in robbing and beating more freedmen.[34]

December of 1866 found several members of the Taylor gang on the San Antonio River not far from the San Antonio-Indianola Road. Jesus Gonzales,

Charles Glascock, Alex Reed, Tom and Bill Dodd, John and Jim Wright, and John Edwards rode up the river. About midnight, they came to a Tejano's home. They broke into the house and robbed the man. Alex Reed claimed to have gotten $115. Getting the money was not easy; the man's wife was game for a fight. John Wright made short work of her. He grabbed a butcher knife and cut the woman, wounding her severely. Then, the raiders were off to Karnes County to hide once again.[35]

Members of the gang remained active as a new year dawned. In January 1867, under the cover of darkness, Tom Dodd and Jim Wright stole four mules from a rural wagon yard near Helena in Karnes County, afterward fleeing to Gonzales County. They needed to dispose of the mules quickly before the rightful owner had time to alert area lawmen. They sold all four to a man called "Colonel Peoples," whose place was on the Guadalupe below Gonzales. Like Dodd and Wright, Buck Taylor and his band slipped back into the area and caused mayhem in both DeWitt and Victoria counties. According to Victoria's Freedmen's Bureau Agent, Buck's "band of outlaws," then working out of Yorktown, were endangering the lives of both whites and blacks. They made "pillaging" expeditions hurting both the citizens of the two counties and solitary travelers whom the gang stopped and robbed. The Victoria agent believed that if a cavalry squad would sweep the area, Buck and his men might be brought to heel.[36] Yet other Taylor raiders were operating in Lavaca County, the Bureau Agent in Hallettsville saying that the whole county was out of control because a "great majority of the people living in this section are a wild, low, wandering set [who have] no respect for man or God and bitterly oppose the United States Government."[37]

Concurrently, freedpeople, native Unionists, and army troops continued to have difficult and dangerous times. Bureau Agent Capt. W. H. Heinstand, stationed in Hallettsville, Lavaca County, wrote that in January 1867, Henry Kelly and other Taylor men had ridden into town, had gone to the saloon, and had started drinking. After he had gotten genteelly drunk, Kelly went out into the street and began tormenting a young freedman, hurling insult after insult at the youngster. Kelly then drew a knife and tried to kill the teenager. The freedman saved himself by running into Heinstand's office. Next, Kelly and his men surrounded the Bureau man's headquarters and threatened to burn the building down, thereby uttering two death threats. One of Kelly's men grabbed a freedgirl and tried to publicly rape her. The girl's mother fought back, however, and the youngster saved herself by running away. That night, Kelly and the others "visited" a Unionist, got into his home, and shot the place up, apparently just to spread terror, for no one in the home was wounded or killed. The next day, Kelly and friends caused more devilment until members of Heinstand's personal guards arrived from their county patrol, whereupon the cowardly Taylor raiders scattered rather than the face battle-tested professional soldiers who had lately won the Civil War. But, unless intimidated by military men who outnumbered them at the scene, Kelly and the others continued to threaten area freedpeople and generally spread terror. For that reason, in March Heinstand requested more troops.[38]

Concurrently, the politics and the governing of Texas underwent revolutionary changes that altered the nature of the Taylor crime ring. By January 1867, the national Republican party, dominated by those called "Radical Republicans," had taken control of Reconstruction away from the inept President Andrew Johnson, a Tennessean who had pro-white Southern sentiments. Then came the First Reconstruction Act on March 2, 1867. It was followed by the Second Reconstruction Act, which passed Congress on March 23 and added details not found in the first. Congress passed a third bill on July 19, allowing district commanders to remove office holders who impeded the process of Reconstruction. General Sheridan took advantage of the third law to remove the conservative ex-Confederate Throckmorton, who wanted few rights extended to the freedpeople beyond recognition of their physical freedom. The Unionist Elisha Pease replaced him. According to the new laws, civil government in Texas and the rest of the South was dissolved. The Republicans set up five military districts; Texas and Louisiana comprised the Fifth District. In all districts, major generals took charge of troops of occupation and set about fulfilling the terms of the Reconstruction Acts. General Sheridan became the first commander of the Fifth District. In turn, Sheridan appointed General Griffin to head the Department of Texas.

As in the rest of the South, in Texas the Reconstruction process included ratifying the Fourteenth Amendment and registering all adult males to vote, their number including the new freedmen. However, all potential voters had to take the "iron clad" oath, each person swearing that he had never been an official of the federal government and then renounced his federal oath and joined the Confederacy. Not everyone could truthfully take such an oath, and some men were disfranchised. Next would come elections to a new state constitutional convention wherein a democratic constitution would ratify the Thirteenth Amendment, which bans slavery. Then, popular elections were to follow. When the newly installed state government began to function, the troops of occupation would withdraw. When Congress passed the Reconstruction Acts, the South received a clear signal that ex-Confederate rule must end. However, many die-hard Rebels were most determined to remain in control. They continued to battle the Yankees, the freedpeople, and the native white Unionists. Since the Taylors had already been dubbed the "Southern party," the clan could now, once again, wrap itself in the Confederate flag, give lip service to the "Lost Cause," and continue using their crime ring to amass more wealth.[39]

Almost immediately, the Taylors' opposition to what was perceived as "Yankee rule" merged with the larger fight to defeat the Reconstruction process. The situation in Taylor Country became even more chaotic than before. For example, by mid-February 1867, Rebels in Calhoun County were threatening to murder white Union men if they did not leave the area. As well, former Confederates threatened to kill the teacher of Indianola's black school. Similarly, in Goliad County, brigands threatened to shoot the county officials, including a judge, and all other Union men. The raiders tried twice to assassinate the teacher of the Freedmen's Bureau school in Goliad town. Failing at that, the desperadoes threatened to keep trying until they were successful, prompting the teacher to request troops, for at the time there were none in the county.[40]

Taylor men caused another incident in Bastrop County in February. Led by Charlie Taylor, the raiders assaulted and robbed several freedmen who were riding along on the stage road. Afterward, one of the gang shot a harmless gypsy woman, a transient, wounding her severely. Next, after going into Webberville, the desperadoes found one man willing to fight back. After one of their number shot him, the wounded man retaliated and killed one of the men. Losing heart, Taylor and the other raiders scampered away, preferring not to truck with someone who could defend himself. According to the Bastrop County sheriff, notable citizens of the area well knew the identity of the marauders but were afraid to come forward for fear of being killed.[41]

The peaceable folk of Lavaca County were little better off, thanks to Taylor ally Henry Kelly who continued to cause chaos. Called "a dangerous man" by one observer, Kelly threatened the life of local Freedmen's Bureau Agent Heinstand, who feared for his life, especially since Kelly usually ran with a pack of malefactors, all members of the Taylor gang. Headquarters granted the agent's request for more men and sent him a squad of soldiers to reinforce others who were members of his personal guard. Now having more men, Heinstand searched for and found Kelly, whom he sent to the Columbus jail, for the one in Hallettsville was most unsound. Although Kelly was already a known felon, the immediate reason that Heinstand arrested him was that he (with another "desperate man") had broken into a freedman's house, robbed him, and at knife-point raped his teenaged daughter. However, a Columbus judge allowed Kelly to post bond; the rapist walked away a free man.[42]

Henry Kelly and his men were in Hallettsville again before the month of March expired. Calling Kelly a "desperate character," Bureau Agent Heinstand reported that he and his Taylor crowd of "roughs" had ridden into town and gotten drunk again and had cursed the United States government generally and Heinstand personally. Staggering out into the street, Kelly again threatened to clean out Heinstand's guard, now numbering fifteen men, and to take control of Lavaca County. Next, the "roughs" headed back to the saloon. After another drinking bout, Kelly grabbed a freedgirl and raped her. Heinstand was powerless to stop the crime because many of his soldiers were on patrol elsewhere. As well, the Taylor men were more numerous and more heavily armed than the Bureau man's small squad.[43]

More trouble with the Taylor raiders would come soon.

CHAPTER TWO

Continuing Mayhem

MORE violence occurred in South Texas as the year 1867 swept by. Much of it could be traced directly to the Taylor ring. For example, on March 17, raider Bateman Bell rode into Bastrop with several of the gang. Before the day had passed, Bell, who had been drinking, had harsh words with Unionist John Catchings, the result being that Bell tried to beat Catchings to death. Local lawmen interfered. They arrested Bell and charged him with assault with intent to murder. However, the authorities released him after he posted a $1,200 bond. Bell was busy again just six days later. He assaulted freedman Guilford Harrison on Bastrop's main street, hitting and kicking him. When Harrison took advantage of an opportunity to run away, Bell grabbed a club and chased him, intending to kill him, but the desperado could not catch his prey. A few days later, Bell caught Catchings again, this time killing him before riding out of town with other Taylor raiders. A hard case, Bell had five area indictments against him for horse theft and cattle rustling, but he paid a total bail of $4,300 on all charges so that he could remain on the loose and could continue to operate as part of the Taylor ring. It is interesting that Bell was part of the riffraff of the area but could still come up with $4,300, which suggests that he had rich backers or that he himself was making money "hand over fist" when he rode with the Taylors.[1]

DeWitt County also experienced chaos. On April 11, 1867, Lavaca County's Thomas Dodd, who often worked for the Taylors, and two cohorts approached the ferry across the Guadalupe River. Hungry, the trio went to the house of a freedman, found two women at home, and forced them to prepare a meal. All three whites had been drinking, but Dodd was the only one who became drunk. And a mean drunk he was. He became violent and overbearing toward the women even as they worked to satisfy the demands of their unwelcome guests. Dodd then threatened to shoot one of his companions, only to have the other one talk him out of that rash course. Then a small black boy, age five or six, started to climb up on one of the window sills of the cabin, whereupon Dodd drew a sixgun and fired at the boy, missing him by only a few inches. Shortly thereafter, a teenage black named Wintz approached the home, popping two quirts as he walked. Dodd took great exception to the popping quirts and asked the youngster why he was popping them. The young fellow said he was doing it just for fun, but the answer did not please the drunkard who told the youngster that "I have a damned good notion to shoot you. By God, I believe I will."[2]

Dodd grabbed his double-barrel shotgun and fired a round directly at Wintz's chest. Blown backward, the teenager died instantly because some of the buckshot penetrated his heart. The murderer still wanted to eat, but his companions convinced him that they must flee, for the law might appear. They mounted up, rode to the ferry, crossed the river, and cut the fastenings of the boat, causing it to drift downstream. That act effectively prevented any pursuit, and the three men went hungrily on their way. A group of irate DeWitt County citizens petitioned the governor, explaining what happened and asking him to put a reward on Dodd's head, but the man was not apprehended even though they gave a good description of him. He was about twenty-one years old and weighed about 160 pounds. He had a light complexion, blue eyes, and light hair that was almost red.[3]

Soon Tom Dodd caused more trouble. Riding with Charlie Taylor, John Thompson (alias John Tope), and Jim and John Wright in April 1867, he attempted to rob an Army commissary train whose men were camped near a farmer's house not far from Gonzales. But barking dogs alerted the squad of soldiers guarding the wagons. The troopers foiled the desperadoes' plans of a sneak attack; nevertheless, the brigands began shooting at the soldiers, who quickly returned fire. While the military men were thus tied down, Dodd managed to steal three of the farmer's mules. All the raiders then galloped away with the mules in tow. They rode to Creed Taylor's ranch in Wilson County where they hid for a time. The mules? Tom Dodd sold two, and Bill Dodd bartered the other one for various items.[4]

The Taylor gang's murderous careers did not go unnoticed by the DeWitt County Sheriff's Office. The sheriff assigned the young Deputy Sheriff William "Bill" Sutton the task of tracking the clan and their raiders. The youngster was a Southerner, the son of Jack Sutton of Tennessee who came to Texas in 1842. Bill was born in the Lone Star State in Fayette County near LaGrange on October 20, 1846. When he was still quite young, his father embarked on a trading journey, but he disappeared and was never heard from again. Indians may well have ended his life. His mother later remarried, and William McDonald became his stepfather. By 1850, Bill had moved with his family to DeWitt County where his stepfather established a farm near Clinton. Along with his older brother James, Bill helped McDonald develop his land by serving as a field hand.[5]

When the Civil War began, the seventeen-year-old Billy joined the Confederate army. He seemed to have had an uneventful military experience without undue hardships, and he came home alive and well. He soon became a deputy sheriff in addition to becoming a cattleman in the era of the South Texas open range. In December 1869, he established a place near the DeWitt-Victoria County line on the south bank of Irish Creek on the Victoria-Gonzales Road. An impressive looking young man, Sutton was about six feet tall. Blue-eyed with a fair complexion, he had light curly hair and a slight mustache. In 1871, he married his stepfather's daughter Laura McDonald, with whom he had grown up. From 1865 onward, he was on the lookout for Buck and the other Taylors who committed crimes.[6]

Sutton had compassion for the freedpeople, most of whom were mired in poverty and had to cope with white violence, too. Compared to the rest of Texas, the extent of racial crimes in Taylor Country seemed similar as the days of 1866 and 1867 rolled by. For example, Freedmen's Bureau Agent Capt. Edwin Miller, stationed in Victoria, believed that race relations in his subdistrict were good overall in 1866, but he mentioned that recently a murderer had killed one freedman while several whites had staged a race riot and assaulted several black men, the cause of the altercation unknown. Miller reported in January 1867 that race relations seemed to have turned for the worst because of attacks by young men like Hays and Doughboy Taylor on freedpeople. The attacks at times defied logic, for they were tampering with white society's cheap labor pool. Indeed, Miller maintained that young men such as Hays and Doughboy holding Rebel sentiments caused much more trouble than the older generations. Writing from Victoria, Miller told superiors that when problems came up, the fault usually lay with "half grown rowdies," a comment referring to the fact that mostly younger men committed most of the acts of violence. Some older men knew better.[7]

Soon, rowdy Doughboy was into mischief again. On April 15, 1867, he attended a horse race in DeWitt County. After losing a bet, he had an argument with William North, a freedman. Although he now owed North money because of their mutual betting, Doughboy refused to pay. When North argued, Taylor assaulted the man, beating him severely. But Taylor raiders usually settled arguments with guns, and Doughboy's disagreement was no exception. To add to North's terror, not to mention his pain, Doughboy shot the man in the thigh, took the money wagered, and fled the vicinity, only to pop up later at a race in another area.[8]

William "Bill" Sutton
and Laura McDonald
Sutton on their
wedding day (1871).
Courtesy Sharon Barnes,
Director, Regional History
Center at the Victoria
College/University of
Houston at Victoria Library

On May 24, 1867, Thomas Dodd was again causing trouble in Clinton. After getting drunk, he decided to "test his ability as a marksman," whereupon he looked about until he spotted a freedman at whom he fired. After Dodd missed the shot, the freedman ran away. Dodd wanted to test himself further. Looking about again, he spotted a small freedgirl and shot at her, too, before deciding it was a good time to leave town. Had Dodd been sober, he likely would have killed both of his targets. Shortly after the renegade's target practice, one Davis, a Taylor man, caused grief in Fort Bend County by killing a freedman for no apparent reason except racial hatred. Authorities found and arrested Davis, took him to Columbus, and tossed him in jail. However, he escaped soon after being indicted for his crime.[9]

Shortly after the latest shootings, Lavaca County Deputy Sheriff Jack

Helm had occasion to track horse thieves. Leaving from Hallettsville, Helm went all the way to the Red River before losing the trail of the robbers as they escaped into Indian Territory. He reported to the military that the entire interior of Texas was alive with terrorist Klan groups and organized bands of outlaw raiders, all of whom were responsible for the general breakdown of law and order. Indeed, often those gangs and terrorists cooperated with one another to spread their mayhem. Helm related that a major band operated in Lavaca, DeWitt, and adjacent counties that numbered at least two hundred men. He was referring to the Taylor ring when he mentioned that all belonged to a "secret organization" for the purposes of cattle rustling and horse theft.[10]

The crime ring was also operating in Lampasas, Bastrop, Brazoria, and Colorado counties. Continuing, Helm said that operating in Bell County was one gang he numbered at about a dozen. He counted separate fourteen-member bands in Bosque and McLennan counties even though they probably did not ride with the Taylors. Worse, a band numbering about twenty-five infested Johnson County. As he moved from Johnson County to the Red River, such raiders were organized in every county that he traversed. Civil officers, Helm said, could not contend with such men because the desperadoes ran in their packs and usually outnumbered—and could therefore trample on—the posses of county sheriffs and town marshals. Helm insisted that such bands did not have political motives even if they claimed to support the South's "Lost Cause." Rather, they were common criminals, rabble who only used the Confederacy's defeat as a smoke screen to make themselves appear as honorable. Their ruse worked to a degree; Helm pointed out that in any area, some of the common folk with Rebel sympathies always helped the marauders. As well, such criminals continued to do work that the Democrats wanted done: destabilize and bring chaos to Texas.[11]

Helm had no sooner returned home when people from both Lavaca and DeWitt counties beseeched him to take more action to bring the area's desperadoes to heel. The men of the two counties petitioned General Griffin to give Helm a special appointment that would allow him to go after all raiders wherever they might be; in other words, they wanted him to have special jurisdiction that would cut across county lines. Further, the petitioners wanted the general to assign to Helm a special military "police force" to help him corral lawbreakers wherever found. Although the wishes of the petitioners were not granted, their proposal was a precursor of the State Police that the Texas Republican Party organized later. McLennan County's D. D. Stubblefield and Captain James Emerson, stationed at Waco, added their voices to those coming from the Lavaca and DeWitt petitioners. Stubblefield and Emerson both believed that Helm could be most effective on a regional level if the military command would support him.[12]

According to an anonymous writer who contacted military authorities in mid-1867, the Taylors stepped up both their cattle rustling and their war against anyone who opposed them. They had begun a "reign of terror," said the informant, that was "complete and absolute." Killings became the order of the day. According to one observer, "death by gunshot" was the usual coroner's report. Meanwhile, Creed Taylor denied it all and wrote biting letters to military authorities criticizing those whom the Taylors persecuted. Other than spinning one falsehood after another, Creed remained behind the scenes, preferring to have his sons and their men do the dirty work necessary for the continuing success of the ring.[13]

More trouble came fast. Writing from Seguin in early July, Freedmen's Bureau Agent Maj. George W. Smith reported a horrific act perpetrated by "the Crede Taylor band of outlaws." In late April, at Lavernia in Wilson County, Buck, Martin, and Charlie Taylor, along with Jim Wright and a couple more men ventured onto a property where a black sharecropper lived. In the pay of area whites, they intended to run him off so his employer could claim that he broke his labor contract. That way, the employer could claim all the crops. The Taylor men jumped their horses into the sharecropper's front yard, and when he asked them off his place, they lashed him with their quirts, stinging him with every blow. The man tried to escape; he ran into one field and then through another as the malefactors pursued, all the while shooting at the man. After riding him down, Buck told the man to lie down on his stomach. Next, the horsemen cut loose with their weapons. They fired repeatedly at the man, hitting him several times in the head and several times in the body. According to Smith, the freedman's face was not recognizable once the savages were finished. The murderers left only a mass of goo.[14]

After the killing, Buck and his men remained in Lavernia for several days, defying the local peace officer and daring him to try to arrest them. Then, the raiders pulled out for San Antonio. Agent Smith investigated the incident, discovered a few facts, but disgustedly wrote superiors that most people in town, including those who saw the crime, refused to talk with him. Yet, Smith already knew generally about the Taylor clan's crimes. In Wilson County, they numbered about twenty-five men, and Creed Taylor directed them, said Smith. They spread terror throughout the county. Smith held Creed to be as guilty as the men who murdered the Lavernia freedman. Meanwhile, other gang members attacked other blacks, the aim being the same: run the blacks off so the white landlords could claim their share of crops.[15]

Later, the authorities located Creed Taylor and questioned him about the

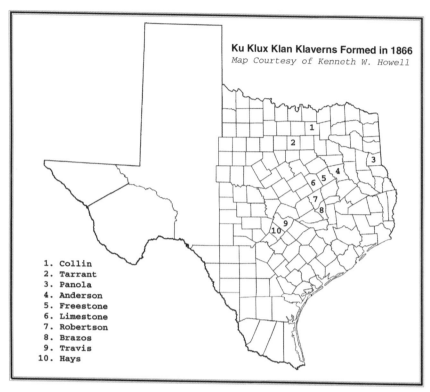

Ku Klux Klan Klaverns Formed in 1866
Map Courtesy of Kenneth W. Howell

1. Collin
2. Tarrant
3. Panola
4. Anderson
5. Freestone
6. Limestone
7. Robertson
8. Brazos
9. Travis
10. Hays

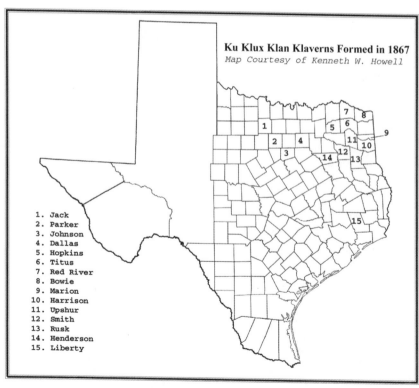

Ku Klux Klan Klaverns Formed in 1867
Map Courtesy of Kenneth W. Howell

1. Jack
2. Parker
3. Johnson
4. Dallas
5. Hopkins
6. Titus
7. Red River
8. Bowie
9. Marion
10. Harrison
11. Upshur
12. Smith
13. Rusk
14. Henderson
15. Liberty

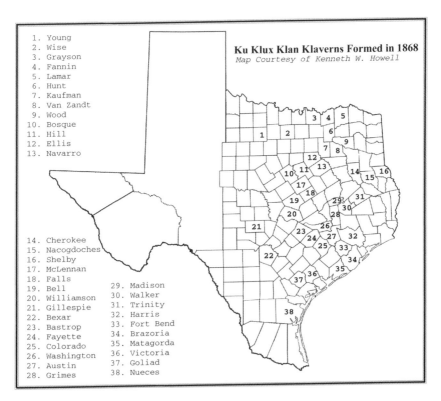

1. Young
2. Wise
3. Grayson
4. Fannin
5. Lamar
6. Hunt
7. Kaufman
8. Van Zandt
9. Wood
10. Bosque
11. Hill
12. Ellis
13. Navarro

14. Cherokee
15. Nacogdoches
16. Shelby
17. McLennan
18. Falls
19. Bell
20. Williamson
21. Gillespie
22. Bexar
23. Bastrop
24. Fayette
25. Colorado
26. Washington
27. Austin
28. Grimes

29. Madison
30. Walker
31. Trinity
32. Harris
33. Fort Bend
34. Brazoria
35. Matagorda
36. Victoria
37. Goliad
38. Nueces

Ku Klux Klan Klaverns Formed in 1868
Map Courtesy of Kenneth W. Howell

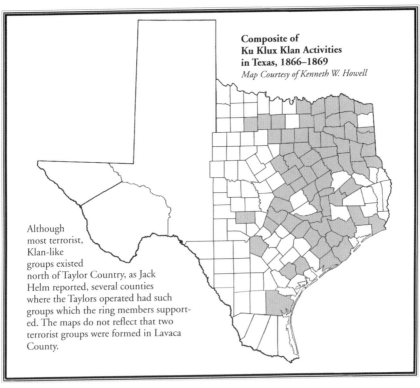

Composite of Ku Klux Klan Activities in Texas, 1866–1869
Map Courtesy of Kenneth W. Howell

Although most terrorist, Klan-like groups existed north of Taylor Country, as Jack Helm reported, several counties where the Taylors operated had such groups which the ring members supported. The maps do not reflect that two terrorist groups were formed in Lavaca County.

Lavernia killing. He said that while the Lavernia tragedy was occurring, he was nowhere near. He was riding from his Wilson County place to his spread in San Saba County that was managed by one of his kinsmen. On the road a number of men, some his relatives, some his employees, overtook him. Then Creed named the heart of the Taylor crime ring, of course not admitting that fact: He listed Doughboy, Hays, and Charlie Taylor; T. C. and George West; John Bunch; David Thorp; Rufus Weaver; Jim Wright; and David and William "Ran" Spencer. According to Creed, his friend Harry Standard had ridden up and informed him that the authorities in Lavernia had accused some of his "party" of the murder. Creed said he questioned the men in camp, whereupon Charlie Taylor spun a tale. He said he had been in Lavernia and he rode into a freedman's yard to light his pipe. On the face of it, Charlie's statement was ridiculous if not downright stupid. He could have stopped on the road to light the pipe. Yet, as he explained, the freedman took exception to Charlie being in his yard and grabbed a hoe intending to strike him.[16]

Only then, in self-defense, did the righteous renegade draw his sixgun and club the black man with it. Then the freedman ran into a field while Taylor and Wright pursued. But he stopped and pulled a knife, whereupon the two white men shot him to death. According to Creed, the action that Charlie and Wright took was clearly self-defense.[17] The military authorities believed Creed not a twit. They continued to search for the murderers. Indeed, General Griffin ordered his subordinates to go after the "band of outlaws" and to use "extreme measures" if necessary, adding that the band had to be "destroyed." The general told his men to seize any property that belonged to gang members and to consider the property as payments for fines.[18]

While various men in the Taylor ring were escaping the law, George Blackburn of the ring aroused authorities in Goliad County, while Jim and John Dodd and another Taylor man were causing chaos in Seguin, Guadalupe County. On July 16, 1867, Blackburn assaulted with intent to kill Mitchell Walton. Then, later the same day Blackburn and cohort William Brocken assaulted with intent to kill a Mrs. Cofter, but the causes of the twin attacks are not known. Just a little later, two of the Dodd brothers, along with an unnamed friend, were riding through Seguin when they noticed a small freedgirl looking out a window. The girl was crying. Not willing to face her tears, all three desperadoes drew their handguns and fired at the girl, one shot grazing her forehead. She was fated to live, for the brigands rode away while cursing their bad marksmanship.[19]

Hays Taylor and a hired gunman caused mayhem in DeWitt County in August 1867. After riding into Clinton, Hays had a disagreement with freedman William North, cause unknown but perhaps related to his brother's debt to North, which Doughboy refused to pay before he assaulted and shot the man. Just as his brother had earlier done, Hays assaulted and battered the man before shooting him; the freedman died a short time later. When he saw North down, another black man quickly ran to local Bureau Agent Hiram Clark and told him what had happened. Clark went to the scene intending to investigate and perhaps to arrest Hays if the charges appeared true, but Taylor vaulted atop his horse and rode away before Clark could take effective action.[20]

Almost simultaneously, Taylor gunman Henry Westfall caused more chaos in Clinton. After he used foul language when he addressed a group of freedwomen, an elderly black lady dared rebuke him for vulgarity. Westfall took great exception to being rebuked; he beat the old woman severely. A few days later, he assaulted yet another black woman. He not only struck her with his fists, he also produced a cane knife and cut her, leaving a horrible wound. Authorities could not establish a motive for Westfall's second attack. With lawmen now after him, the desperado left DeWitt County and rode for Brazoria County, where he immediately caused trouble again by assaulting with intent to kill the freedman Richard Blackburn.[21]

While Hays, Doughboy, Buck, and Martin Taylor and gang members like Westfall were looking over their shoulders every day to avoid authorities, in August 1867, other Taylor raiders added to the chaos. They marked two outspoken Victoria County freedmen—James Wilkerson and the youngster Martin Dickinson—for death because they had become informants to the military authorities. Upon learning that they were targets, the two blacks fled the vicinity, but the raiders, numbering thirteen gunmen, caught up with them in Goliad County. The murderer Wiley Pridgen—the brother of lawyer Bolivar J. Pridgen, a firm Taylor man who had been retained by Creed Taylor to protect his family's interests and who would soon become a member of the Texas Legislature—led what was called a "vigilance committee." Its members included James Patterson whom a grand jury had already indicted for murders committed in Victoria and Harris counties and for a robbery committed in DeWitt County.[22]

The "committee" soon caught its quarry. Along with the others, Patterson shot Wilkinson to death on a road near Goliad, the man dying from multiple gunshot wounds, but young Dickinson managed to flee. He rode into the military post in Goliad town and sought protection. After he told Capt. P. C. Holcomb of the affray, the officer took the field with a squad and managed to captured three of the shooters: A. G. Brown, Jordan Perkins, and Henry Thompson. But most of the party, including Pridgen, escaped. However, as Holcomb told Gen. J. J. Reynolds, he doubted that the civil authorities would convict the three murderers, for the area remained awash with Confederate sympathizers. Later, just as Holcomb predicted, a judge of a civil court allowed the felons low bail and released them to once more bedevil Unionists and freedpeople.[23]

Such chaos led several Victoria County residents to petition Capt. P. A. Lathrop, now commanding the post of Victoria. They complained about the "bad state of affairs" in their county. In turn, Lathrop complained to state headquarters that he could do but little. He only had infantrymen, and they were widely scattered across his district. He told superiors that he could be effective if he had just a "few mounted men." If headquarters could not give him cavalry, he asked if he could accept offers of citizens to loan him horses, up to ten in number.[24] The situation of military men all across the interior of Texas mirrored Lathrop's plight.

The "vigilantes," still led by Wiley Pridgen, targeted DeWitt County's Seabury Phillips for special treatment. The gang had assaulted freedman Seabury's wife who went to Goliad to make a complaint. Officials there told her to take the complaint to Victoria. Instead, she wrote a letter, and her husband rode toward the new destination to deliver it. But along the way, Pridgen, leading a group of about twenty-five men, attacked him about dark on the Yorktown-Victoria Road. Seabury knew to let his mount run, and run it did. The gang pursued for five or six miles until the would-be victim managed to lose them. He forgot his Victoria business and returned home, later sending a youngster to deliver the letter. Still later, Pridgen and gang threatened to kill him just as they would have if they had caught up to him on the road. Philips complained to the authorities and asked for some protection lest the vandals return and finish their mission to eliminate him.[25]

Pridgen was not the only man in the Taylor ring causing havoc. Recruiting more men, the raiders—led by Buck, Hays, and Doughboy (after he returned to the area) and Bob F. Civas—became bolder and openly challenged military and civil authorities, white Unionists, and freedpeople who tried to exercise their new liberties. Such developments convinced five worried women from Yorktown in DeWitt County to write their influential friend Theo Hertzberg, a politician in San Antonio. They asked him to contact military leaders there to lobby for sending troops to the Yorktown area. Led by Henrietta Frey and Nora Gugenheim, the women reported that the Taylor gang's atrocities included the recent murder of white Unionist Edmond Edwards and his son Walter. Yet the civil officials refused to bring the killers to justice. Although the sheriff tried to gather a posse to bring the Taylors in, Buck and Martin threatened area civilians, saying that anyone who supported the sheriff would suffer immediate death.[26]

According to the women from Yorktown, Buck, his cousin Martin, and some Taylor raiders were forever up to no good in and around their town.

Yorktown was the scene of much action related to the Taylor ring. Pictured here are structures in downtown Yorktown that date from the Reconstruction era.

Of all the gang members, the women considered Martin to be the most dangerous, for he seemed to have a "murderer's personality." The ladies reported that the gang had lately beaten a man who taught in the freedmen's school in the area and that they had earlier robbed a number of travelers. Led by Buck and Martin, the gang was still determined to eliminate anyone who opposed them. That determination caused them to be indicted for the attempted murder of a man named Meyers who incurred the wrath of the raiders for cause unknown. The Taylors went to Meyers's home and tried to kill both him and his wife, but when Buck shot at the man, his gun misfired, whereupon Meyers's wife fainted while the would-be victim took advantage of the misfire to run to a neighbor's house to seek a weapon and ask for help. Next, the Taylors fired on women and children who had heard the commotion and rushed to Mrs. Meyers's assistance, but when the Taylors rode away, there were no fatalities. The renegades next sought Unionist Edmond Edwards and his son, Walter, mentioned previously. After setting up an ambush, the raiders shot and killed both father and son. After the twin murders, one woebegone Unionist exclaimed that every day decent folk were confronted by and forced to cope with the dangerous "band of banditti" who "defied all the laws and duties of civilization."[27]

The Yorktown women held that it was truly horrible for settlers on the frontier to be victims of Indian depredations, but they needed military protection, too. The ladies insisted that the Taylor gang, whose chief "occupation" was "theft and murder," made it unsafe and truly horrible for citizens of the interior who needed help to stop the lawlessness. The women wanted help but reported that the renegades would be hard to catch because their supporters warned them anytime troopers or other authorities were near.[28]

The same month that the Yorktown women complained about their plight, Gen. Winfield Scott Hancock, the new commander of the Fifth Military District, took action that defied logic and greatly harmed the peaceful folk of Texas by hamstringing the forces of law and order. A pre-war Democrat with Southern sympathies, Hancock issued General Order 40 on November 29, 1867. It required military commanders to turn over all prisoners held and any caught later to civil authorities for trial. The order virtually guaranteed that many prisoners would go free, never having to pay any penalties if their only targets were white Unionists, military men, or freedpeople. According to the Texas Legislature's Special Committee on Lawlessness and Violence, prior to Hancock's order some malefactors had to at least think twice before committing their crimes because of the fear that the military might arrest them and then haul them before a military commission for trial. The special committee pointed out that the murder and robbery rates went up tremendously after field commanders implemented General Order 40. The committee complained that Hancock "turned a deaf ear" to the cries of white Unionists and freedpeople when they notified him of ill treatment. As well, Hancock seemed not to care when raiders attacked his own men, attacks that often took the form of cold-blooded murder. Terrorists and raiders like the Taylor bunch stepped up their activities because they knew that they had little to fear from the authorities.[29]

As late as the end of 1867, ex-Rebels were still in control of Taylor Country. In Lavaca and Calhoun counties, for example, the old secessionists controlled the courts. In DeWitt County several former Confederates were in positions of power. The same was true for Victoria County where a Rebel posing as a Union man became county judge while having three indictments against him for cattle rustling and one for horse theft. As well, Unionists in Goliad made complaints, some asking that the military authorities remove Rebel county officials and replace them with loyal men. Otherwise, the county would remain out of control. The Goliad Union League's A. M. Boatright, the mayor of Goliad town, told General Reynolds that a total "house cleaning" was necessary if law and order was to be restored. As well, the mayor said a Klan group was operating in his county, its disguised members committing mayhem. Likewise, men with Confederate sympathies controlled Karnes County, for voters elected them on the same ticket with

Democrat Throckmorton. That was most important, for one of Creed Taylor's main ranching operations was there, and it was there that others in the crime ring hid when necessary. However, the raiders were active in all the counties mentioned previously.[30]

Agent Hiram Clark's district saw yet more trouble on September 20, 1867, in DeWitt County. The killer Wiley Pridgen of Thomston argued with Neill Brown of Mission Valley about a horse. Pridgen was riding it, but it was one of Brown's horses that had been stolen earlier. The two men exchanged hard words, after which Pridgen drew a gun, fired it once, and shot Brown stone dead. Clark hurried to the scene, arrested Pridgen, and later labeled the shooting a "cold-blooded murder," for Brown was armed but had not drawn his weapon. Later, Wiley managed to escape from Clinton's rather porous makeshift jail. Into the future, he remained in the Taylor ring and continued to cause chaos. But, according to at least one source, Brown's widow raised her young son with but one purpose. She told him everything that had happened to his father on the day of his death. She raised her son to kill the man who murdered her husband, his father. Eventually, the boy-become-man did exactly that.[31]

General Phillip Sheridan, who replaced Hancock as commander of the Fifth Military District, confirmed that Rebels controlled Taylor Country as well as the rest of settled Texas. Reporting to the War Department in November 1867, he averred that general lawlessness prevailed in the Lone Star State and that attempts to undermine the national government were rife. He added that "nearly every civil functionary, from the Governor [Throckmorton] on down, had been soldiers or aiders and abettors in the Rebellion, and that in nearly all cases they had been elected on Confederate grounds, and solely for services rendered in their attempts to destroy the general Government. In fact, many, if not all, had advertized when they were candidates, their service in this respect as a meritorious appeal for votes."[32]

In November 1867, Creed, Hays, and Doughboy Taylor, along with in-law R. W. "Ran" Spencer and gang members James Cooke, Fred Pell, and George Kellison, rode to Mason County and set up their camp at Centennial Springs in the hills not far from Fort Mason. They began a rustling operation, stealing other people's cattle and selling them to a contractor. For a diversion, they went into Mason town to participate in horse races, their horses pitted against those owned by Jim Crosby and B. F. Gooch. Creed had a new horse named Cotton-eye and believed that the steed was fast enough to win a goodly sum of money during the competitions. After they arrived in town a day early, the younger men headed for a local saloon while Creed rode to his nephew George Bird's farm to visit.[33]

After Creed was on his way, an altercation occurred between the thieves and a group of troopers who belonged to the Fourth United States Cavalry stationed at Fort Mason. Hays had an argument with a black sergeant, John McDougall, the exact cause of the disagreement unknown. The sergeant may well have recognized the Taylor brothers and their brother-in-law Spencer since all three were known felons. When the sergeant tried to draw his gun, likely to arrest the young men, Doughboy drew faster and used his sixgun to club McDougall to the ground. Then, he, Hays, and Spencer held their guns on the entire group of troopers, obviously for the purpose of controlling them and coming out of the fracas alive. From inside a store, the post commander Maj. John A. Thompson heard the loud voices and the scuffling outside. Going out to end the disturbance, he drew his gun and tried to arrest the Taylor men. Hays, Doughboy, and Spencer then shot Thompson multiple times before Hays fired a bullet that struck the major in the right cheek before cutting his carotid artery, causing a fatal hemorrhage. The major's distraught wife was one of the eyewitnesses of the killing. Her wails continued as she got on her knees, cradled her husband's head in her arms, and watched him bleed to death.[34]

Just as Thompson was falling, Sergeant McDougall struggled to his feet while hearing the widow's mournful cries. He again tried to draw his revolver, whereupon Spencer shot him, the bullet hitting the sergeant in the upper arm. Then, Hays fired a lethal round, and the target fell dead with a hole in his head. Some sources held that a third soldier also died in the gunplay, but that report cannot be verified. The gang continued to hold off retaliation by training their guns on the remaining handful of troopers. The renegades walked backward to reach their horses, mounted them, and made a fast getaway. The confused and leaderless Yankees could not effectively mount a chase. The two terrible Taylors, Spencer, and other gang members first rode to Bird's farm where they talked with Creed, who always aided other Taylors in their criminal deeds. He told his sons "to get away as fast as possible," before the Yankees showed up. As fast as their horses would carry them, the killers rode to Honey Creek Rocks, an area of rough country about six miles away. They remained hidden there for three days. They only ventured forth at night, going to a friend's ranch to secure food and water. On the third night, Creed met the boys and explained his plan. He had hired his friend George Gamel as a guide to escort the killers safely out of the area. Gamel took them as far as Crab Apple Creek in Gillespie County before he turned back for home. Shortly, the malefactors scattered, trying to throw the authorities off their trail. Their tactics were good, for early scouts turned up no leads. Soon, however, Hays and Doughboy rejoined their father at their old operation on the Ecleto in Karnes County. Troopers came to Creed's spread but could not find the young guns who were now sleeping in the bush and who appeared in the open only when friends told them it was safe to do so.[35]

Thompson's murder spurred authorities to take more action. First, an investigation confirmed the identity of the killers. As well, military personnel learned that both Taylor brothers lived on their father's ranch on the Ecleto, while Spencer lived in Helena. Orders went out from military headquarters in San Antonio to track down and to arrest not only Doughboy, Hays, and Spencer, but also Buck and Martin Taylor who had last been seen in DeWitt County. Indeed, Buck now had a new charge pending against him. He sought and found freedman E. Selfridge because the man had given military authorities information about Buck's murders and robberies. When Buck found the man, he quickly drew a gun and shot Selfridge in the arm and neck; however, the freedman survived. Commanders put Lts. Charles A. Vernou and William V. Wolfe in charge of about sixty men whose job it was to search for the desperadoes. As was becoming common, the troopers made a thorough scout but could not find their quarry, for the men knew to flee the area of their crimes and ride into another county where they slept in the bush and adopted aliases.[36]

Soon, however, military officials learned that the Taylors had left Karnes County and had fled to Creed's ranch in Wilson County. In mid-November, commanders ordered Maj. George W. Smith to make a thorough scout. Lieutenant Vernou was Smith's second in command. With about fifty men, Smith and Vernou intended to find the murderers of Thompson and to find and arrest Buck and Martin and any men with them. Leaving San Antonio on November 16, the squad rode to Seguin. They reached the ranch the next day but found none of their quarry. They found two women and a man on the place. The latter was a hired hand, tending to the stock on the spread. All three appeared innocent. The detail let them be after the man told Smith that the Taylors had left and had gone to their operation in San Saba County. The major's men searched the house and confiscated four weapons found within. Smith also took four fresh horses that his officers needed. Then the detail rode to Kelly's Stage Stand on the San Antonio–Yorktown Road, for the major had received intelligence that Buck and Martin Taylor were in that area. Once there, the detail did not find the Taylors but did arrest T. C. West, who had in the previous summer helped the Taylor gang murder the freedman in Lavernia.

Equally important, Smith learned where Buck was living. The major hired the guide Sol Brown who led him and a detachment of fifteen men to Buck's place. But, unknown to Smith, his guide was a Taylor man. In the early morning at dawn, Brown indeed led them to the place but took the most obvious, exposed route possible. When Smith realized what Brown had done, he decided that there was little to do but charge the place. Smith and a few men stormed into the house only to find Buck gone. However, his wife was there, and Smith noted that she had just made her and her husband's breakfast, which was still hot and sitting on the kitchen table. He noted that the guide, Brown, had make a clean getaway while the troopers were concentrating on the house. The wife told Smith very little, but she did say that Buck had escaped out the back door and quickly mounted his horse, sans saddle or bridle.

According to the wife, Buck had earlier told her that he would never be taken alive. He reminded her that when a captain and his squad had earlier tried to take him, he had killed the captain and three of his men. Before leaving his wife, Buck said he could probably kill three or four of Smith's men but he preferred to fight another day when he held the advantage. After learning all that he could, Smith took Buck's shotgun, saddle, and bridle and directed his men to Watt Anderson's house near Yorktown, Anderson being Buck's father-in-law. Also suspected of a murder, he had hidden members of the Taylor gang previously. Anderson was not home. People in the area refused to give Smith any information for fear of reprisals. However, one brave soul volunteered to Smith that while he did not know the whereabouts of Buck or Anderson, he knew that Charlie Taylor, Jim Wright, and the brothers Mat and Clint Peace were making their headquarters in the Yorktown area, but the informer did not know the exact place.[37]

At that point, Smith knew that his scout was a failure. Disgusted, he led his detail back to San Antonio. However, he detached five men to go to Gonzales town to try to find and arrest Ed Glover, a crime ring member who was wanted for the murder of a freedman and the attempted murder of another one, both from Seguin. The squad found Glover's place, but, as was becoming typical, the man was not at home. The troopers confiscated a sixgun, a rifle, and a shotgun before leaving. Reporting to his superior, Smith mentioned that he had heard that Martin Taylor was in Atascosa County and that he had sent a few men to investigate, but the squad had no success.[38]

Almost concurrent with Smith's failed scout, Horton in Hallettsville had another clash with Taylor man Henry Kelly, described by some later pro-Confederate historians as a "fine upstanding citizen." October 20, 1867, was a day of entertainment for Lavaca County folks and all visitors from elsewhere. That day, horse races thrilled the crowd that assembled just outside town. Unfortunately, heavy betting was accompanied by heavier drinking on the part of some men. During the day, Kelly got drunk, as usual, and started bedeviling a freedman, cause unknown. The "fine upstanding citizen" assaulted the black fellow, beating him severely. Horton learned of the incident, found Kelly, and had his squad subdue him. The Bureau Agent then arrested him on a charge of assault and battery. Horton turned the brigand over to civil authorities. He should not have, for Kelly quickly escaped jail, commandeered a mount, and spurred the steed away, heading for the safe havens of parts unknown.[39]

While Kelly was causing havoc in Lavaca County, Taylor man W. J. A. Bell was deviling Bastrop County while another Taylor raider, Ben F. Prior, raised hell in Walker County. On November 11, Bell rode into Bastrop town and went about the place looking for Bureau Agent Byron Porter. Seeing the agent crossing a street, Bell waylaid him. With a loaded sixgun in his hand, Bell threatened to kill the agent. However, Bell must have been intimidated by the professional soldier, for Porter managed to wrest the gun from him, place him under arrest, and toss him into the Bastrop jail, from whence the renegade quickly escaped. Almost simultaneously, Prior—conspiring with cohorts J. O. Stevens, Richard Slades, and Thomas B. Slades—assaulted with intent to kill another Bureau Agent. The raiders attacked the man simply because he represented Yankee authority and was doing a good job as the local Bureau man.[40]

Although Taylor men seemed to always escape from the grasp of the law, military authorities from Fort Inge heard interesting news on December 3, 1867. An informer told officers that two men, one matching the description of Doughboy, had just passed through nearby Uvalde, heading south toward Mexico. On receiving the news, Capt. E. J. Conway dispatched a lieutenant and ten troopers to track down the two strangers. The squad found Doughboy after he stopped for the night at the Turkey Creek settlement on the El Paso Road. Although Taylor managed to make a break for the nearby woods, the lieutenant confiscated his horse, saddle, weapons, and various personal items. The squad then returned to Fort Inge but left two of their number in a hidden place in case Taylor returned to reclaim the horse and other property. Indeed, Doughboy returned at first light the next day. The two troopers arrested him and marched him to Fort Inge. Although he stoutly denied that he was Doughboy Taylor, Captain Conway was not fooled and knew that his men had corralled one of the key leaders of the Taylor gang. However, once the young murderer was placed in the hands of civilian authorities, he managed an easy escape.[41] He would soon cause trouble again.

Open Warfare

LTHOUGH Doughboy remained on the loose, the Taylor gang was reduced by one in a bizarre development. Lawmen in Clinton arrested one McClannahan who was wanted for horse theft; he also had an indictment pending against him in Lavaca County and had earlier broken out of jail in Gonzales. To make sure that he did not escape, deputies chained him in the basement of the jail, one that had only one entrance, a trap door in the first floor. After enduring confinement for a time, McClannahan wrote to some Taylor men that if they did not rescue him, he would turn state's witness and implicate various of the ring's men in a laundry list of crimes. The Taylor men, however, refused to truck with such a turncoat. On the night of January 19, 1868, several of them overpowered a guard, got into the jail, found and opened the trap door, and shot McClannahan to death after using a "fire ball" to illuminate the basement. The man was in chains, could not move about, and made an easy target.[1]

Almost simultaneously, Lieutenant J. D. Verney, after completing an assignment, stopped in Helena for a night's rest before going on to San Antonio. While there, he talked with a brother-in-law of one of the Taylors. The man had loose lips. He told Verney that the clan intended to assassinate Major Smith because he dogged the murderers of Major Thompson. He threatened to arrest Doughboy and Hays if he could find them. That being the case, the leadership of the entire Taylor ring, including Buck and Martin Taylor, marked Smith for death. The lieutenant knew it was his duty to help a fellow officer by alerting him to "the danger that is awaiting you at the hands of these outlaws and murderers . . . [whose] record is definitely black and infamous . . . [I] strongly advise you to do all in your power to protect yourself from a similar fate like that of the lamented Maj. Thompson."

Verney continued, saying that in November 1867, near Yorktown in DeWitt County, a party of Taylor men received an erroneous tip that Smith would be a passenger on a stage to San Antonio. They stopped the stage and forced all passengers out. They inspected them closely, trying to determine if Smith was among their number. Verney concluded that "there is not the least doubt but that there are at least 8 or 12 of these outlaws banded together for the purpose of taking your life."[2]

While Smith faced murder threats, another officer, Byron Porter, the Freedmen's Bureau agent headquartered in Bastrop, also had difficulties. W. J. A. Bell, who frequently rode for the Taylors, threatened to kill Porter. As mentioned earlier, in December 1867, he had assaulted Porter and threatened him by waving a loaded gun in his face. Porter managed to wrest the gun from Bell and arrested him for assault with intent to kill. As per General Order no. 40, Porter turned Bell over to civil authorities. His trial became a farce. Bell plead "not guilty," even as his attorney was working on a plea bargain: Bell would admit to the reduced charge of aggravated assault. The district attorney accepted the compromise; a judge fined Bell $100 and released him, whereupon, one of the first things the marauder did was to threaten yet again to kill Porter. That local authorities treated Bell gingerly is in part explicable: He was related to the county sheriff. Porter wrote headquarters saying that his life was not worth straw, especially since his superiors had transferred his personal guard to another post. Alone with no support, Porter was much afraid of Bell, for the brigand might well succeed in killing him. According to Bastrop's John Schutze, Porter had plenty of reason to worry. The man had heard Bell repeatedly say that he was going to kill Porter along with several Bastrop residents, their number including the ethnic German, Charles Kleinert.[3]

In March Charlie Taylor and others caused so much trouble in Yorktown that locals armed themselves and drove the Taylor men out of town. But, once out in the countryside, the raiders joined Buck Taylor and committed yet more devilry. Victoria and Goliad counties were little better off. Buck Taylor, James Thompson (alias James Tope), and other raiders caused grief in Caldwell, Gonzales, and Guadalupe counties. It was clear that the crime ring operated throughout Taylor Country, with desperadoes spilling into all the area's counties.[4]

Another Taylor man, John Gorman, gave Bastrop County more grief. Protected by some of the ring, he savaged Justice of the Peace John Kiesnick of Serbin by knifing him in the side, intending to kill him. But one of the judge's ribs partially deflected the blade of the bowie knife, thereby saving his life. Gorman and others had broken into Kiesnick's house where Gorman did the stabbing. The renegades left, believing that the judge would soon die.

Of course, the sheriff failed to arrest the killer, partially because he was always accompanied by several heavily armed men. A few days later, Gorman's knife was busy again; this time, it stabbed another man in the arm, after which the felon left town in company of other desperadoes. The terrorism prompted Governor Elisha Pease to appeal to Gen. J. J. Reynolds, commander of the Department of Texas, Pease saying that Gorman belonged to a "band of out-laws . . . who live[d] in the woods" and attacked area people, especially the Germans, in the small community of Serbin.[5]

Next, unidentified assailants shot freedman Nathan Rector in the back, killing him. They stole his horse and gun and then set Rector's body on fire, probably to hide his identity, but the fire went out after the killers left. W. J. A. Bell and his cohorts were suspected of the crime. Following the death of Rector, murderers killed five more men in the county. According to one resident a "gloom" had "spread over the entire community." Following the chaos in Bastrop County, military authorities took action. They ordered Capt. C. S. Roberts and a detail of seven cavalrymen to conduct an investi-gation. The captain found and arrested Bell, took him to the post at Austin, and tossed him into a cell, while recommending that a full "campaign" be made in Bastrop County, for depredations there continued.[6]

Despite apparently being able to terrorize DeWitt County at will, Buck and Martin Taylor eventually left the area because they feared being caught. The twin terrors soon popped up in Panola County, one of Buck's old haunts. In early March 1868, they attacked blacks who were attending a Cotillion. They killed or wounded seven party-goers by shooting indiscriminately into the crowd. Before leaving the area, the dastardly duo shot several more freed-men. In part, their violence may have been politically motivated, for new statewide elections were coming soon. Former Confederates wanted to sup-press the blacks' right to vote by intimidating them, and the Taylors' activi-ties served that purpose. Such motivation existed all across settled Texas as Unionists and former Rebels fought for political control. In DeWitt and Victoria counties and in the rest of Taylor Country, many whites greatly opposed giving blacks the right to vote and were determined to stop them. Alternately, Buck and Martin probably did not worry about politics. They attacked blacks, sometimes with a motive of robbery and sometimes out of sheer irrational racial hatred.[7]

Buck and Martin Taylor continued their errant ways. They surfaced in Bastrop County in late March 1868. Buck, for one, immediately got into trouble while trying to spread more terror. Charlie Taylor, James Sharpe, W. J. A. Bell, Jack Connor, and ten other desperadoes in the Taylor gang created even more chaos. They moved back into DeWitt County where they rustled an untold number of cattle and stole about one hundred horses. After selling to a "contractor," they hauled away a goodly sum of money. The ranchers who lost stock complained to the county authorities. One was Dick Whittset who suffered great losses. He rode into Clinton and complained to local lawmen about his purloined herd. Sheriff Jack Miller gave Deputy Bill Sutton the duty of organizing a posse and going after the culprits. When Sutton and his men began chasing them, the gang fled. Some of the raiders moved north into chaotic Bastrop County and joined Buck Taylor.[8]

Since February 1867, Bastrop had been virtually out of control, and Charlie Taylor did not help the situation. His gang of marauders assaulted and robbed freedmen while also rustling cattle and stealing horses. According to a Freedmen's Bureau Agent, civil authorities either could not or would not try to restore law and order: Such was a hard job since, like others in the ring, Charlie Taylor moved from one county to another in South Texas to escape lawmen. Charlie, for one, continued his career of robbery and murder. March 1868 found him and the gang again in the Bastrop area, where they hid after doing more of their DeWitt County "business," including robbing and murdering at least one freedman. Pursued by Bastrop's lawmen, the desperadoes slipped back into DeWitt. In addition to other crimes, the gang stole a number of cattle from a DeWitt County widow named Thomas who lived on Thompson's Creek. Charlie Taylor personally robbed the woman of a number of household goods worth a tidy sum of money. But the authorities were on the move. As fate would have it, DeWitt Deputy Sheriff Sutton was a personal friend of the widow. He knew that she was alone and defenseless when the Taylor gang struck and deprived her of her goods and livelihood.[9]

Sutton wanted to right a wrong, to find Thomas's cattle, and to arrest the rustlers if possible. The DeWitt County Sheriff organized a posse of about fifteen men in Clinton, the members intending to capture or kill the raiders and to recover the stolen stock and the widow's other property. Setting out from Clinton, the posse tracked the rustlers but soon found that the raiders had split up. The sheriff then split the posse, and the men followed both trails. The sheriff led one group, Sutton the other. Sutton and seven other men tracked the malefactors to Bastrop town. Altogether, fourteen members of the Taylor gang had slipped into the town ahead of the posse. When the lawmen reached the outskirts of town, they began looking for the felons.[10]

After the posse reached Main Street, its members continued looking about for their quarry. Although a number of the gang escaped detection because the men from DeWitt did not have good descriptions of them, a posseman identified Charlie Taylor and James Sharpe, both of whom happened to be sitting on the porch of a general store. The posse demanded that the rustlers surrender immediately. Instead of giving up, the two felons filled their hands with guns. With scant regard for innocent people in and around the store, Taylor and Sharpe began shooting at the posse the second they heard the lawmen's demands. Sutton and his men responded in kind with shotguns and pistols. Peppered seventeen times, mostly with buckshot, Taylor died at the scene. Wounded, Sharpe surrendered but later suffered the same fate.[11]

Unfortunately, during the melee stray shots killed a young child and wounded an adult, both members of the local Lange family of Germans. Freedmen's Bureau agent Byron Porter was most critical of the posse's actions, holding that they should have given consideration to the safety of harmless civilians before they shouted the words that began the gun battle. Porter believed that it was only good fortune that the shooters had not wounded or killed other innocents. Sutton could only argue that he and his men constituted legal authority in hot pursuit of criminals and that the brigands, after all, had initiated the battle by shooting first.

The posse intended to take Sharpe back to Clinton, but near Lockhart, he made a break for freedom, whereupon posse members shot him dead. They left Sharpe's body where it fell on the roadside; some Lockhart men buried the corpse the next day. Ex-Rebels made the charge that the posse had murdered Sharpe, but that fact could not be substantiated. No legal action was forthcoming. Bastrop County officials later tried to indict Sutton for murder, holding him responsible for the death of the German child, but a grand jury ruled no bill.[12]

While the lawmen could congratulate each other for ridding the world of two renegades, in a quick search before they left Bastrop, the posse could not find Bell, Connor, or any other Taylor men. But, shortly after the posse left, Bell and Connor once again came to the attention of the townspeople. On Saturday, March 28, 1868, the two brigands committed acts that Bureau Agent Porter later investigated. Because freedman Priestly Lucius did not show them due deference, Bell and Connor assaulted the man on a town street. Looking for safety or at least for help, Lucius ran into a store. Bell and Connor followed and tried to shoot the black man in the back, but the store owner interfered, giving Lucius a chance to run again, this time down the middle of the street. Still following, the brigands mounted their horses, rode down the street, and got off several shots at Lucius with their sixguns, paying no heed to other people who were nearby. But, for all their firepower, they did not hit Lucius or anyone else.[13]

In the confusion, the raiders lost sight of their target but kept riding up and down the street. Bell had his revolver cocked and dared anyone to arrest him. Shortly, his relation, Sheriff John P. Jones, made a feeble attempt to do just that. Connor left, but Bell kept riding to and fro for about an hour. That gave the sheriff time to recruit a posse. Collectively, the men overwhelmed Bell and put him in jail. The Taylor man immediately posted bond and disappeared for the rest of the day. The next morning, Sunday, he was again with Connor, and the dastardly duo started looking for Lucius, whom they did not find. In the afternoon, they left Bastrop for parts unknown. Agent Porter complained that Sheriff Jones was worthless, for he was a former Confederate who in the past had sided with the men in the Taylor gang who had committed the recent outrages. The Bureau man later told superiors that if Bell and Connor ever faced a judge and a jury of their peers, the trial would be "as great a farce as previous ones where freedmen were the victims." Porter concluded, saying that "there is no decrease in the bitter feeling of the whites toward the blacks. Many murders and outrages have been committed on the blacks during [this] month."[14]

Bastrop's Schutze echoed the sentiments of the Bureau man, saying that Bell belonged to a numerous gang who would "support him if force should be used against him." Schutze was talking about elements of the Taylor ring but did not have all the pieces needed to understand the enormity of the puzzle.[15] Soon, matters got even worse when Bateman Bell and others in the Taylor ring started sweeping the county, stealing horses and robbing and killing freedmen. Bateman Bell, who may have been related to W. J. A. Bell, had caused mayhem in Bastrop County earlier when he went out of control. Before being run out of the county, Bateman had thirteen indictments against him: six for misdemeanors, six for horse theft, and one for the murder of John Catchings. Then, he returned to the county with the Taylor raiders to commit the current crimes.[16]

W. J. A. Bell remained in the area, causing trouble. April found him still working with the crime ring while bedeviling Unionists and freedpeople. One target was the eldery James E. Brady, a veteran of the United States Navy and a retired frontier ranger who once served the Republic of Texas. When the Civil War came, Brady proved to be a Nationalist whose loyalty remained with the United States. That he was a Unionist was the reason why Bell attacked him, for Bell had often called him a "Yankee spy." On Tuesday, April 28, Bell confronted Brady on a Bastrop street and cursed him, calling him a "son-of-a-bitch" among other endearments. Seventy years old and in ill health, Brady ignored the remarks and tried to walk around Bell and head toward the river. Bell followed him there and then grabbed his neck and tried to strangle him while saying: "Porter has escaped me but you shall not do so . . . I have caught you and I am now going to murder you on this spot . . . no one will ever know who killed you." Bell did not anticipate that, exactly then, some boys who had been playing by the river saw him killing the old man, whereupon the boys screamed and raised an alarm.

Summoning his strength while Bell was distracted, Brady managed to escape and walk rapidly back to the main street before Bell caught him. When the desperado tried to draw his sixgun, Brady grappled with him and prevented that. But Bell grabbed a rock and hit the old man in the head. Just then brave bystanders interfered with Bell long enough for the old man to get into the post office. Just as Bell fired his gun, Brady slammed the door and threw himself beside an adjacent wall and thereby saved his life. Next, Bell threw rocks at the door. He held off the crowd outside by waving his handgun and threatening to kill anyone who moved against him, but as more people arrived at the scene, he gave up his nefarious purpose and fled. Temporarily saved, Brady knew that to appeal to the civil authorities would avail him nothing, for Bell had been tried for other crimes before with no result. Indeed, Sheriff Jones even occasionally deputized him, a move that let him run wild at will. The woebegone Brady appealed to General Reynolds to send troops to Bastrop; it was the old man's last hope.[17]

In March and April 1868, military leaders in Taylor Country turned attention to the bad state of affairs that existed along the San Antonio–Indianola Road. Members of the Taylor ring, often numbering thirty or more men, robbed army trains using the road and waylaid civilians, robbing all, killing some. The problem was such that Reynolds ordered Gen. John Mason to tour the region, to gain intelligence, and to find a solution to the problem. After a three-month effort, Mason reported that a far-flung crime ring, led by the Taylors, was operating along the road. "There is no doubt," he said, "but there is an organized gang of desperadoes who at present infest the road . . . committing acts of violence at different points."[18]

Although Mason learned the names of various men in the Taylor gang, he said that even if the army could arrest them, the civil authorities would do nothing with them, for they either favored their violence or feared assassination if they opposed any members of Creed's raiders. To illustrate the point, the general summarized the saga of highwayman James Thompson, one of Creed's men who used the alias Jim Tope. Lawmen caught Thompson/Tope in Bexar County twice for stealing mules, but ex-Rebel officials let him go both times despite the confessions he made. On his second tour of duty in jail, he named names and implicated assorted members of Taylor's men, yet he was still turned loose, much to Mason's disgust. Democratic officials allowed such violence because it continued to serve their purpose to reclaim the state government at first opportunity.[19]

While Thompson/Tope continued his nefarious career, Hays Taylor came to General Mason's attention. An informant told the general that Hays had recently been in San Antonio looking for Lt. Charles Vernou. As mentioned earlier, after the murder of Major Thompson in Mason, the lieutenant had tracked the Taylors and intended to arrest them. Vernou was still looking for the murderers, and Hays believed that the ring had to be free of the meddlesome officer. Hays decided to kill him. To save Vernou, other military men, and innocent travelers on the San Antonio–Indianola Road, Mason suggested that area lawmen, aided by the military, recruit a large force of civilian volunteers, perhaps as many as fifty. The volunteers should patrol the road and "clear the country" of the Taylor gang. Mason wanted military tribunals to try anyone caught because civil judges and juries usually let the felons go, believing as they did that the roughs represented the Confederacy and were only continuing to make life unsafe for Yankees, white Unionists, and freedpeople. Along with W. B. Moore of the *San Antonio Express*—who researched and complied a list of felons for the army—the general asked that the names of all informants be kept in utmost secrecy to prevent retaliations that could be as severe as assassinations. Along with Mason, Officer Adam Wickes serving in San Antonio wanted something done. He agreed that the situation had to be improved since the army was losing lives as well as commissary stores. Moreover, the command at Indianola suffered from a lack of supplies whenever raiders bushwhacked a train. In time, two special civilian patrols, one headed by Jack Helm, began policing the road and its environs, and trouble in the area decreased.[20]

The biggest problem on the road was the stretch from San Antonio to Helena in Karnes County, part of Taylor Country. Thompson/Tope and up to thirty more men operated there. Sometimes members of the gang wearing army garb impersonated military officers. At other times, they impersonated civilian lawmen and wore silver stars on their vests. That allowed them to come close to their quarry without great risks. Then, once within range, the highwaymen's job was much easier. The problem became so bad that the area's Republican newspapers ran column after column, complaining and laying blame. The editor of the *San Antonio Express,* for example, wondered in print why the authorities caught men like Thompson/Tope and then turned them over to Rebel-dominated local officials who let them go. According to the editor, Karnes County was not the only trouble spot. The gang was spilling into Gonzales and Guadalupe counties. In those areas, county officials professed loyalty to the national government to gain offices but once in control facilitated the work of desperadoes. The editor mentioned Ed Glover by name, holding that he and other Taylor men were running amok in both counties. DeWitt County, too, continued to see its travail.[21]

Continuing their violent careers throughout much of 1868, the Taylor raiders seemed to have their way as they roamed, rustled cattle and horses, and generally spread terror. Like Sheriff Jones of Bastrop, many civil authorities had neither the desire nor the manpower means to corral them, for they represented the Confederate resistance to Reconstruction policies that tried to protect white Unionists like Sutton (although Sutton had fought for the Confederacy during the war) and others and to bestow basic civil rights upon the freedpeople. Although victims looked to the military for relief, most commanders at local posts did not have the manpower to enforce law and order in the vast land that was eastern and southern Texas, especially when more troops were needed on the West Texas Indian frontier and along the Mexican border.[22]

The shortage of manpower was illustrated by a later crisis that Col. Samuel H. Starr, commanding a post in faraway Tyler in Smith County, found himself facing. He received orders to transfer ten men to posts in each of Kaufman, Henderson, Van Zandt, and Anderson counties—a total of forty men. Starr had to remind his superiors that he only had forty-one enlisted men at his post. Thus, if he transferred the number that headquarters demanded, he would be left with but one private. At posts in South Texas, in counties like DeWitt, Karnes, Goliad, and Lavaca, the manpower supply was not noticeably better, with post commanders often powerless to go after lawbreakers, especially if they rode in packs, for they continued to outnumber the troopers at the scene.[23]

Despite the manpower problem, or perhaps because of it, in mid-1868, military authorities decided to crack down on lawlessness around the state. That decision greatly affected the Taylor gang. First, General Reynolds recruited a number of "Special Policemen," some also being called "detectives." They functioned as auxiliaries of the army. One of the recruits was Charles S. Bell. A Union veteran of the Civil War who attained the rank of captain, Bell was an imposing fellow. Standing more than six feet tall, he was slender, had light hair and blue eyes, and sported a flowing beard. Originally a journalist who had been a frequent contributor to the *New York Ledger,* Bell became especially noted during the war as a Union scout and a spy who at times donned Confederate garb and infiltrated the ranks of the enemy to gain intelligence. He served under both U. S. Grant and William Tecumseh Sherman. Captured in the Mississippi theater in 1863, he escaped before reaching the prison in Richmond, Virginia, whereupon he returned to his command and continued to give valuable military service until the war ended.[24]

Usually calling himself a "detective," Bell early on was approached by the intrepid Jack Helm, another fellow who stood more than six feet tall. A deputy sheriff of Lavaca County and one of Reynolds's special agents, Helm had a dark complexion, black eyes, and black hair. He was a stocky man whom Bell thought "well formed." Helm claimed to be a sincere Unionist who was more than willing to take on lawless men and end their reign. At the time, Bell—and the military authorities he answered to—had no way of knowing that Helm was an opportunist who might well render valuable service but who was only interested in power and prestige. Indeed, during the war, he lived in Northeast Texas and identified with the Confederates. As such, he persecuted Unionists in the region. Among other nefarious acts, he was primarily responsible for the lynching of the Hembys and Howards, five prominent men in the region who had been accused of but were innocent of treason against the Confederacy.[25]

By June 1868, Bell and Helm were making plans to bring the Taylors to justice. By the end of the month, Helm took the field with about fifty men, some troopers, some civilians. One goal was to bring in the murderers of Major Thompson of Fort Mason. In early July, military authorities, backed by the U.S. Secretary of War, offered a $1,000 reward for the apprehension of the murderers Doughboy and Hays Taylor along with Ran Spencer. Thompson's sorrowful wife put up an additional $500 reward for the killers. After several months of searching for the three renegades yielded no clues as to their whereabouts, Gen. R. C. Buchanan, now commanding the Fifth Military District, upped the army's reward to $1,500. Buchanan held the wanted men responsible for crimes ranging from murder to assaults with intent to kill, from brazen robberies of freedmen to stock rustling.[26]

In trying to catch members of the Taylor ring, lawmen like Bell and Helm had great difficulty. First, otherwise uninvolved citizens, most having Confederate sympathies, continued to warn raiders like the Taylors when any authorities were near. As well, ex-Rebel Democrats kept a constant stream of complaints against the investigators roaring like an avalanche into General Reynolds's office. Although Bell defended himself in private behind the scenes, Helm made his case public by writing newspaper columns and by giving interviews to news correspondents.[27]

Even as a crackdown was underway, some members of the Taylor ring remained busy. Hays, Doughboy, and Martin Taylor—along with Dave Morris (Martin Taylor's father-in-law), Edward Glover, and Jim Wright—worked on a Creed Taylor operation on the San Miguel River near the Laredo-Fort Ewell Road. In April and May 1868, while the army was gearing up for a full-scale campaign against lawlessness, Taylor men gathered three herds of beeves, seventy-five head belonging to Creed. They rounded up another 625 head that had other brands. Obviously, they stole that 625, but they believed that if they quickly sold the cattle, their crime would not be detected. After forcing a "Mr. Hill" to corral the herd, the thieves waited for cattle-buyer Reed Weisiger with whom the gang was going to do business. Led by Hays and Doughboy, the rustlers believed they were so much feared that no one in the area dared oppose them.[28]

According to Hill, a virtual prisoner who had to allow the raiders to stay at his place, the Taylor men's favorite amusement was to frighten his family by getting drunk and shooting over the family home from the other side of the San Miguel. At other times, they rode roughshod over his front yard and trampled his vegetable garden in the back yard. In addition to Hill, the vicinity's West family gave information to Bell on the horrible ways of the gang. However, other settlers warned Bell that if he did find any of the rustlers and arrest them, most likely the remainder of the gang would kill the Hills and the Wests, for the desperadoes' spies would know those two families gave the information to use against the Taylor outfit.[29]

Nevertheless, after learning that some members of the gang came to the Hill place each morning to attend the cattle, Detective Bell, Jim Cox, and Henry Ragland seized the Hill house at dawn one day and waited while the Hills in unison told Bell that the Taylors would kill him along with his two cohorts. One family member told Bell that the raiders were "desperate men" who would not allow themselves to be taken alive. The source added that after Bell and his men were dead, the villains would kill the entire Hill family. Bell later said that the family's experience pointed out why desperadoes were so hard to catch in Texas. Most of the sober sorts were deathly afraid of men like Creed, Hays, Doughboy, Buck, and Martin Taylor. All of them, Officer Bell held, were born killers who would murder anyone standing in the way of their profit-making schemes.[30]

Despite the risks, Bell and his men remained in the house, and shortly after dawn on a sparkling day in May 1868, Hays and Martin Taylor, along with Morris and others, came to attend the cattle. When they were within twenty yards of the house, Bell, Cox, and Ragland rushed out with "cocked pieces," demanded immediate surrender, and got ready to kill the renegades if they resisted. According the Bell, "Hays Taylor blanched white and slid off his horse," as did the others. Bell's men secured all the prisoners, except Martin Taylor, in a locked storehouse. Then, with Martin in tow, Bell headed for what he later called a "favorite haunt" of Doughboy, a supposedly hidden place on the Nueces. But a search of the area failed to turn up any desperadoes.[31]

However, Bell had drug Martin along for a different purpose. He forced the renegade to allow him to talk with a Mrs. Beall, a cousin of the Taylor clan. Fearing for his life, Martin did what the detective demanded, and Beall never guessed that Martin was a prisoner. Rather, Martin presented Bell, who had only a sidearm, as a good friend of the family. The woman spoke frankly and gave the detective information about the whereabouts of the other Taylors and about their present doings. Next, Bell returned to the Hill place, retrieved the other prisoners, and marched them toward Pleasanton in Atascosa County, a place garrisoned by Lt. H. Taylor and ten men. The charges Bell intended to file against his wards included everything from cattle rustling to murder and attempted murder. However, the party never reached Pleasanton. Rather, about twenty miles from Oakville, a dozen or so heavily armed men confronted Bell after he and his men had made camp for the night.[32]

In the dark with clouds obscuring the moon, Bell did not recognize any of the men. Believing correctly that the group intended to lynch the prisoners, Bell stood squarely in front of them, the move signaling that he would protect them. Then, the prisoners did the most logical thing: They turned and started running away. Bell preferred that they escape rather than die at the hands of an illegal mob, and he tried to stop the vigilantes' pursuit only to be hit hard on the head by a rifle barrel and pushed out of the way. A man appearing to be the leader approached him and suggested that "I [Bell] should leave and say nothing," adding that "good people appreciated my actions but [their] safety demanded the death of such men as I had captured." Later, the special officer reflected that even decent people—when forced to live with insecurity and violence all around them, forced to live in fear of mortal retaliation if they defended themselves, their families, and their properties—would take the law into their own hands to save themselves when the authorities could not give them security.[33]

The detective gave up his resistance, later explaining that the odds against him were too great to overcome. As he, Cox, and Ragland settled back into their camp, they heard shots in the night and well knew what the gunfire meant. After an interval, the three heard more rapid firing, a fact suggesting that at least one prisoner was still alive and was making a run for it. Later, Bell was much surprised when he learned that several prisoners, including the Taylors, had escaped. He called it a "miracle."[34]

Soon, Bell returned to Laredo, hoping to find the murderer Thompson/Tope, the shooter who had killed one man in Austin and another in Rockport. Bell learned that Thompson/Tope and several other Taylor men were off with a herd of stolen beeves, driving them into the interior of Mexico. Knowing that the targets would soon return, Bell bided his time. Conversely, if Thompson and the others had decided to stay in Mexico, Bell had official letters for the governor of Nueva Leon for their extradition. Likewise, the detective's intelligence told him that the murderer Henderson was at Mier, and the detective believed he had a chance to corral him, too. Unfortunately, like many another chase, Bell came away from Laredo empty-handed, for the brigands had good communications, too. According to one observer, the Taylors now had a vast spy network that kept them informed of the doings of any of the authorities looking for them. And, when warned, they knew when and where to flee.[35]

Meanwhile, political developments had an impact on law enforcement after Congressional Reconstruction began. After Congress took control, it was mandatory that each Confederate state, save Tennessee, write a new constitution that, among other provisions, gave freedmen the right to vote. Also most important, when the Reconstruction Convention convened in 1868, delegates addressed the problem of rampant crime, including robbery and murder, committed by common desperadoes like the Taylor ring and by terrorist Klan groups that operated in at least seventy-seven counties in the Lone Star State. The delegates resolved that $25,000 of state money should be set aside to fight crime. They intended that some of the money should be used to hire more detectives to ferret out lawbreakers and that some should be used as reward money for their apprehension. In their resolution, the delegates also asked the commander of the Fifth Military District to establish military commissions to try captured offenders, as others had earlier suggested. Republican delegates believed that military trials were necessary because ex-Rebel judges and juries almost never convicted law breakers if Yankee soldiers, white Unionists, or freedpeople were the only victims.[36]

In late September through early October, Capt. A. Steelhammar mounted a search for Doughboy and Hays Taylor. The captain and his men eventually found the two in company of other desperadoes, and a gunfight erupted. Although the detail wounded two of their men, both Taylors along with Dick Chisholm slipped away, leaving their wounded, one of whom soon died, to fall into Steelhammar's hands. The captain released the dead body to the man's family, who held a funeral. The Taylors were criminals, but they had grit. Doughboy, Hays, and Chisholm brazenly attended the funeral despite knowing that troopers were near. When the three raiders left, they told the man's family that they would kill every army officer or enlisted man who came their way. According to one report, every attempt to corral the malefactors only made them more desperate.[37]

The mayhem the Taylor ring caused in their region continued to be mirrored across the interior of Texas where Klan-like groups and outlaws had the proverbial field day against the authorities. Such was the judgment of General Reynolds and the newspaperman/Republican politician James Newcomb of San Antonio when they reported to the Constitutional Convention. Reynolds wrote of the Klan and outlaw bands. The isolated, rural areas were the hardest hit, not the major cities and towns that had army garrisons. According to Newcomb, almost the entire area of settled Texas was in a "state of outlawry." He maintained that white Union men and freedmen had little protection. Murdering them became the "order of the day." He suggested that the Lone Star needed more outside help. He wanted Congress to declare martial law from the Sabine to the Mexican border.[38]

Although Hays Taylor and others in the crime ring were continuing their

murderous careers, the authorities had some success. Another Taylor supporter soon fell. Frank Frisbie had a farm near Gonzales where he retained
black sharecroppers to work his land. Lawmen sought both Frank and his
son on myriad charges, including their participation as members of the
Taylor band. On October 2, 1868, at about 8 P.M., Goliad County Deputy
Sheriff Henry Board and his deputized nephew Zacariah Loven surprised
Frank Jr. at the Frisbie home. When the lawmen came close, the family's
dogs alerted Frank Jr. that something was awry. When he stepped outside, he
saw a black sharecropper's wife and asked her if she had seen anyone. After
she said "no," Frank continued to look about. Apparently afraid of giving his
quarry a chance to defend himself, Board fired a double barrel shotgun blast
at him and, seconds later, fired the other barrel. Although Frank Jr. briefly
survived, the wounds were fatal. He died on October 27. Although Frisbie's
mother termed the attack "outright murder," authorities refused to bring
charges, for Board was a legal authority and had shot a felon, a fugitive who
had indictments pending against him.[39]

While other officials were trying to catch members of the Taylor ring,
the military command ordered Lieutenant Vernou into the field again. His
superiors told him to tour the interior of the state and to make a comprehen-
sive report. That accomplished, Reynolds released Vernou's October report
to the press. From Austin moving north, Vernou found that many areas were
virtually out of control. Armed outlaw bands and Klan-like terrorist groups
abounded. Without realizing it, the lieutenant commented on the actions of
one of the Taylor gang. When he reached Hillsboro in Hill County, locals
told him about gang member Ed Glover's brother Jim's recent activities in
their area. Jim had lately shot two freedmen, one of whom shortly died. He
rode with a "gang of desperadoes," who were other members of the Taylor marauders. The band apparently had little to do except "rob and shoot
negroes." The raiders did not live in one place; rather, they roamed to and
fro in the county, committing mayhem whenever they chose. They did not
work. They "live[d] upon what they succeed in stealing." The county sheriff
and his men finally drove the raiders from Hill County, but they simply
moved into Johnson County and continued their depredations. However,
the Hill County sheriff rode into the latter county and managed to capture
Jim Glover, but the other raiders got away. The sheriff took Glover back
to Hillsboro and pitched him in a cell from which the brigand managed a
quick escape. Later, like his brother Ed, he turned up again in the midst of
the Taylor gang.[40]

Despite the apparent success of varied members of the crime ring, on
Christmas Eve of 1868, a Taylor man fell. Long a wanted man, Buck Taylor,
along with the raider Dick Chisholm and others, appeared in Clinton, ap-

parently there to watch a Christmas program presented at the courthouse. Arriving early, Buck and Dick decided to visit a saloon for some refreshments, a decision that led to immediate disaster, for DeWitt County Deputy Sheriff Sutton and his friend "Doc" White were already there. Traditional accounts say that Sutton was seated, with his hat pulled over his eyes, while dosing off. Since he appeared to be alone, Taylor and Chisholm apparently believed they had little to fear. Buck walked up close to Sutton and reportedly whispered in his ear: "If the sun goes down on you in DeWitt County, we'll kill you."[41]

Then, as the two outlaws walked toward the saloon door, Sutton reportedly stood up and asked: "Why wait until sundown?" So it was on Christmas Eve that all three men drew their guns and fired, but so did White who came to Sutton's defense. When the imbroglio ended, White was unharmed, and Sutton was still standing despite a serious shoulder wound. Buck Taylor lay dead on the saloon floor, thereby paying the supreme price for challenging the lawmen. Chisholm managed to bolt from the saloon and to escape while White gave attention to Sutton's wound. In part because of protests from ex-Rebels, authorities put Sutton and White on trial for murder, but a jury cleared them by ruling self-defense. Later a lawman himself, Lewis Delony was only a boy, but he saw the shooting and always remembered the details, including the fact that the felons had attacked a lawman.[42]

Despite Buck's death, the Taylor ring made sure that more trouble followed soon.

CHAPTER FOUR

More Murder and Mayhem

T HE Taylor gang remained active as the winter months of 1868 gave way to a new year. Hays and Doughboy Taylor along with Ran Spencer were in the field, defying any authority to bring them to justice. Their defiance was understandable, for, as in the past, the Taylor men often outnumbered the lawmen sent to arrest them. By January 1869, the Taylor forces had broadened their areas of attack on Unionists and freedpeople. The new different elements of the raiders now operated in both Lavaca and Colorado counties in addition to other areas like Goliad, Karnes, and Gonzales counties. In Lavaca County, two new Klan organizations sprang up, with evidence suggesting that the Taylor element founded the groups.[1]

Disguised men attacked freedman Jacob Aakman on February 4, shooting into his cabin repeatedly with no thought for the safety of the man's wife and children. The terrorists attacked other blacks as well. But local authorities in Hallettsville declined to pursue the brigands, claiming that they did not have enough volunteers to form a posse. Sheriff W. H. Coleman was willing to track the malefactors, and the local military command trusted his sincerity, but he simply lacked the personnel to be effective. Shortly, citizens demanded that the army increase the troop strength of the post of Hallettsville, a demand that was not met. In Colorado County reports were similar, with the area's freedpeople also coming under attack.[2]

Problems became so severe in Goliad County that Judge M. Kreible wrote the influential A. H. Jordan asking him to contact the post of Helena with the message that Goliad needed troops. The judge asked for at least twenty-five to thirty men "if not a full company." The reason? A wing of the Taylor ring now operated openly in the county. The brigands were nothing but a "set of scoundrels who . . . depreciated upon the people, defying civil authority." The county sheriff and his deputies could not arrest them, said the judge, because the desperadoes always outnumbered the officers and were willing to fight to protect each other. The Taylor men were "desperate wretches" who would come to heel only if enough military men could be sent to Goliad County. The judge said he wanted to convene his court on the fourth Monday of February, but he could not do so safely without troops to support him.[3]

Simultaneously, Taylor men were stirring up the citizens of Gonzales and DeWitt counties. In the latter place, Buck Roland had recently shot and killed a freedman. In the former, the seventeen-year-old George Johnson had murdered a man. However, Jack Helm was optimistic when he reported to Governor Pease. After noting that various officers had killed several of the Taylor gang, Helm assured Pease that he and his men were on the trail of Roland and Johnson.[4]

There were more Taylor men in Calhoun and Lavaca counties by February 1869. In the former area, they took delight in coming into Indianola at night, getting drunk, and shooting into various stores and houses in the main part of town. According to the physician H. Rosecrans, "a state of anarchy" prevailed because of the Taylors' actions. "Rough" men flocked to the town's saloons, and every one was a "Rebel." Each was heavily armed. Begging for a squad of military men, Rosecrans said he believed that once the military arrived, the men of the town would volunteer to help the troopers. In Hallettsville the story was much the same. County Judge A. K. Foster reported that he had every confidence in the county sheriff and his deputies, but the sheriff's small contingent was no match for the Taylor renegades. Further, the judge averred that the gang had attacked, robbed, and assaulted several area freedmen.[5]

To add to the chaos in the county, the two Klan-like terrorist groups remained active. Men in disguise tormented yet more blacks. All Judge Foster could do was advise the freedmen to secure arms to protect themselves since civil authorities were powerless. Within two weeks, other freedpeople reported similar assaults. Concurrently, members of one of the terrorist groups approached a black sharecropper at home and destroyed all his farm implements. Authorities suspected that the Kelly brothers were among the leaders of that violent group. Concluding, the judge asked for troops to protect the county's residents.[6]

While Lavaca and Calhoun counties were in turmoil, more trouble was afoot in DeWitt. On February 19, Helm reported that he was after a number of murderers, some of whom slipped away and left the county. But the lawman also reported that "several [more] of the Taylor party have been killed," and that had a good effect among the residents.[7] However, the county remained under threat. Near Yorktown, an area resident reported that assailants, possibly Taylor men, had attacked a five-member family of blacks whose home was just outside town on the Gonzales Road. The felons forced their way into the family's house and shot elderly one-armed Tom Banks in the knee twice, further crippling him. Banks was fated to live, but he was abed for weeks while recovering from his wounds. They fired at his wife, Hanna, and she took a bullet in the foot. The attackers shot their daughter Harriet in the leg. Their sons tried to fight back, but the raiders shot and killed one in the house and took the second outside, found a live oak tree, and hanged him from it. The Banks family's ordeal was explicable, given the fact that they worked for lawman Joe Tumlinson and family; the descriptions of the leaders of the violent bunch fit several of the Taylors. In addition, some raiders had threatened white Unionists in the area, one of whom wrote to Pres. U. S. Grant, telling him that unless he would intervene, many loyal men would be forced to leave the region and seek safety in less violent climes.[8]

Other Taylor men may have been active in Victoria County where Sheriff W. W. Hammed spoke of "desperate cases" and "desperadoes" before appealing to military authorities for at least twenty troopers. The brigands ran in packs, said the sheriff, and law officers could not bring them to heel. The felons had evaded arrest for quite some time, Hammed concluded.[9]

Meanwhile, Detective Bell and Special Agent Helm continued their pursuit of different elements of the Taylor gang, but the lawmen had more than one difficulty, just has they had in the past. Otherwise uninvolved civilians, most of them having Confederate sympathies, continued to warn the raiders when any authorities were near. Second, ex-Rebel Democrats kept up an ongoing stream of complaints that flowed into General Reynolds's office like a flood. Helm tried to deflect such criticisms. He continued to write newspaper columns to explain and to justify his actions and those of Detective Bell.[10]

Given their superior manpower, by early February 1869, the Taylor forces broadened their areas of attack on white Unionists and freedmen. Some members of the Taylor ring renewed operations in Mason and Gillespie counties, just as they had in the past. In the winter of 1869, complaints of lawlessness in the two counties became legion. Of particular concern to some area settlers was the wholesale slaughter of "mavericks" solely for their hides, with the hunters leaving the carcasses to rot on the ground. Even small calves fell before the onslaught of the hunters. The shooters often did not quibble when they found branded cattle; they killed and skinned them, too. Many sources implicated the Taylors as being chief among the perpetrators, thus giving the authorities more reasons to hound the gang. Ranchers complained that they were losing thousands of dollars due to the illegal slaughter of their herds. They demanded that the high command transfer more troopers to

Fort Mason and that the new forces be deployed to go after the Taylor men who were decimating the herds.[11]

Shortly, Jack Helm, whom the Taylors had already threatened to kill, assembled a posse and went after the malefactors and their hired gunfighters. Helm learned that about forty raiders had collected at one place but then broke into squads of from five to fifteen and scattered themselves throughout several counties, including DeWitt. Helm took part of his men and personally pursued desperado Jim Bell who now called DeWitt County home. The Helm forces managed to capture him and others, all of whom later tried to escape, whereupon their guards killed all of them except Jim Bell, who got away. The number of the prisoners "shot while trying to escape" drew criticism. It appeared that too many of Helm's captives seemed to die that way. Nevertheless, the lawman was reducing the outlaw population of the area. In his defense, some observers pointed out that the authorities chased desperate characters who would risk their lives in escape attempts rather than face long prison terms or, perhaps, their date with a hangman.[12]

Using the alias James Weaver, Jim Taylor—destined to become a co-leader of the crime ring—continued his criminal career after breaking out of the Austin jail. Actually, Taylor's wife had bribed a guard with $300 in $20 gold pieces to let her husband go. Then, she continued as always to spy for the ring and to pass pertinent information to her husband. As Weaver, Jim Taylor slipped into Bastrop County with fourteen of his men and camped in an area near Walnut and Cedar creeks. The man were wearing stolen army uniforms to confuse both lawmen and the general public. With little to fear, the raiders went about their business of stealing stock, mostly cattle. When not working, Weaver/Taylor and some of his men developed the habit of riding into Bastrop town heavily armed to get drunk and generally to raise hell. Further, they threatened to kill anyone who challenged them. Local lawmen and the local Freedmen's Bureau Agent could do little; they were always outnumbered at the scene. The Taylors' abuses led Bastrop Judge William T. Allen to make repeated requests for troops to bring the raiders to heel.[13] Although the Taylor crime ring apparently had its way in Bastrop County, Special Detective Bell was soon after Jim Taylor and his men. However, Bell was confused about aliases. Writing superiors, he said that Weaver used the alias of Jim Taylor when, in fact, the true identity was the reverse. Despite temporary confusion, Bell tracked Taylor to a point about twenty miles from Gonzales town where he secured the assistance of Helm, who served as the detective's scout and guide. Later, Bell complimented Helm, saying that he was invaluable as a scout because he knew Texas all the way from the Red River to the Rio Grande. As well, Helm brought three more men with him: T. J. Lane, W. M. Crenshaw, and T. Neill. Now a posse numbering five, the lawmen continued to trail Taylor. His tracks moved north to Bastrop County and then back southward into Caldwell County. On the chase went, into Gillespie County where the lawmen learned that Taylor had been joined by the desperado Frank Wilcox, a man like Taylor; that is, Wilcox was noted as being a spectacular horse thief and cattle rustler. Led by Helm, the posse rode to the Wilcox place, which was on a creek that was a tributary of the Pedernales. There, the lawmen found him, a man named Gilmore, and two teenaged boys who were attending a herd of four hundred stolen cattle. Although Wilcox denied being a Taylor partisan, the posse arrested all four for cattle rustling.[14]

After Bell repeatedly questioned Wilcox, the felon finally admitted that he rode with Jim Taylor, who had gone back to Bastrop County to contact other members of the ring. Jim needed at least five more men to help drive another stolen herd westward into New Mexico. After tracking that herd to Blanco County, Detective Bell learned that the route the Taylor men would take was the usual one—westward to forts Mason and McKavitt. Cowboy brigands were moving northward with other Taylor herds, destination Kansas. Detective Bell held that most of the cattle in all the herds were stolen. The Taylor gang, Bell averred, were stealing cattle in broad daylight, literally in front of the owners, who were powerless because the gang members were always heavily armed. According to Bell, since 1867 the rustlers had had their way all over Central and South Texas. As he was reporting on Wilcox and his stolen herd, Bell sent word to his superiors about the latest activities of Hays and Doughboy Taylor along with their cohort Ran Spencer. They "lurked" in the vicinity of Helena in Karnes County. They were still making a living by stealing horses. Bell spoke of a few other Taylor gang members. Ben Lane and the Gibson brothers, Short and Sam, murderers all, were somewhere in Lavaca County.[15] Yet, despite Bell's intelligence, neither civil nor military officials could catch any of the thieves and murderers.

By the first week of June 1869, Special Officer Bell was hot on the trail of two of the Taylor gang, Frank Frisbie, whose son had already been killed, and Dick Chisholm, who had been with Buck Taylor when Sutton killed him. Both men were acclaimed horse thieves and cattle rustlers. In addition to Bell's search for them, Frisbie and Chisholm were still dogged by the Unionist Deputy Sheriff Henry Board and Zacariah Loven, the two men who had earlier killed Frank Frisbie Jr. The Unionists incurred the hatred of Frisbie and Chisholm simply because they were indeed loyal to the United States and because they tried to help area's hard-pressed freedpeople. The authorities had trouble bringing such men as Frisbie and Chisholm to justice because many area citizens still believed that such men still fought for old Dixie. Some civilians continued to aid ring members by giving them supplies, by providing safe, hidden harbors, and by divulging information about the movement of any troopers or lawmen looking for them. When it was safe to do so, Frisbie and Chisholm often stayed at the home of Frisbie's wife, Matilda, a place that Officer Bell identified as a "regular den of thieves."[16]

Other than the killing of Frank Frisbie Jr., there had been earlier trouble between Frisbie and Board and Board's brother William. Indeed, Frisbie had threatened to kill them both, and it seems that Frisbie's wife was willing to help him fulfill that goal. She used some ruse to lure William to the Frisbie place where Frisbie and several other members of the ring surprised him. The villains immediately opened up with shotguns and revolvers. Even as he was being shot, the victim managed to get atop his horse and make an escape. He was terribly wounded but survived.[17] Henry Board, then, had good reasons for wanting to bring in both malefactors.

As events proved, Frisbie and Chisholm shared the Taylors' hatred for freedpeople. According to Detective Bell, they assaulted blacks on several occasions, the ex-slaves giving them no provocation whatsoever. The two brigands had no respect for property as they demonstrated in an incident at a Mr. Plank's farm north of Concrete. Frisbie and Chisholm rode onto the farm and destroyed Plank's fruit orchards. They wrecked a number of farm implements and stole various others. Then, they assaulted several of the freedpeople who worked for Plank. The farmer was a Unionist who was good to his workers, which probably were the twin motives for the attack. However, Henry Board, assisted by Lovin, both men armed with writs and warrants in their hands, finally tracked Frisbie. When cornered at his wife's place and asked to surrender, Frisbie fought back, firing repeatedly with a sixgun in each hand. Board and Lovin returned effective rounds that killed him. The Taylor gang thereby lost one more of its members. What about Chisholm, who was also wanted? He disappeared and was nowhere to be found.[18]

After the death of Frisbie, Board and Lovin found that they were in much trouble. A grand jury, most of the jurors being former Rebels, returned murder indictments against both men. Both left the area and went into hiding. Special Officer Bell complained to superiors that "as the Frisbie party have been allowed their way at Clinton, that bills of indictment have been found against Board and Lovin, which ought, of rights, be quashed." Bell said that the two men had "legally rid the world of a monster, and should be allowed to return [home]. So badly are affairs by the grand juries in this county," Bell asserted, "that every man who kills a desperado is sure of being indicted." He pleaded with superiors to intervene, saying that "I am perfectly satisfied that the killing of Frisbie was justifiable."[19] Bell could have added that most of the "desperadoes" were ex-Confederates who now did the work of the Democratic party, and most of the victims were white Unionists or blacks.

Bell argued that if the Henry Board and Lovin had money, an attorney could no doubt win a not guilty verdict from a trial jury, but Bell added that both were poor men from poor families; they could not raise the money to pay for an expensive defense. Luckily for the two harassed men, the military indeed intervened and cleared them of any wrongdoing, a judgment that allowed them to return home and resume their roles as loyal Nationalists.[20]

While Special Detective Bell was focused on the above-mentioned desperadoes, Lt. William Thompson, post commander at Helena, was having misgivings about the authorities' campaign to bring in lawbreakers. He told superiors that Hays and Doughboy Taylor, along with Edward Glover, had sent out a call for some of their raiders to concentrate until a force of at least twenty-five men had gathered, all "thieves and murderers," to hear Thompson tell it. He said they intended to ride into Clinton, storm the jail, and liberate the Wofford brothers who had been confined there. Additionally, the Taylors and Glover had targeted certain men in authority for death: Joe Tumlinson, Helm, Sutton, Cox, and "Doc" White. Already, said Lieutenant Thompson, violent attempts on their lives forced them, along with several other officers, to take to the woods at night. Already, they feared being attacked by night riders, and it appeared that the renegades were ready to dispose of them for good. The lieutenant lamented that his small command could not help the civil authorities, for the Taylor gang was larger than his meager forces. As of June 22, Thompson said he had only seven men fit for duty, adding that "the present condition of affairs being of such a nature I would respectfully request that [more] troops be sent immediately."[21]

About two weeks later, Thompson was pleading to his superiors again, saying that Taylor assassins were still after Tumlinson and Helm particularly and that his command was still too small to protect them. The lieutenant was hearing rumors daily of a coming armageddon that would clean out the authorities altogether. He said he dealt often with people who "prayed" that troops would come to save the day. But he also reported that the Taylors were receiving more and more reinforcements from "all parts of the country." He said the Taylor party had indeed taken over the Clinton jail and had liberated the Wofford brothers, who were now at large and likely riding with the Taylors to give their forces yet more manpower. Other desperate men were concentrating, said Thompson, including a number of "villains" from Lockhart. He added that if his superiors did not send reinforcements, the peaceful folk of the region would be forced to leave their homes and seek protection from a larger garrison.[22]

On a more positive note, Thompson reported that Helm and his men, helped by a posse of civilians who had heretofore remained uninvolved, had captured several desperadoes and sent them to the same Clinton jail that the

Wofford brothers had just vacated. Almost immediately, the prisoners tried to escape the porous jail, but their guards shot them to death. Thompson thought it significant that DeWitt County citizens had helped corral the evil-doers, but he feared that their posse would eventually break apart if the military could not render meaningful assistance. The consequences of the civilians disbanding would be tremendous. The "villains" would control the entire county, said Thompson. He also reported that DeWitt County Sheriff W. A. Jacobs had had to find Helm to seek protection, else the Taylor raiders would kill him, which, indeed, they later did.[23]

In early June, Helm went to Austin where he visited with General Reynolds and lobbied for more military help. After he returned to Clinton, Helm learned that still more violent men were concentrating. They were determined to protect the Taylors and to help them take control of DeWitt County. Helm confirmed that the sheriff of DeWitt was indeed sleeping in the woods for safety and that the turmoil was spilling into Victoria County. Helm reported that on two occasions elements of the Taylor gang had tried to storm the jail in Victoria, the county seat, and liberate two other ring members held there. The Taylors had also threatened the lives of all the men who had helped Helm and Detective Bell.[24]

Helm determined to fight back. He joined Sheriff Jacobs of DeWitt County, and together they raised about forty men for a posse and "moved on the enemy," as Helm put it. However, the Taylors' tactic at first confused the lawmen. As they had done earlier, the raiders broke into three squads, each one going its own way. The deconcentration obviously left each squad more open to attack even though small groups could travel faster and could hide more easily. Still, Sheriff Jacobs took advantage of the deconcentration by capturing key Taylor leaders Jim Bell and a man named Moore. Helm detached six men to take Bell and Moore to the Clinton jail, but the two raiders attempted to escape, and the lawmen killed them. The next night Helm and his men attacked one squad of desperadoes but had little success. First, the members of the group scattered into dense woods while rain came in torrents, turned dirt roads into bogs, and stopped further pursuit. Nevertheless, Helm was optimistic, for he had heard that the Taylor gang would surrender if the military promised that they would be tried in civil court. The Taylors believed that a jury of their pro-Confederate peers would rule in their favor regardless of their offenses. Still, as he wrote General Reynolds, Helm hoped for the best and believed that trials would end the turmoil. However, he wanted the general's advice before the Taylors surrendered.[25] As events proved, members of the Taylor gang had little intention of surrendering. Perhaps ring leaders floated the possibility to buy time and to conceal their real purposes: They still intended to kill Helm, Detective Bell, and other lawmen who bedeviled them.

Even as marked men, Helm and Bell continued to pursue the despera-does. In particular, Bell decided to focus on Ran Spencer, one of the killers of Major Thompson, and Joe Clarke, another member of the Taylor circle. He heard that both raiders had popped up in Concrete, possibly looking for the Boards and Lovin, no doubt to kill them and avenge their friends, the Fris-bies. However, Bell was at Helena at the time and thereby missed a chance to capture the two renegades. Meanwhile, Helm complained that on a trip back from Austin, he found "armed parties" banding together for the sole purpose of "protecting the Taylor party against the authorities," of whom he was one. The gun rather than the law ruled the day, he said. Continuing, Helm added that the desperadoes had made two more attempts to storm the Clinton jail and to free several cohorts incarcerated there, whom the authorities charged with horse stealing.[26]

By the summer of 1869, Helm and Bell were still doing all they could to corral the members of the crime ring. They received the aid of W. A. Jacobs of Goliad County, whom the Taylors had threatened. The brother of DeW-itt's Sheriff George Jacobs, W. A. helped the lawmen recruit posses on vari-ous occasions. But after conferring with both civilian and military leaders in the area, Helm learned that at least two score of men had banded together to serve and to protect the Taylors. He found that the raiders still intended to kill Officer Bell and the men assisting him. When he made contact with Jacobs, Helm found that the man was seldom home and that he slept in the woods at night for fear of a raid by Taylor partisans.[27]

Yet, with Helm as a driving force, Jacobs and lawman Joseph Tumlinson helped raise a party of about thirty volunteers who wanted to end the tur-moil in Taylor Country. Helm intended to wipe out lawlessness in the entire region from the Guadalupe River to the Nueces. With the civilians behind him, he managed to arrest two of the gang's leaders, whom a DeWitt County grand jury indicted for horse theft, among other charges. Helm dispatched six guards to take the brigands to the Clinton jail. En route, the two prisoners made a break for freedom, and the guards killed them. But, eliminating two men was not enough to stop the Taylor gang's activities.[28] Moreover, when ring members congregated, they still outnumbered Helm and his volunteers, who were mostly otherwise pacific citizens without military experience; they were no match for professional killers.

To raise more men, Helm, Jacobs, and Tumlinson appealed to Lieuten-ant Thompson, still commanding at the post of Helena. In June and July, the lawmen virtually begged him to send elements of his command to help corral the raiders. But the officer had only a personal guard and could not spare men to assist the local officers. Thompson contacted his superiors again, asking for more troops, telling them the situation was desperate, most especially be-cause the Taylors were receiving reinforcements. The lieutenant asserted that the desperado Jim Miller had brought twenty-five men to join the Taylors' forces, a development that added even more firepower that could be aimed at peace officers and soldiers. Thompson added that more messengers still came daily, asking the lieutenant for help. His superiors promised more troops, but as of July 7, none had arrived. Also significant, the lieutenant mentioned that two raiders who had been in the Clinton jail had escaped, remained at large, and were rounding up more men to help Taylor deal a death blow to Helm, Jacobs, Tumlinson, and their volunteers. As well, another violent group from Lockhart had arrived and had reinforced the Taylors.[29]

About the only good news Thompson had to report was that in the countryside Jack Helm and W. A. Jacobs had arrested two more brigands for multiple murders. Helped by civilians, Helm sent the prisoners under guard toward Clinton. En route they attempted to escape, and the guards shot and killed them, thus reducing the ranks of the area's desperadoes by two more. That had a good effect on the morale of the peaceable folk in the area, said Thompson, but he warned that if the military did not act soon to take stronger action to protect the loyal citizens, the civilians might disband and allow the lawless Taylors to control the region. Thompson ended his report begging for enough men to either kill the Taylors or to put them to flight.[30]

As the campaign against lawlessness proceeded, the authorities suffered a terrible blow. In the summer of 1869, the Peace brothers, Clint and Mat, of the Taylor ring became determined to kill Sheriff George Jacobs, a proverbial thorn in the side of the ring members. The brothers brought James Stapp, another Taylor man, into their conspiracy. Having no charges against him, Stapp was able to move freely and to talk to authorities, something the Peace brothers could not do, for a grand jury had already handed down indictments on them. Stapp contacted Jacobs and claimed that thieves had stolen a horse from him. The sheriff went to the Stapp place and started an investigation. In retrospect, he made a deadly mistake by going alone. Talk turned to the Peace brothers, with Stapp claiming that he knew where they were. Luring the sheriff into a life-threatening situation, Stapp led Jacobs to a thick copse of trees not far from Stapp's home and told him that the brothers were camped about midway into the grove, one that became more like a thicket as one walked through it. Advancing slowly and not knowing of Stapp's collusion with the brothers, Jacobs had just reached the fringe of the thicket when, from hidden places, the Peaces opened up and shot him to death.[31]

Going in small squads, other Taylor raiders were still hoping to find Helm, Tumlinson, and Cox in an insecure situation and kill them all. Although the plan fell through because the lawmen proved to be both careful and elusive, Jacobs's death was bad enough. Not only was the sheriff an effective leader out to clean up his region, but he was also someone whom the harmless, hapless, law-abiding citizens trusted. After they murdered the sheriff, the Peace brothers rode to John Choate's ranch in San Patricio County. Firmly in the Taylor camp, Choate agreed to help the two murderers after they told him that vigilantes were persecuting them without cause.[32]

Choate rode many miles just to see Tumlinson. Choate told him about the supposedly harmless Peace brothers and asked him to join the Taylors against Helm and his men. Tumlinson refused, for he knew the Peace brothers to be murderers, whereupon Choate threatened the old ranger, promising him that he would die shortly because of his refusal. Choate's next stop was Creed Taylor's place in DeWitt County. He stayed about three days and went into Yorktown each day in company with Hays Taylor and other desperadoes. After he left Creed's place, Choate went to Jim Bell's house where he gathered some of the dead man's clothes, weapons, and other items that he took back to his San Patricio ranch to give to the Peace boys. When he arrived home, Choate found that a number of Taylor men had gathered there around the brothers. The Broolans, Doughtys, Perrys, Gormans, and a man named Fulcrod were there with about forty or so other men, almost all having indictments against them in the various counties throughout Taylor Country. The men scattered after learning that Helm and his posse were in the area. Choate gave the Peaces $150 and told them to ride to Galveston and go into hiding there. Instead, the brothers went to the Stapp place, perhaps to persuade Stapp to go with them.[33]

But what of Stapp? Lieutenant Thompson held that he was as guilty of the Jacobs murder as the Peace boys. A civilian posse of seven or eight men from Helena went to the Stapp place and found not only him but Clint and Mat Peace, too. The officers arrested the three malefactors and started them on the road to Goliad. About half an hour later, settlers nearby heard rapid-fire shooting. Several banded together and went to investigate. They found Stapp near the road stone dead with multiple wounds made by shotguns and revolvers. The Peace boys got away, but a trail of blood indicated that at least one was seriously wounded. Lieutenant Thompson believed that because so much blood was found around the scene of the shooting that one of the brothers must be dead or would soon be. Also interesting, Thompson later talked with Stapp's wife, and she did not recognize any of the men in the posse that killed her husband. It is unknown if the woman simply spoke the truth when asked a direct question or if she made the claim fearing that she would herself be killed if she divulged any names.[34]

Meanwhile, Helm took up the chase for others in the Taylor ring. Knowing that he was after them again, gang members scattered in small groups of from five to fifteen men. Helm and his men captured several of the desperadoes while looking for the Peace brothers. He was not the only authority determined to find the Peace boys. Operating for the military, Lieutenant Thompson of the post of Helena took to the field, but he failed to find any of the Taylor band.[35]

One man who escaped Thompson was ring member George Tennille, who may established an operation independent of the Taylors. Called a "thief on a big scale" by one of his contemporaries, Tennille hired a group of Hispanic cowboys and paid them to steal horses in Texas and to run them to Mexico and sell them. While there, they stole horses and drove them back to Texas for sale, thereby creating a type of revolving-door prosperity for Tennille.[36]

While Tennille was prospering, military leaders were still looking for Doughboy Taylor and any other raider-rustlers they could find. A Unionist spotted Doughboy in Webberville near Austin. Sources reported that Taylor planned to come into Austin to join a poker game on a Saturday night. One informant relayed that message to Special Officer M. P. Hunnicutt who, like Detective Bell, had been searching for Doughboy. Most grateful for the information, Hunnicutt believed that he would have an excellent chance of arresting the renegade when he ventured into town. However, Sheriff Pratt of Travis County spoke to others about the lawman's plan, and an unidentified party warned Taylor who, of course, did not come into Austin. Instead, he left the vicinity of Webberville. He probably headed back toward Taylor Country to hide in Wilson County.[37]

While tracking Doughboy, Detective Bell had some good luck. With Hunnicutt and a small posse accompanying him, Bell found Doughboy, James Cook, and George Kellison north of Austin and immediately charged them. In a running gun battle fought on horseback, Bell and his men wounded Doughboy, shooting him in the shoulder. But all three felons had fast horses and escaped the posse. All three made for North Texas to hide there for a time. Bell and his men pursued after the detective telegrammed authorities in Bastrop and LaGrange, for he believed that the raiders would cross the Colorado River at one of those two points. Bell asked local lawmen to be on the lookout for the three villains and to arrest them if possible. Yet, despite Bell's hopes, all three men disappeared, and authorities at neither Bastrop nor LaGrange had a chance to corral them.[38]

While Hunnicutt, Bell, and their men were in the field, General Reynolds issued Special Order No. 7. It required Capt. T. M. K. Smith, then at the post of Corpus Christi, to take the field with a squad of troopers and to investigate doings in DeWitt and San Patricio counties that involved the Taylor ring generally and the Peace brothers particularly. The captain was to search for members of the ring and to try to find Officer Helm. Reynolds ordered Smith to investigate the recent deaths of John Choate and his son

Crockett, but as events proved, the deaths of the Choates was explicable. According to Smith, they belonged to the Taylor ring, and John Choate had threatened Joe Tumlinson's life in July while both were in Yorktown. An officer of the law, Tumlinson, of course, had refused to help him protect the Peace boys, while warning the Choates to leave the Taylor band if they wanted to live. John Choate exclaimed that he and the Taylors could gather enough men to completely wipe out Helm, Tumlinson, and their posses.[39]

Helm and his men were camped near Yorktown when he learned about Choate's threats. He decided to steer his posse toward the Choate ranch in San Patricio County. According to his intelligence reports, not only had the Choates returned to their ranch, but also several Taylors—including Creed, Hays, and Doughboy—were there, along with the Peace brothers. The informant said that various other raiders were there, the number including Frank Skidmore and William Kirtner. Although the intelligence proved spurious, Helm readied a simple plan to flush his quarry out of the Choate ranch house. He directed Detective Bell to take fifteen men and go on a scout to the Choate ranch. Bell moved out on August 19, reached the ranch on Sunday morning, August 22, and awaited Helm's movement. After Bell and his men left camp, Helm led the rest of the posse on an indirect path to the neighborhood of the ranch and then surrounded Choate's house, thereby preventing all possibilities of escape as well as stopping any others in the ring from communicating with the now trapped people in the ranch house. Once a runner told him that all his men, including Bell's contingent, were in place, Helm hailed the house, asking for surrender.[40]

Helm had no way of knowing that only John and Crockett Choate, their wives, and the two young guns, Skidmore and Kirtner, were the only people inside. Henry Choate and William Casion were hiding in nearby woods. Earlier, Helm had learned that various members of the Taylor bunch were there, but he did not know that most of them had scattered. Despite the small number of men, these members of the Taylor circle were forted up, barricaded in, and ready to fight in a place that was battle-ready. The Choates had cut loop-holes for firing weapons on every side of the house. They had dug secret passages from one room to another so that men could move around without showing themselves and becoming easy targets. The family had stored enough water and food to withstand a siege of up to fifty days. The Choates had stockpiled five hundred shotgun shells, two hundred Spencer rifle cartridges, and assorted ammunition for handguns. Helm later found fourteen guns in the place.[41]

Even as the lawmen were demanding surrender, the party in the house opened up with shotguns and rifles. The men inside fought gamely, desperately. Crockett Choate fired from a chink hole between the logs, his aim was true, and a posseman named Kuykendall became the first man to die in the affray. Helm's men returned fire until he gave an order to storm the house; whereupon, Officer Bell and a few others charged, the first result being the almost instant death of Crockett Choate as Bell shot him repeatedly when he fired into the chink hole that Crockett was shooting through. As well, one lawman fired a shot that mortally wounded Kirtner, who shortly died. Someone shot Skidmore who was destined to survive the shootout, but his wound was severe.[42]

After the posse gained control, John Choate came out of the house holding his wife in front of him as a shield while saying, "I'll surrender, I'll surrender. Where is Jack Helm? I want to surrender to him."[43] Choate continued to advance through the yard while still keeping his wife in front of him. Either most brave or foolhardy, Helm left his cover and started walking toward Choate, who began walking toward him. When the brigand was about ten feet from the lawman, he raised a revolver from behind his wife's back, took aim at Helm, and fired. Incredibly, he missed his target. Likely, he was nervous and had hurried his shot, wanting to kill Helm before the lawman could return fire. Instead, Helm raised his gun and pulled the trigger, but he was mindful of the woman, whom he did not want to kill. Consequently, the posse leader only had a shot at one of Choate's legs; he took it, wounding his enemy. After being hit, Choate shoved his wife away, left her lying in the dirt, and limped back toward the house. Why Helm did not fire a second shot is unknown. Perhaps, the woman was still in the line of fire, and he did not want to take a chance and perhaps shoot her by mistake; meanwhile, Choate ran inside and barricaded the door once again. Helm then ordered Sergeant Louis Peyton to take his four-men squad and secure Choate. The troopers stormed the house, broke down the door, and fought through the barricade. In a move that would be his last, John Choate shot at the men. They returned fire and killed him.[44] Working together, the military men and the civilian posse had eliminated more of the Taylor ring.

In September 1869, Maj. George H. Crosman, now commanding at Helena, received what he believed to be reliable information about the whereabouts of Taylor men Buck Roland, James Patterson, Mat Peace, Jim Wright, Fred Pell, and one other man. Grand juries had indicted all of the rogues for crimes ranging from robbery to murder. Crosman placed Maj. James Callahan and three enlisted men on detached duty to go after them. Callahan found fifteen civilian volunteers among area Unionists who constituted a makeshift posse that accompanied him and his small squad. Riding out of Helena, Callahan and his posse scouted extensively, but they did not find any of the felons.[45]

CHAPTER FIVE

Rampant Lawlessness

A S Helm, Bell, and their men disposed of the Choates, Captain Smith was carrying out his orders from General Reynolds. Once he reached the town of San Patricio, he found that people were greatly excited. Someone told Smith that Jack Helm had moved to "Round Lake" with at least two dozen men. When Smith and his escort reached the place, they questioned Helm, who produced several military documents, along with items from the courts, to prove his authority. In addition to representing the military, he was also a Lavaca County Deputy Sheriff, and he produced evidence of that, too. According to his orders, Helm had permission to issue summons if he needed help. He had the power to arrest any "suspicious" men and known members of the Taylor ring. He had the authority to disarm any men carrying shotguns and revolvers and to use the weapons to arm his citizen soldiers. As he looked about Helm's camp, Smith noted that he and his escort were not the only troopers there. He saw four members of the Fourth United States Cavalry, one being Sergeant Peyton, the other three being privates. They had come from the post at Helena to assist Helm's force and to find and join Joe Tumlinson's men. Clearly, the military and civilian officials remained confused about chain of command and authority. Incredibly, Smith had not known that Helm was acting within the law. That Smith had been suspicious of Helm and Bell represented a breakdown of communication.[1]

The next morning the Helm contingent, now numbering about forty men, went into San Patricio, where Captain Smith began questioning anyone who had knowledge of the Taylors' whereabouts. Smith also sent a small detachment to Choate's ranch, about sixteen miles from town, to question anyone remaining there. The detachment returned the next day with Henry Choate and William Cashion who had hidden during the battle there. Smith wrote superiors that the Taylors had to be defeated and that while Helm and Tumlinson's forces were often brutal, they were in the process of ridding the area of "thieves and murderers [the Taylor band]."[2]

While Smith was looking for members of the ring, Bell took to the field again. When he was in Helena on August 8, 1869, he learned that some of the Taylors were hiding in the chaparral about thirty miles north of town. Before pursuing them, Bell wrote a superior, saying that he, Helm, and Tumlinson were apparently effective. While they had not captured or killed that many Taylor men, Bell asserted that a general stampede of criminals was taking place; they were running to other parts of the state or to Mexico to avoid arrest or death. He reported that he already knew that various members of the Taylor ring could be found in Bell, Milam, Washington, Karnes, and Lafayette counties, in addition to DeWitt and Gonzales counties. Bell said he had led a raid on the Taylors' camp in Karnes but could not corral any raiders because leaders Hays and Doughboy changed their locations so often they were hard to track.[3]

As well, Bell commented on Helm and Tumlinson. They had now re-cruited about one hundred men, including some troopers from the post of Helena, and were sweeping DeWitt and adjacent counties, mainly looking for cattle rustlers and horse thieves, whereas military authorities had told Bell to concentrate on murderers and others who committed violent crimes. By early August, Helm and Tumlinson's forces had killed eleven and wounded four supposed thieves. Bell averred that Helm, Tumlinson, and their forces had not killed even "one honest man." Still somewhat critical, Bell wished that the two lawmen and the posses would concentrate more on felons with capital offenses lodged against them.[4]

Meanwhile, the people of Lavaca County became desperate. According to petitioners, horse thieves and robbers virtually held the county hostage. They asked that the military give Jack Helm the authority to pursue and to arrest renegades wherever found, even if outside the county. More than thirty-five men signed their request in the hope of relief.[5]

In an August report, Bell wrote about the Peace brothers, who had mur-dered Sheriff Jacobs, and about their comrades who were supposed to assas-sinate Helm, Tumlinson, and Cox. In July Helm found and arrested the Peace brothers, but they escaped on the trail, rode south, reached the border at Eagle Pass, and found safe haven in Old Mexico after crossing the Rio Grande. Bell considered the whole affair a disaster, for if Helm's men had done a proper job, the brothers would be in a jail awaiting trial. Yet the brothers had taken risky action and managed to get away with it. They were two *not* killed while trying to escape.[6]

Detective Bell remained busy. To his superiors, he explained the case of DeWitt County's James Lunsford who sometimes rode with the Taylors. Accused of killing a man in 1866, Lunsford spent more than a year in the Clinton jail before being released on a $3,000 bond. Bell found him in Lockhart, Caldwell County, and arrested him. But after seeing Lunsford's papers, Bell released him, for he was not wanted for any new crime. Nevertheless, Helm's men later found and arrested him. He became another of the men who were killed while trying to escape.[7] Bell next outlined the tale of George Blackburn and Reuben Purcell, both of whom had once been members of Helm's posse. But when Helm received intelligence alleging that both men were ex-Confederate raiders and thieves, Helm and his men attacked them, the result being the death of Purcell and the severe wounding of Blackburn. Meanwhile, Bell reported that Tumlinson was worthy of respect, having captured many criminals before, during, and after the Civil War. Now he was responsible for recruiting most of the men in the posse but turned overall command to Helm.[8]

One of the men trying to corral the Taylors was rancher John W. Littleton of Helena, an ex-sheriff of Karnes County. He was a former Texas Ranger who fought with distinction during both the Cortina War and the Civil War. He was one who was losing cattle and horses to the Taylor ring, and he wanted to bring its members to heel. He well knew the Taylors' reputations as cold-blooded killers, but he decided to go after them nevertheless. On the one hand, Littleton wanted to help the authorities reduce crime in the region; on the other hand, the reward for the murderers of Major Thompson was now up to $2,000 apiece. Looking for the killers, Littleton joined forces with William "Bill" Stannard. The two men began scouting, hoping to find their quarry. They had a major problem, however. They could not keep all their movements a secret. Soon, Taylor sympathizers informed the desperadoes about their plans. The Taylors ordered several men to spy on the two bounty hunters and to monitor and report all their movements.[9]

Although the Taylors sometimes laughed at how easy it was to elude regular authorities, including army personnel, the clan felt differently about Littleton, who was a bonafide military hero because of his valor in battle. The Taylors respected and feared him because he was courageous, persistent, and resourceful. Apparently, he was a man who would fight the devil himself should he ever run across Old Scratch. Understanding that ring members would be watching them, Littleton and Stannard were forewarned and for a time did not give the band any opportunities to strike. The hunters usually traveled by night. Often they were in the company of lawmen and therefore made hard targets. However, Littleton's routine changed when an emergency business meeting in San Antonio required his presence. He did not want to go alone; he asked Stannard to make the trip with him for their common protection. They set out in a buggy, for Littleton was too heavy to ride horseback for long distances. They traveled at night, both to avoid the hot summer days and the Taylors' scouts. From Stannard's home in Riddleville, they drove up the Ecleto to Nockenut in Wilson County; there they took the Old Gonzales Road that General Santa Anna's soldiers had cut in 1835. They reached San Antonio without incident and remained there about a week while Littleton attended his business meetings.[10]

On their return trip, Littleton and Stannard had no trouble until they were about ten miles from Nockenut at a place called the "sandies" where sand turned the road into a potential quagmire and slowed their buggy. As well, they had to negotiate a forest that bordered on being a thicket. Although they could not know it, Hays Taylor had earlier learned from spies about the route the two men had taken to San Antonio. He gambled that they would return by the same route. Indeed, they did, and they died for that decision. But, before the ambush, a fifteen-year-old youngster from Gonzales County, William Lewis, came upon the Taylors' camp in the "sandies." The boy was searching for his runaway horse when he stumbled into the raiders' camp. Present were Hays and Doughboy. Also encamped were Ran Spencer, Buck Roland, Jeff Clark, Fred Pell, and others, the entire bunch determined to kill Littleton and Stannard. The villains told Lewis that they were hunting for horses. Since Lewis was doing the same, the men offered to take the teenager with them. The next morning, one of the men asked Lewis to go into Leesburg to get them something to eat but also to ask about Littleton's movements. The boy rode to Leesburg and went into a store. He bought a can of oysters and a box of sardines, some ham, and some crackers. He asked the merchant about Littleton's whereabouts. Told that Littleton had gone to San Antonio, the boy returned to the camp, whereupon the entire group saddled up and rode for the head of the Ecleto where they made camp and awaited the return of Littleton and Stannard.[11]

Again sent off to find food the next day, Lewis could not find any nearby houses. As he was returning to camp empty-handed, he heard gunshots from about four hundred yards away. He ran into the camp and saw all the men hurriedly reloading their guns. They said they had just shot Littleton and Stannard. Yet, the two men were still in their buggy and were running away. During the ambush, Littleton and Stannard realized their plight when they saw about a half dozen men on horseback thundering toward them. With Hays Taylor in the lead, each of the horsemen had a sixgun or shotgun in hand. Both Littleton and Stannard reached for their weapons, but their guns were on the floorboard of the buggy under the seat. They could not come up with their weapons in time to make a fight of it. Instead, the Taylor raiders shot two more of their foes to death.

Upon reloading their guns, the murderers scrambled upon their horses, and with Hays in the lead, they caught the buggy. Hays grabbed the reins and stopped the horses. Upon their examination, the raiders saw immediately that Littleton was dead. A bullet had struck him on the right side of his head above his right ear and penetrated his brain. Shotgun buckshot had also hit him in his right breast and right leg. Upon being shot, Littleton cried "murder" at least twice. Stannard made not a sound but fell out of the wagon when Hays stopped it. Later, Doughboy took credit for killing Littleton because he fired the shot into his head. Ran Spencer argued, claiming to have shot him first in the breast when he fired both barrels of his shotgun at him. Jeff Clark claimed that his shotgun blast had ended Stannard's days; however, Stannard's groan proved that he was still alive. Without much ado, Doughboy finished what Clark started by approaching the prone, bleeding man. He used his sixgun to shoot Stannard in the head. After the killings, the desperadoes told Lewis that they would never be taken alive and would kill anyone who tried to arrest them. Because the boy appeared to be harmless, the men allowed him to leave unmolested.[12]

Still searching for the Taylors, Detective Bell was in Yorktown by early August. Shortly, he found Helm near the junction of the San Antonio River and Coleto Creek. Helm commanded about one hundred men in his posse, and the group was still on the trail looking for thieves. Bell and his men left Helm's camp and struck out for Karnes County after learning that some of the Taylor men had been sighted there. The raiders continued to move frequently, but Bell believed their days were numbered because citizens had again banded together to track them. Bell learned that many of the band had moved to Ecleto Creek in Karnes County near Creed Taylor's place. Bell and his men—twenty civilian volunteers and two troopers from the Fourth Cavalry—began moving that way. The detective had no way of knowing that Hays and Doughboy Taylor had already planned to abandon the area and move south of the Rio Grande.[13]

However, Hays and Doughboy delayed their trip to Mexico, and that decision proved to be most costly. They decided to steal a large horse herd to drive before them. After selling them south of the border, the brothers' profits would allow them to live in splendor at least temporarily. Bell, Helm, and their posse approached Creed Taylor's home at night, got into the place, and placed Creed and family under house arrest while waiting for Hays and Doughboy to show themselves. Bell posted some of his men in the weeds here and there around the house. Although the two hotspurs were now sleeping well hidden in the woods near the house, the lawmen expected them to return in the morn for their breakfasts. The next day, Doughboy indeed returned, but he was alone. Bell and his men spotted him. When he was within gun range, they demanded surrender. Instead, he drew a gun, whereupon the posse opened fire. Doughboy took a ball in a shoulder but returned fire while running toward a fence. He jumped it and disappeared into a cornfield.

Hearing the shots and knowing that Doughboy was probably in danger, Hays Taylor, Henry Westfall, and some others working the stolen horse herd rode in the direction of the sounds. Reaching the scene of battle, the alarmed Hays immediately understood his brother's peril. Determined to save his sibling, he charged the Bell contingent, as did Westfall and the others, all firing their guns as they rode. Hays managed to kill one of the posse members with a shot to the head, but Bell and his men returned fire and sprinkled him with lead. A posseman hit Hays in the arm with a shotgun blast, that arm shattering; a sixgun ball did damage by burying itself in Hays's breast. Several other blasts hit him, yet he remained on his horse. Knowing that he was seriously wounded, Hays attempted to run. He wheeled his mount away, but Bell and some of his men pursued. About 200 yards from Creed's place, while still chasing the felon, Bell fired an accurate round that slammed into Hays's skull. Knocked off his saddle, he was stone dead when his body hit the ground.[14]

Simultaneously, the Bell men wounded Henry Westfall, who took a ball in his breast. But he did not go down. The lawmen shot Westfall twice more before shooting his horse out from under him, after which he fled afoot. As the madness continued, Doughboy managed to slip out of the cornfield and to make it to a horse. But some of the lawmen saw him as he tried to escape and shot his horse out from under him. Doughboy rolled on the ground but popped up shooting his weapon. The wounded Westfall, still running, finally found a horse and sprang atop it, spurring the steed onward. Westfall was a thief and a murderer, but he had sand. In a dramatic show of loyalty, while knowing that he was exposing himself to lethal fire, Westfall galloped toward Doughboy, who jumped on the horse behind the saddle. The two killers made a clean escape, with Doughboy firing on the posse to keep them at bay while also spitting blood, that fact showing how seriously the lawmen had wounded him.[15]

After the bloody encounter, members of the Taylor gang who had participated in the shootout scattered, but Bell and Helm arrested Creed Taylor for aiding and abetting murder, horse theft, and cattle rustling. They did not abuse Creed, but they had no respect for him; they took him to the post of Helena's guardhouse and pitched him in. Creed remained there, held without bond, while Helm wrote General Reynolds to inform him of the development before asking the general to divide all reward money for killing Hays equally among the entire posse, as all had taken part in the scout, the attack, and the victory.[16] In reporting to Capt. C. E. Morse, Bell had much negative to say about Creed, holding that "he is the worst living man in this country. His life has been one of robbery and murder in the past, but for several years he has used his sons."[17] Writing Reynolds, Bell added that Creed was "a very bad man" who should be detained and put on trial.[18]

Even as Helm and Bell achieved success, critics condemned their supposedly harsh actions. Former Confederates charged that Helm, particularly, was guilty of the outright murder of a number of prisoners. Worse, as early as June 1870, J. L. Haynes, a Republican, accused Helm of killing thirty-one men and then using their supposed attempts to escape as justification for shooting them. Haynes failed to mention that most of the criminals that Helm and Bell went after were of the most malicious kind. Wanted for murder, cattle rustling, and horse theft, many men, as mentioned earlier, indeed tried to escape rather than face a certain execution or a long prison term. Some desperadoes were willing to fight and perhaps to die rather than face legal consequences. Theirs was an either-or world. They would fight for their freedom, or they would die in the attempt. As well, records divulged that more men did indeed successfully escape than officers killed during attempted escapes.[19]

For the killers, the odds seemed on their side when they decided to flee from lawmen. Nevertheless, authorities ordered Special Officer M. P. Hunnicutt to ride to Karnes County to investigate the deaths of several members of the Taylor crime ring: the Choates, John and Crockett; Purcell; Stapp; Moore; Jim Bell; James Rutland; William Kirtner; and James and Dobe Poole. Hunnicutt reported that a DeWitt grand jury had indicted Purcell for cattle rustling and horse theft. Helm found him in Goliad County and tried to arrest him. Taking great exception to being corralled, Purcell fired a double barrel shotgun at Helm and his posse; the posse returned fire and filled the rustler's body with lead. A last shot knocked him off his horse; he was dead before he hit the ground. In all the other cases, Hunnicutt found that Helm acted legally when presented with violent, armed men who made threats or who took hostile action. Hunnicutt's investigation cleared Helm of wrongdoing.[20]

Concurrently, the Rebel faction in the area turned attention to Creed Taylor and his arrest. As August turned into September, the authorities continued to hold him in the Helena garrison's guardhouse. He was held for fully one month without legal charges being filed. Rather, he remained there because of the allegations that he was the leader of the Taylor ring and consorted with known felons, aiding and abetting their criminal activities. In the time span of about a dozen days, Creed—still posturing as an old hero of the Texas Revolution—impressed Lieutenant Thompson, second in command at Helena, as being honest and forthcoming. The misguided Thompson therefore lobbied his superior to recommend that Creed be released. Further, Thomas H. Stribling of San Antonio wrote General Reynolds on Creed's behalf. Stribling pointed out that local authorities had filed no formal charges and that Taylor was an elderly man who supposedly could not control grown sons and should not be punished for being their father.[21]

Stribling, of course, failed to mention that Creed himself was a rustler and saw his sons frequently to coordinate his activities with theirs. Moreover, his sons and others in his employ committed known criminal acts. Notwithstanding the facts, Post Commander Capt. George W. Crosman verified that Creed was being held but that no charges had been filed. The captain explained that District Attorney Wadsworth, whom the Taylors bribed, had appealed for Taylor's release which was eventually accomplished; however, Creed had to raise a $10,000 peace bond. One of the five men who helped raise the bond was Colin Campbell, who ran the crime ring's operations in San Saba County. For Creed to regain his freedom, conditions applied: He would cooperate with the military and civilian authorities; he would keep the peace; and, specifically, he would not seek revenge for any wrongs, real, alleged, or imaginary, done to his family. Further, he could use firearms or other weapons only in self-defense.[22]

With his bond posted on September 18, 1869, Creed returned to his Wilson County ranch and continued to help direct the Taylor crime ring and its war on lawmen. He plotted how to avenge the death of his son Hays and how to help Doughboy in the cattle-rustling, horse-stealing business. As best he could, Crosman continued to monitor Creed and those people who visited him. Specifically, the captain ordered a detachment commanded by Sergeant Thomas C. Curtis to stay near Creed's ranch and to patrol the immediate area every day. Creed was to molest no one, but Crossman ordered Curtis to protect him from any hostile acts. Men like Captain Curtis and Lieutenant Thompson did not realize the harm that they had done in releasing Creed. They did not know that he directed the disastrous course that the extended Taylor bunch was taking. He worried little, however, because he had many killers on his payroll. He paid for them with the ill-gotten gains that he made from stealing so many horses and cattle. Moreover, military supervision soon lapsed because of manpower shortages, and Creed was free to do whatever he pleased.[23]

Soon after Hays's death, Bell, Helm, and their posse moved into Goliad County, looking for men with prices on their heads as well as trying to catch cattle rustlers in the act. They found two desperadoes whom they killed when their quarry refused to submit to arrest. They found and killed another rustler when he pulled a weapon and tried to make a fight of it. All three of the men killed often rode with the Taylor gang.[24]

Creed Taylor, a
founder of the Taylor
crime ring, in his
later years.
Courtesy Sharon Barnes,
Director, Regional
History Center, Victoria
College/University of
Houston at Victoria Library

Bell and Helm were also looking for Doughboy, who was still on the run. He was in Crockett in early September, camped just off the Huntsville Road not far from town. He remained there for four days; however, local lawmen who saw him did not recognize him. They did not have a description of him until one of their number read accounts of his nefarious doing in the *Galveston Daily News* and *Flake's Daily Bulletin.* Shortly, the district clerk of Houston County, J. P. Delespine, reported that on September 8, 1869, an informant told of the whereabouts of Doughboy, James Cook, and George Kellison, all of whom authorities called "desperadoes" and members of the Taylor gang. A citizen's posse coalesced and took to the field near Pennington, a settlement about fifteen miles from Crockett.

That night the posse tracked the renegades and at sunrise the next day

found them having breakfast with William Connor, another raider. The posse hailed the house, demanding surrender. When no answer came, the lawmen opened fire with shotguns and handguns. One of the shooters got lucky with a ball that killed Kellison, but Taylor and Cook made a dash for an open log house firing their revolvers as they ran. The lawmen fired their shotguns repeatedly at the log cabin until the murderers surrendered, Doughboy now having been shot twice in one of his shoulders. Someone among the posse secured both men with ropes, after which the entire group headed for Pennington. In all the fighting and its confusion, Connor managed to slip away. From Pennington, the lawmen took Taylor and Cook to Crockett and tossed them into one of the county sheriff's cells. However, the two felons soon escaped and rode into the vast nowhere.[25]

Simultaneously, Detective Bell was still in the field on the trail of gang member Ran Spencer, one of the murderers of Major Thompson back in 1867. The intrepid Bell followed the man from South Texas all the way to Denton County in Northeast Texas. First, the lawman learned that his quarry had been staying with Jake Miller, a Taylor man who lived on Cowhouse Creek in Coryell County. Once there, Bell arrested four of the Taylor gang, but Spencer was not among them. Learning that Ran had an uncle who lived in Upshur County and had hidden there after he murdered Major Thompson, Bell moved into Upshur. He found Spencer at his uncle's house in late September, but Bell was alone at the time, whereas Spencer was in the company of his two cousins and uncle. Outnumbered, Bell had to bide his time.[26]

Spencer left his uncle's place and moved generally northward until he arrived in Denton County. He may have been trying to get to Indian Territory to hide, for the town of Denton was only about forty miles south of the Red River. Helped by County Sheriff B. E. Greenlee and two volunteers (John V. Dickson and James Bennett), Bell succeeded in finding and arresting Spencer in the early morning of September 26. While the desperado was still asleep, Bell rushed him with a cocked shotgun. Quickly awake and staring at the wrong end of the gun, Spencer knew that to surrender was to save his life. Bell put him in irons immediately. The detective and the sheriff then accompanied Spencer on the trip back to Austin to hand him to authorities there. Both men and their two volunteers shared equally in the civil and military rewards for the capture. As for Spencer, he freely admitted to Bell and the sheriff that he was present when the Taylor boys murdered Thompson and that he left the scene with them, but he denied firing a shot although eyewitnesses said otherwise. He added that he had gotten away from the self-destructive Taylors at first opportunity and had not seen them since.[27]

Meanwhile, Helm was hard at work. At one point in September, he had moved into Lavaca County while scouting for brigands. He organized

a posse of local men to help track malefactors. That action came to the attention of Lavaca County Judge A. K. Foster, who called Helm the leader of
a "band of regulators," a most unflattering statement implying that Helm had
no authority when indeed he did. Hearing of the judge's protest, Captain
Charles A. Wikoff, post commander at Columbus, became agitated. He notified Lt. C. E. Morse, the Acting Assistant Adjutant General and Secretary
of Civil Affairs in Austin, that he, Wikoff, would arrest any armed band that
came into his command territory unless he received orders to the contrary.
Clearly, there was still a lack of communication and coordination between
Fifth Military District headquarters and local military and civilian authorities. That some authorities worked at cross-purposes created additional headaches for Helm.[28]

Meanwhile, as Bell was celebrating a victory while he and Greenlee drug
Spencer toward Austin, the acute manpower shortage that both civil and military authorities suffered made itself felt once again in Taylor Country. Cav-
alry Capt. G. G. Huntt, now commanding at Helena, ran afoul of General
Order No. 185, issued in October. It directed him to scatter thirty of his men
about the country. He was to send ten to Gonzales, ten to DeWitt, and ten to
Refugio because the Taylor rustlers had been operating in all three counties.
Horrified by the order, Huntt told superiors that if he obeyed, he would have
only nineteen men left to guard his prisoners, store house, and water supply.
His men would have the additional duty of caring for and feeding sixty-five
horses. Such complaints and cries for more troopers continued to be a common lament of most post commanders all across the interior of Texas.[29]

While Huntt was worrying about his manpower and the possibility of
attack by the Taylor raiders, Joe Tumlinson learned from an informant that
Mat and Clint Peace had returned from Mexico. Several people had seen
them in and around Columbus. He passed the information on to Lieutenant
Thompson, who took to the field. Out of Helena in early October, he directed his small detachment to Yorktown where he raised a citizens' posse to
help him. Then, the party rode for Columbus. Once there, Thompson questioned the locals and collected information about the brothers. He intended
to bring them in for the murder of Sheriff Jacobs. He learned that they were
raising (rustling) a herd for a relative, one Cole, a man of "bad reput," according to one informant. When the lieutenant and his men reached the
Cole place, they learned that he and the Peace boys had left. They were driving their stolen herd toward St. Felipi. The posse immediately pursued and
found Cole and the herd near the Brazos River, but the Peace brothers were
not to be taken. They had received intelligence that the posse, including men
in uniform, was on the way. Thompson believed that the missing brothers
were on the way to Galveston where Mat Peace's wife lived. After dismiss-

ing most of the posse, Thompson, Tumlinson, and two others headed for Galveston. After reaching the city, the lieutenant went to local police chief, one McCormick, and told him of the mission, whereupon McCormick immediately sabotaged Thompson's efforts by having an informant alert Mat Peace of the pursuers' presence. The murderous brothers had ample time to escape. Further, the man named Fulcrod, who had eighteen indictments against him, was with the brothers, and he escaped, too. With no leads, Thompson and the others returned to Helena with nothing to show for their recent efforts. Soon, the lieutenant received word that Clint Peace had been seen in Liberty County, and he was again off in another pursuit, yet another one that yielded no fruit.[30]

While Thompson was in the field, authorities in DeWitt County learned the location of a number of Taylor men who had slipped into their county. Deputy Sheriff William Faust and Capt. H. G. Wood, with a small posse, left Yorktown looking for Taylor raider Chris Kirlicks Jr., who had murdered a man named Lockhart in Houston in September. Subsequently, a grand jury indicted him. He and his extended family had a farm about four miles southwest of Yorktown. His home was a logical starting place for a search. After their short trip on a late October night, the authorities, including Tumlinson's men James Cox and W. R. Russell, surrounded the house before Faust and Woods went inside to search it. Chris Kirlicks Sr. and George Kirlicks opened the door, spoke with Woods and Faust, and allowed a search, guiding the men through the house. Although they could not know it, the posse members missed the hiding place where Chris Kirlicks Jr. and John Kirlicks were secreted. Then, while they were still inside, George and William Kirlicks, who had been in another hiding place about six hundred yards away, approached the house and slipped inside. Now, five family members had temporary superiority. They used their advantage. John Kirlicks drew his revolver and fired, the blast wounding Captain Woods mortally; he died a short time later. Quickly after the shot, Faust grabbed John and his gun, and the two men grappled. John Kirlicks won the struggle and shot Faust to death.[31]

Wary of the lawmen outside, one of the malefactors extinguished all lights in the house. All then grabbed weapons before bursting out of the place. They ran to their horses, firing at the posse as they went. Although the lawmen returned fire, the action was not effective. Once mounted, the five men rode quickly through the posse whose members had dismounted. All five escaped, but a trail of blood indicated that one was seriously wounded. After camping at the site for the night, at dawn the posse pursued the Taylor raiders. At 2 P.M., the authorities found and arrested Chris Kirlicks Sr. and William Kirlicks and took them to the Yorktown jail. At nightfall, a detach-

ment with the prisoners in tow took off for Clinton, for the county seat's jail
was more secure than the one in Yorktown. Near Clinton, however, a group
of men in disguises confronted the undermanned posse and took the prisoners but a short way into a nearby copse of trees and shot them to death. The
posse retreated to Yorktown, but the next day Cox and Russell went back to
the scene to get the corpses and deliver them to their families.[32]

The four gang members who escaped rode south on fast horses. They went
through San Antonio and rode on toward Eagle Pass and the Rio Grande.
Clearly, they planned to go across the Mexican border to escape retribution.
Shortly, they were seen in Castroville, which confirmed the authorities' guess
about Old Mexico. Then in San Antonio, Special Officer Bell took up the
chase once he learned of the development. He hoped that dressed in plain
clothes, he could cross the border, find the men, and bring them back, something no uniformed man could do. Still, little came from the chase, and the
brigands began enjoying life because they were safely out of the reach of the
Texas authorities.[33]

In his next missive to headquarters, Bell reported that the young killer
John Wesley Hardin and a small band of men had been spotted in Taylor
Country, this perhaps being the first time that Hardin had ventured so far
south. He did not stay long, but Hardin, his band, the surviving Kirlicks,
and other desperadoes would one day return and add more firepower to the
Taylor arsenal.[34]

After failing to find any of the Kirlicks clan, Bell received a communication from military headquarters in November, listing the quarry among the
Taylor men that Bell was to go after next: Doughboy Taylor, Jim Wright,
Buck Roland, and Jim Cook. All four were wanted for murder. After talking
to an informant, Bell left Austin on a mission to find Wright. First, the detective went to Pleasanton in Atascosa County, for that was Wright's home area.
Next, he sought out Peter Tumlinson who had a ranch about seven miles
north of the town. Upon talking with him, Bell became highly dissatisfied
with what he heard. The rancher had just returned from a visit to Austin
and a meeting with General Reynolds. In their conversation Reynolds and
Tumlinson had discussed the case against Wright in some detail. A key detail
involved James Thompson, still using the alias James Tope, whom Austin authorities had arrested in 1867 for several murders. Confined in San Antonio,
he told one of his guards that Jim Wright was his partner in crime and a party
to the murders. Returning home, Tumlinson told everyone he knew about
those details. He even sought out Wright and told him! Disgusted, Bell ask
Tumlinson why he gave the information to the felon. Tumlinson averred that
he wanted to gain Wright's trust so that he could learn the desperado's plans.
In essence, Tumlinson had warned Wright who had ample time to flee before

Bell could find him. Later calling Tumlinson "a fool or a knave or both," Bell lamented that Wright would be much harder to catch, for he was on the run and now knew the authorities were actively looking for him. Indeed, Wright, accompanied by his brother Riall, crossed the Rio Grande at Eagle Pass and thereby cheated justice.[35]

Bell next went to Helena, where he heard news of Creed Taylor. In a local saloon, Bell talked with Dist. Atty. J. Wadsworth on November 12, 1869. Wadsworth got genteelly drunk, and his tongue got looser with each swallow. He confessed that Creed had bribed him to help get out of the military lockup in Helena. The bribe consisted of $100 in gold and a quality horse. The animal was, of course, a stolen one that belonged to a rancher in Lavaca County, but it went through many hands before it reached Wadsworth. John Glover originally stole it and gave it to Doughboy Taylor who gave it to his wife who gave it to Creed who gave it to Wadsworth as part of the bribe. The disgusted and somewhat confused Bell confiscated the animal and assigned one of his men to return it to its owner.[36]

Bell next gave a report to his superior that made it appear that most men in South Texas might belong to the Taylor gang. The Peace brothers were now south of the Rio Grande, as were many others who were most afraid that Bell might pick up their trail. On the banks of the River Frio during another scout, Bell learned that Bill Thompson—who had committed a murder in Austin and several others around the state—was at Fort Ewell running a store. Bell said another brigand wanted for murder, Jim Weaver (Bell did not know that "Weaver" was the alias that Doughboy was now using), had escaped into Mexico, as did Sam and Drew Hassley, who had killed a soldier in Bell County in 1868 (one day all four would return and add their guns to the Taylors' firepower). Bell learned that murderer Ben Hinds, who had ridden with the Taylors, was now in Bell County. Other desperadoes, the detective said, were roaming in the country from the Nueces to the Rio Grande. Informants told him that one wing of the Taylor bunch was concentrating along the Nueces.[37]

To scout the region, Bell recruited the steadfast James Cox as a guide and Henry Ragland as an interpreter, and the three, in the manner of cow hunters, headed south into the chapparal below San Antonio. They were ready to fight, if necessary. All three had a shotgun and two sixguns apiece. The trio intended to visit all the "notorious" places from Edinburg to Eagle Pass, believing that they could go where uniformed soldiers could not. He could have enlisted troopers, said Bell to a superior, but the mission needed "finesse." Most brigands would tolerate three harmless-looking cow hunters, whereas they would kill troopers. Information gained from the scout was mixed. Jim Wright was on the Frio when Bell and party were not, prompting the detective to assert that "these outlaws seldom stay in one place too long." They continued to commit their crimes in one place, then run to another area to hide and to assume aliases. Still, Bell learned that Doughboy Taylor and James Cook had escaped jail in Houston County, where they had been lodged after committing depredations. Once free, they rode south. An observer spotted the desperate duo just north of the Rio Grande; clearly, they were joining some of their friends in Old Mexico.[38]

After uncovering a smuggling ring in South Texas and chasing a murderer from San Marcos—actions having nothing to do with the Taylor ring—Bell learned that Wright was, indeed, in Mexico. So was Thompson, the murderer of William Burke and other men, who was in Monterey and whom Bell expected to pop up in Laredo at any time. Gang members Jim Hamilton, Jim Henderson, Buck Roland, the Peace brothers—all were hiding south of the Rio Grande. At one point, Bell crossed the big river and moved about three miles southward, hoping to find some of the desperadoes. But he feared going further without official authorization. A little later, the detective's pipeline of intelligence told him that Doughboy Taylor had returned to Texas and was hiding along the San Miguel River not far from the Laredo–Fort Ewell Road. Bell had to curse his luck, however, when he learned that Martin Taylor, Doughboy's cousin, had just paid a visit to Creed Taylor on his Wilson County ranch, but lawmen missed Martin altogether.[39]

Nevertheless, Bell determined to go after Martin Taylor and Taylor's father-in-law, David Morris, who was riding with him. Again the detective set out with Cox and Ragland. Reaching a small hamlet on the Laredo–Fort Ewell Road near the San Miguel, Bell learned that Martin had been in the area. Locals there feared Taylor because of his bad reputation, one that included an assault with intent to murder charge in DeWitt County. Bell continued his scouting for known murderers but did not find Taylor. However, he learned that Doughboy had recently been seen along the Ecleto.[40]

In early December 1869 while he was in Austin, Bell received news that Jim Wright had taken up residence in Rio Grande City, one of the oldest towns in South Texas, which had become an international port and a key cattle center. That made the area good cattle rustling territory. As well, an observer had seen a man fitting the description of Chris Kirlicks Jr., who was on the Frio when he was spotted. Near there, Kirlicks stole a fresh horse, leaving behind another stolen one that he had ridden almost to death.[41] However, Bell decided to go after Doughboy, whom an informant had seen on one of the ranches of Colin Campbell, a Taylor man. The spread was on the Ecleto, about twenty miles northwest of Yorktown. Before he left Austin, Bell learned more about Doughboy's whereabouts. An informer had seen him on the Elm Fork of the Ecleto, "armed to the teeth" and riding for his father's ranch in Karnes County, another indication that Creed Taylor, old hero that he had been, was deep into rustling and assorted other crimes. Once Dough-boy reached the area, he told one man that he "had come back to Karnes County to stay and that he wanted to be at peace with everybody."[42]

Apparently, young Doughboy believed that if he promised to be good and to stop killing men, rustling cattle, and stealing horses, everyone would forgive all his previous crimes. Along with military authorities in Austin, Bell was otherwise minded and took off after the young murderer. However, once he reached Karnes, the lawman could not find his quarry, for despite his pledge to remain on his father's place, Doughboy was nowhere about when Bell conducted a search. Once he was back in the county, the detective received much good information on others in the Taylor ring. Earlier, in late November, Moses Taylor, who helped run Creed's stock ranch operations in San Saba County, popped up on the Cibolo near Sutherland Springs in Wilson County in the company of Fred Pell and Buck Roland, other of Creed's men. Bell surmised that Doughboy had met Moses there and had re-turned to San Saba County with him, for that county was a rural, out-of-the-way place where he could lose himself, a place where he would not be seen by anyone who could identify him. At the time, Creed also left Karnes and headed for Columbus with a cattle herd, many head of which may have been stolen by his men.[43]

A fount of knowledge, Officer Bell learned that the Peace brothers were once again in San Patricio County, near the town of the same name. Bell put Joe Tumlinson in charge of a posse and asked the men to find and ar-rest the boys for the earlier murder of Sheriff Jacobs. Next, Bell reported to superiors that an informant had seen the two Gorman brothers—originally from Goliad—in Indianola, the informant believing that the brothers were going home. Bell alerted Goliad County officials. He warned Tumlinson to be vigilant, for the Gormans had earlier promised to kill him.[44]

Soon catching a stage for Austin, Bell himself became most alarmed when three heavily armed horsemen emerged from the chaparral and began following the stage closely for several miles. Knowing that assassins were af-ter him, Bell crawled out one of the carriage doors, bounced atop the stage, crawled to the driver's seat, and armed the driver with his spare revolver while he pulled two more. Having a gun in each hand, Bell pointed the weapons toward the three riders, who first advanced toward but then retreated from the stage several times as if trying to decide whether they should face the lawman's guns or break off. The would-be assassins ultimately decided that facing Bell's guns would be folly and ended their pursuit. The stage made it safely to San Antonio and thence went on to Austin.[45]

After arriving in Austin, Bell told superiors that he feared danger was imminent in DeWitt County south of Clinton. He believed that, led by Creed and other Taylors, the ring members were thirsting for revenge, for many of their number were now dead, in jail, or scattered all over South Texas and northern Mexico. Bell listed several of the targets for revenge: himself, Joe Tumlinson, Helm, Cox, Ragland, Bill Sutton, and others. However, DeWitt County voters had elected Jack Helm sheriff, and the detective hoped that Helm and his posses could hold the Taylors in check. But, Creed had just sold a herd in Mexico and had plenty of money. Bell knew that he would use some of the new wealth to hire more gunfighters who would hunt down and kill his enemies, those of his sons, and those of the rest of the extended Taylor clan. Bell had actually learned of Creed's plans when he was in the post office of San Antonio. He overheard two of Creed's friends talking and laughing about the situation. They did not know Bell, and, in retrospect, they were quite foolish. They gave away the Taylors' plans to go to war with the authorities. Bell thus had time to prepare.[46]

CHAPTER SIX

Lawmen Closing In

IN January 1870, Detective Bell continued his quest to find and arrest Doughboy Taylor. Knowing that the Taylors were having him followed, Bell changed directions several times coming out of Austin and wound up in Waco after losing a spy. He received word that George Pierce, a desperado who ran with both the Hamilton gang and the Taylors, was in Webberville. Acting alone, Bell went there and managed to arrest Pierce. Although threatened several times by Hamilton and Taylor men, Bell got his ward to Austin's jail and removed one more villain from the Texas landscape.[1]

Despite that small success, conditions in Victoria, Gonzales, and Karnes counties seemed to deteriorate rapidly because members of the crime ring stepped up activities in those areas. A Victoria Republican office holder, W. J. Neely, told Gov. E. J. Davis that the county needed troops because it was "not possible for an officer to arrest offenders in this county unless he has a posse" that outnumbered the criminals. Neely requested at least ten troopers to help the county sheriff do his job. Then the situation was made worse when the sheriff resigned rather than continue to fight the Taylor raiders. The desperadoes were concentrated in one part of the county, and they outnumbered lawmen, who dared not interfere with them. No one stepped forward to take the sheriff's place; as well, the town of Victoria did not even have a justice of the peace.

Gonzales resident L. M. Shockley echoed Neely's concern. Shockley had recently returned from a trip to Karnes County and reported that it was out of control. Civil law was powerless, Shockley complained, adding that even peaceful men in Karnes had to go armed everywhere for fear of new attacks. The farmers wore guns even while they plowed their fields, and many blacks continued to hide in forests at night for fear of the raiders. Like Neely,

Shockley wanted troops to patrol both Karnes and Gonzales counties with civilians serving as guides. He believed that continuous patrols would drive the malefactors to other haunts.[2]

At the end of February, General Reynolds received word of how terrible life had become in DeWitt and Goliad counties. Writing from Myersville, B. O. Stout reported that the Taylor men had no respect for any law that stood in their way. They threatened to kill anyone who opposed them, just as they had murdered Sheriff Jacobs earlier. Stout thanked Reynolds and his men for the protection the army tried to give. He said that the "great mass" of people were law-abiding but that the Taylors' actions destabilized the entire region, with people being too afraid to speak out or even to defend themselves. The Taylor raiders, Stout held, were "rustlers," "robbers," and "thieves." He was afraid they might go to "open warfare" and kill all troopers in the area and any civilians who supported the military. Acknowledging the late elections that brought the Republican party to power, Stout said he looked to Reynolds "and to Governor [E. J.] Davis for support and protection." But, continued Stout, "the robbers believe that your authority will soon be at an end[,] and there will be a change of government[, and] they [Taylor brigands] will have their revenge . . . I do hope and entreat you that you will give your friends protection, that you will not leave them to be murdered."[3] Unfortunately, the prediction about the end of Yankee and Unionist rule proved true. Once E. J. Davis won the governorship, the federals began withdrawing from the state, the exception being those troops on the Indian frontier.

W. A. Jacobs's experience emphasized what Stout had to say. Now living near Clinton in DeWitt County, Jacobs had helped his brother, Sheriff George Jacobs, before Taylor men (the Peace brothers) murdered him. W. A. helped detective Bell and Joe Tumlinson many times by recruiting men for posses and by joining them himself on sundry occasions. His horror story began on March 10, 1870, at approximately 11:40 P.M. Twenty-five men belonging to the Taylor bunch surrounded his house, many of the men wearing Klan-like disguises but claiming to be federal troopers. Some tried to disguise their voices. Yet, Jacobs recognized several men, most from DeWitt County along with some from Lavaca County. The spokesman for the terrorist group threatened to lynch Jacobs while demanding that he come outside, saying that the men would throw fire balls into his home if he refused. After questioning, haranguing, and threatening him for about four hours, the raiders departed. The reason they let him live is a mystery. Thenceforth, the lucky Jacobs began staying away from home at night, the man believing that the terrorists would likely return but would not harm his family if he were not there. An informant explained to him later that if they had caught at home again, the Taylor men would have murdered him. He appealed to the military for protection. Barring that, he asked the post commander at Columbus to ask the sheriffs of DeWitt and Lavaca to arrest the malefactors. Jacobs explained that he was a supporter of Deputy Sheriff Joe Tumlinson and could be reached through him.[4]

While Jacobs was coping with his travail, the first months of 1870 found Bell still chasing Doughboy Taylor after he recruited the incarcerated Ran Spencer to help him. The felon Spencer—who had been with Doughboy and Hays Taylor when they murdered Major Thompson and his sergeant at Mason—received a parole for his assistance. While Spencer was off trying to obtain information, Bell went from Austin to Yorktown and scouted DeWitt County before moving into Goliad County. He had no success, largely because the hunt of the previous summer had gone so well. Those among the Taylor forces were still scattered, most of them much afraid to return to face Bell, Helm, and the military authorities. Soon Bell popped up in San Antonio where, as agreed, Spencer met him and gave a report. Ran had sought out Doughboy's wife, who believed that he was still a Taylor man. She told him that her husband was gone and that James Cook was with him. She produced a letter from Doughboy that he mailed in Palestine, Columbia County, Arkansas, the home of Cook's brother John.[5]

As Doughboy told his wife, when he and Cook escaped from a Houston County jail, they rode into Arkansas. Badly wounded in the shoulder, Doughboy, whose alias was now J. C. Wright (the real James Wright, part of the crime ring, remained in Texas), found a physician to remove two balls from his wounded body. Next, Doughboy's wife produced another letter from her husband, one telling her that he and James were going east, destination Georgia. She was to write Doughboy in care of John Stephens & Company, commission merchants, in Atlanta (Stephens was her uncle). Determined to go to Atlanta at once, Bell hired B. F. Thompson to accompany him, for Bell knew he could not bring Doughboy and Cook in alone.[6] Then began a comedy of errors.

The daunting duo reached Atlanta on February 22, 1870. After explaining his mission to military authorities there, Bell received permission to proceed. He then wrote a letter supposedly from Creed Taylor to J. C. Wright (Doughboy), announcing that Creed had given his messenger (Bell) $250 in gold for Wright. Bell went to Stephens's business office and talked with an employee who claimed that Doughboy had returned to Arkansas. Soon, Stephens arrived, and Bell told him about the letter and the gold while showing the missive and the yellow ore. However, like the employee, Stephens told Bell that "Mr. Wright" was back in Arkansas. The businessman produced a $125 note that "Wright" had signed and asked Bell if he could have $125 of the $250 in gold. The detective claimed that his instructions were to deal only with Wright and give him all the money. Although he did not know it at the time, an informant had told Stephens who he really was, or, rather, who he had been.

A Union scout during the Civil War, Bell at one point operated in Arkansas, but Confederates caught him and imprisoned him at Washington, Arkansas. There, a Confederate officer interrogated him several times. A Georgian, the officer returned to Atlanta after the war. The same man saw the detective enter Stephens's office. While Bell was dealing with the aforementioned employee, the ex-Rebel sought out Stephens and warned him, which accounted for Stephens's lack of cooperation. Stephens—and therefore Taylor and Cook—had discovered Bell's purpose.[7]

Not realizing that he was found out, Bell continued his mission. After telling Stephens that he was leaving for New York City, Bell caught a train for New Orleans. With Thompson, he took a steamboat to Shreveport, thence going to Columbia County by carriage. Questioning people in Magnolia, Bell learned that "Wright" and Cook had gone to Atlanta, Arkansas, which was in the same county. Upon reaching that town, the detective learned that his targets were once again in Palestine, only six miles from Atlanta. Next, someone told him that since their return from Georgia, Wright and Cook had engaged in the most bizarre behavior. In just one week's time, the horrible hearties had committed assault with intent to kill on three separate occasions. Atlanta Justice of the Peace Nathan F. Smith had "Wright" arrested on the first charge with bond set at $100. Unable to get a bondsman, Cook, who had avoided arrest by hiding, deposited the money with a merchant, one Millican, whereupon the judge allowed Wright's release. The next day, Wright and Cook sought out Millican and demanded the money. After they beat him, the businessman complied, largely because they threatened to kill him and "were armed to the teeth" with shotguns and revolvers. After the dastardly duo had threatened to kill yet another man, both Wright and Cook got married! According to Bell, they married good, respectable girls, two cousins named Moore.[8]

The father of the girl Wright (Doughboy) intended to marry immediately took to his sick bed just after he learned of Wright's proposal. As he lay dying, the protective father denounced his future son-in-law, calling him a desperado and a scoundrel. He begged his daughter not to marry him. The father then died in vain, for the headstrong girl later married Wright anyway, but not until more turmoil developed. With their father gone, the girl's brother started objecting to the marriage, whereupon Wright beat him over the head with a sixgun, picked up the girl, threw her over his shoulder, carried her to a buggy, and headed for the nearest judge to perform a ceremony. Shortly after consummating their twin marriages, Wright and Cook discovered that a detective from Texas was near and looking for them; they quickly abandoned their new wives and disappeared, telling the locals they were going back to Atlanta, Georgia.[9]

The determined Bell took off for Georgia once again, arriving in Atlanta on April 2, 1870. He learned that a "strange lady" had arrived at the Stephens's home. She turned out to be none other that Wright's Texas wife. Yet, there was no sign of Wright or Cook. Since Stephens and his family were church-going Catholics, Bell donned a disguise, and from a livery stable, he watched the church on several Sundays, hoping something would turn up. Nothing did. Bell next received intelligence that Wright's Texas wife was leaving Atlanta on the Macon Railroad. Donning another disguise, Bell boarded the train. He hid in the baggage car and searched it. He found her bag checked to Jonesboro, Georgia, a place about twenty-one miles from Atlanta. After a thorough search around Jonesboro, Bell determined that Wright was not there. The detective hired a freedman to look for the renegades after giving him a description of Wright and Cook. Bell then went back to Atlanta where military authorities finally called Stephens in for questioning, but the man was obstinate and insulting. He told his interrogators nothing. Eventually, Stephens's lawyer secured his release. The disappointed and frustrated detective finally gave up the hunt and returned to Texas.[10]

While Bell was on the chase, Joe Tumlinson learned the whereabouts of Martin Taylor and David Morris. Martin had settled on some land in McMullen County about halfway between Tilden and Oakville. Morris's place was near Martin's, about a quarter of a mile away. Tumlinson formed a posse of about a half dozen men and went after both felons. The posse's first stop was the Morris place where they found and arrested Morris. With the prisoner in tow, the posse approached the Taylor place. Although details are scarce, Martin resisted violently, and Morris tried to escape while the lawmen were dealing with him. During the gunfight members of the posse killed both men.[11] The significance of the action was clear: Tumlinson and his men had eliminated two more men of the Taylor ring.

Later in April, Bell was tracking Doughboy again. Believing that he had returned to Texas, the detective went to Galveston, informed the local police of his mission, and received their word that they would look for the desperado. If they caught him, they promised to hold him. Next, Bell went to San Antonio to talk with Ran Spencer, who failed to come to a scheduled meeting. The detective then went to the Kellys' operation in Karnes County about fifteen miles north of Helena (the Kellys also had an operation in Lavaca County). Bell hoped to find his quarry there because the Kellys were firm Taylor men, and two of the Kelly brothers, Henry and William, had indictments against them.

Then came bizarre news. The detective learned that, while running a herd of cattle, Spencer had been struck by lightning and killed. He was at the junction of the San Marcos River with the San Marcos–Bastrop Road when death came. Bell was, of course, disappointed at the loss, for finding Dough-boy would now be more difficult without Spencer's help. Reporting to su-periors, Bell gave the whereabouts of Creed Taylor who now worked out of his ranch in Wilson County. The detective reported that the desperado Jim Weaver (the alias of Jim Taylor) had left Mexico for a quick trip to Bastrop but had already run back to safety south of the Rio Grande. The detective still did not know that "Jim Weaver" was Jim Taylor using an alias. Next, Bell met with Joe Tumlinson. The two men tried to develop a common strategy for coping with the Taylor raiders.[12]

Almost concurrently, the military command developed a plan to pro-tect commissary trains using the San Antonio–Indianola Road—as General Mason had earlier recommended—and to bring law and order to Karnes and DeWitt counties. Obeying General Order No. 11, army officers created a company of civilian volunteers to carry out the twin goals. Two captains commanded the volunteers. The military chose civilian William Elder as one of the captains; he and his thirty-two volunteers received orders to patrol Karnes County west of the San Antonio Road. The military named Jack Helm as the other captain; he and his twenty-nine men had orders to patrol DeWitt County in the vicinity of the Guadalupe River. Armed with military power, Helm and Elder were to police their areas and arrest criminals, be they murderers, robbers, or cattle and horse thieves. Both captains and their men could cross the lines of any counties to pursue and stop lawbreakers.[13]

Shortly after the army established the civilian patrols, authorities had reason to celebrate because the Karnes County Sheriff ridded the world of Fred Pell, whom the *Austin Daily State Journal* called "a member of the Tay-lor gang of banditti." Pell had been in the Taylor squad that murdered Major Thompson in Mason and Littleton and Stannard in the "sandies." A mili-tary patrol had earlier captured Pell, and in May 1870, military commanders turned him over to the sheriff who was escorting the desperado to Helena for trial when the murderer made a break for freedom near Lockhart in Caldwell County. His guards shot him to death. According to the *Journal,* "there were numerous indictments against him for deeds of violence and crime," adding that "thus perished the shedder of blood."[14]

As the patrols began their work, Bell learned from Helm that Doughboy Taylor had returned to Texas. Helm said the raider had appeared in DeWitt County in company of at least ten "very desperate characters from all parts of the state." Shortly, the county statistics for rustled cattle and stolen horses went up. Helm still did not believe that traditional civil law could handle the Taylor men; rather, he knew that military help continued to be critical.

He insisted that more firepower was needed to protect the county. Indeed, Helm had to use his own money to hire personal bodyguards because murder threats against him had become so common.[15] Bell needed bodyguards as well, for the Taylor raiders were after him, too. He also needed his pay because State Sen. B. J. Pridgen, destined to commit several murders, was holding it as a means to pester the lawman. Pridgen, whose brother Wiley was wanted for more than one murder, was a moderate Republican, but his political sympathies seemed to lay with the Democrats. A wealthy, slave-owning planter in the antebellum era, he became a vitriolic opponent of the State Police once the legislature founded that law-and-order organization. Senator Pridgen, in fact, was an active participant of the Taylor crime ring. Indeed, the Taylor clan had earlier retained lawyer Pridgen to represent their interests and to keep the law at bay. Despite the financial problems that Pridgen caused him, Bell continued working in the field trying to locate and to arrest desperadoes.[16]

In June 1870, several newspaper editors reported that unknown parties had killed Bell. Supposedly, the Taylors had found him and ended his multifaceted career. Shortly, however, the detective appeared in Austin, thereby putting the rumor to bed.[17] By the end of Bell's unproductive pursuit of Doughboy, several momentous events had occurred in the Lone Star State. In the state elections of 1869, Republican E. J. Davis, who had served in a provisional appointment, became the new governor, and the voters elected a Republican majority in both houses of the legislature. In February 1870, General Reynolds called a special session of the newly elected legislature, one that reapplied for admission to the Union. Congress readmitted Texas in April, and the Fifth Military District was dissolved; military commanders began pulling their troops out of the interior of the Lone Star State.[18]

In retrospect, when the military withdrew from the interior, Republicans, white and black, were left to the tender mercies of the former Confederates, many of them active in terrorist societies around the state, others of them outlaw raiders like the Taylor band. Those ex-Rebels had no tender mercies. Rather, many determined to use any means necessary to restore Rebels to power and to inaugurate "Redeemer" rule that would last until the 1950s. Although many people did not know it, the new circumstances dictated that the Republicans would hold power for one term only and then be swept out of office. Yet, for the brief time they were in power, they tried to reform the state. Among other improvements, the Republicans gave Texas its first statewide system of public education, practically the only thing that would help the poor masses, black and white, to rise above soul-crushing poverty and, one day, to escape the selfish rule of the upper class. Although it was later replaced, the new Constitution was an improvement while it existed.

As well, Republicans encouraged railroad development, the one area of common ground they had with many Democrats. Despite progress, Republicans still came under attack, especially for the creation of the Texas State Police.[19]

On July 1, 1870, the new Republican legislature created the State Police, and it continued operations until late April 1873, when a newly installed Democratic legislature killed the agency. In lobbying to create such a force, Davis understood that Confederate elements in Texas were still at war. In June 1871, he elaborated, telling the public that "the war is not over yet. I tell you there has been a slow civil war going on here and has been ever since the surrender of the Confederate armies."[20]

Davis wanted a state force that would help county sheriffs suppress crime, especially in areas where local authorities could not act because of manpower shortages or simply chose not to act. Moreover, the new force would be mobile; that is, it could operate in all Texas counties, cutting across all legal jurisdictions. Headed by Adj. Gen. James Davidson, the new force had four captains: E. M. Alexander, Jack Helm, M. P. Hunnicutt, and L. H. McNelly. Eight lieutenants, twenty sergeants, and 125 privates rounded out the force. Although the new organization was never at full strength, especially in the number of privates, every local peace officer was also enrolled and subject to the orders of the adjutant general.[21]

One name that was conspicuously absent from the first roster of the State Police: Special Officer Charles S. Bell. Unionists might well have expected to see his name among the captains or the lieutenants, but such was not the case. Earlier in June 1870, various developments strained Bell's relationship with Jack Helm. Although some ex-Rebel Democrats roundly condemned both men for supposed illegal acts, the real focus early in the year was Bell. A number of Republicans even criticized him, citing the fact that so many men he arrested were "shot while attempting escape." Finally Bell had enough, now believing that his service to Texas had ended in failure. He tendered his resignation as special officer and left the state. He quickly found more work once he relocated to Washington, D.C., where he served as a detective for numerous federal departments, a post he held for several years. He also worked as a detective in Mississippi for a time. However, by 1878 he had developed consumption, the disease forcing him to move to the Soldiers Home in Dayton, Ohio, where he died on Tuesday, February 18, 1879. The record is clear that he tried mightily to fight crime in Texas. After the Redeemers came to power in the 1870s, a movement began to bring Bell back to Texas and charge him with sundry murders, but that plan never materialized because the record revealed that Bell had always acted within the boundaries of the law.[22]

While the Republican legislature was creating the State Police, the solons also reestablished the State Militia. By the end of the year, the force was comprised of 3,500 men spread among thirty-nine companies. The major job of the militiamen was to assist both local authorities and the State Police. Altogether, the new law enforcement agencies made life much harder on terrorist groups, individual criminals, and outlaw bands. More and more, Taylor men were now forced to move frequently just to escape the law. Some went to Old Mexico when policemen or militiamen got on their trail. The Taylor raiders had a much harder time in their cattle-rustling and horse-stealing operations. The frequency of their crimes declined. However, they remained the bane of the free black community's existence, but few sources give details.[23]

To supplement the new law and order agencies, the authorities later recruited a group of twenty "Special Policemen" per county to act as auxiliaries for the regular forces. They could join posses chasing lawbreakers and could make arrests if they found felons. Like the personnel of the regular force, the special policemen could be moved from area to area depending on the needs of different locales. Interestingly, a roster of the State Police as of mid-June 1872 listed Taylor man George Tennille as a special policeman from DeWitt County's Yorktown, but no information exists that provides details of his time with the police. By the end of their first few months of existence, the new organizations seemed to be a rousing success. By December 31, 1870, the police had tracked, found, and arrested 973 fugitives and had returned $30,000 in stolen property to the rightful owners. Still, year-end statistics showed that Texas continued to lead the nation in the number of homicides.[24]

Many former Rebels, along with Democratic newspaper editors, denied that such a force was needed and downplayed the rampant crime occurring in the state. For example, The Democratic *San Antonio Daily Herald* was denying that terrorist groups existed in Texas when in fact such groups had been organized in at least seventy-seven counties. Claiming that only "an unprincipled class of vampyres" had spread untrue rumors about the Klan and similar groups, the editor blamed the Republicans for all the ills in the Lone Star State.[25]

Although criticized by many Democrats, the state policemen were expected to fill the void left by the removal of the army. For evidence that the new force was sorely needed, one only has to examine long-term crime statistics across the state. From 1865 through 1868, for example, violent men committed at least 1,035 homicides, with 486 among the victims freedpeople. However, the figures are gross undercounts because not all counties reported to the state, and some gave only partial returns. Further, between 1865 and 1871, sheriffs reported 4,425 crimes but only 588 arrests, a statewide undercount because many county sheriffs did not submit reports to the state. Despite the magnitude of the problem, by September 1871, state policemen had arrested 3,475 men, the number including 638 for murder or attempted murder and 50 for rape.[26]

About crime generally, many knowledgeable people believed that all the statistics relating to criminal activity were undercounts. Writing U.S. Atty. Gen. George Williams in April 1872, U.S. Attorney for Texas C. E. Garland estimated that the true figure of homicides was probably close to two thousand. Further, Garland reported that from May 23, 1868, to May 23, 1870, villains had committed a total of fifteen hundred homicides. Many of the killings were racially motivated, for whites murdered the large majority of the ex-slaves who died. Seldom did blacks kill other blacks; seldom did blacks kill whites.[27]

Most of the murderers who killed blacks went unpunished. Grand juries handed down only 279 indictments, and petit juries convicted only five men between 1865 and 1869. The situation was even worse in 1870. That year, Texas led the nation in homicides with 323, at least 195 more than any other state. Additionally, in 1870 local lawmen in 108 counties reported to the state. The 108 counties listed a total of 2,790 criminals at large, 702 wanted for murder and 413 for attempted murder. At least 1,017 thieves remained at large. By the end of 1871, statistics reflected that Texas had 4,414 fugitives, including 970 murderers. As well, the state had 641 felons wanted for attempted murder and 1,453 wanted for robbery. Of course, such statistics were definitely undercounts, for, as mentioned, often the robbing and killing of blacks were never reported.[28]

Lax law enforcement at the town and county levels helped explain the crime statistics, for many local authorities had Confederate sympathies and would not arrest their fellows, most especially if the victim had black skin. However, many other problems partially explained the figures. First, just as in the past, jurisdictional confusion often allowed a felon to commit crimes in one county and then ride a far piece to hide in another county while adopting an alias. Even jails were inadequate in most cases. In 1869, for example, only 82 of 152 counties had jails and only 24 of those were termed "secure." Clearly, state intervention to solve law and order problems was necessary.[29] Upon taking office, Gov. E. J. Davis made law and order one of his priorities, and he had enough support to push the aforementioned State Police Bill through the legislature. Yet, the force would remain controversial from its creation to its repeal.[30]

To introduce the State Police, Jack Helm gave an interview to the *Gonzales Index*. Calling himself a "senior captain," he explained that he had the authority to operate anywhere in the Lone Star State but that his primary assignment was to police a district that included thirty-three counties in South Texas from the Brazos River to the Rio Grande, an assignment that kept him in Taylor Country. During the interview, the editor of the *Index* spoke freely, saying that he condemned the law under which Helm had been appointed and that the law was "vindictive." Helm tried to allay the editor's fear, saying that in his district, he would seek out and hire only men of proven reputation for fair dealing, and he would accept no one with a history of crime. While the journalist was still skeptical, he advised his public to give the police a chance, for that might hasten the day that former Confederate Democrats would regain control of the state. For one, the editor of the *Victoria Advocate* disagreed with his colleague from Gonzales. He was impressed with Helm and believed that the force would be used for good.[31]

Many Democrats lambasted the State Police for one reason or another, but the major complaint was tinged with racism. The force was about 60 percent white and 40 percent black with a few ethnic minorities also serving. Former Rebels considered it galling that ex-slaves now had a role in bringing law and order, the role including giving orders to whites. Likewise, most ex-Confederate found it horrifying that black men could arrest and incarcerate whites. Further, those who believed in local control opposed the portion of the law allowing the police to act independently of local authorities when necessary. As well, the critics condemned the new organization because it could cross any county line to pursue suspects and/or to make arrests. That said, some former Confederates became members of the force. In Karnes County, stronghold of the Taylor gang, Helena's own Thomas L. Patton was one such example.[32] In volatile DeWitt County, police assignments and headquarters included the following: Jack Helm, Concrete; R. B. Hudson, James W. Cox, and H. Y. Leftage, Clinton; and Joe Tumlinson, J. B. Taylor, and O. H. Bennett, Yorktown.[33]

Despite the hopes that Republicans had for their administration, Democratic newspaper editors were quick to condemn, the *Houston Telegraph* saying that the naive Davis had been taken in by the "most bitter and unscrupulous Radicals in Texas" who were "evil." The governor should stay out of local affairs, said some of the editors, and he should leave law enforcement to local authorities and the state's court system. "He should let the Militia State Guards and Police rust for the want of employment. . . . We would rescue him from the men who will make his name as infamous as Nero's . . . Pray Over It."[34]

Despite such criticisms, the State Police quickly went to work. After three weeks of existence, the force's men arrested fifty malefactors whom county authorities had been unwilling or unable to arrest. One of the arrests was related to the Taylor gang. The ring's George West killed George Martin in Lavaca County, but policemen found and incarcerated him.[35]

Despite some early success, almost immediately criticism—mostly based on unsubstantiated rumors—of Jack Helm surfaced and did damage to the reputation of the State Police. One of his earliest actions as leader of the new force occurred in Victoria. Helm led a posse into town and took a prisoner out of jail. The unlucky fellow was Taylor man Robert Holliday, who was charged with murder and arson. He had burned the Goliad County Courthouse to destroy evidence and proceedings against members of the crime ring. Earlier, elements of the Taylor ring came into Victoria County determined to rescue Holliday, but the county sheriff kept a strong guard on the jail for four 24-hour days until the Taylor men gave up on their attempt. U.S. Internal Revenue Agent I. R. Kean reported the facts to Governor Davis, adding that since Helm had taken Holliday, the murderer seemed to have just disappeared. Indeed, he was never seen again.[36]

Despite controversy, Helm continued to do his job. In one campaign he went after Henry Westfall, called a member of the "notorious Taylor gang" who had once saved Doughboy in a shoot-out. He had a murder indictment against him for a killing in Wilson County. Helm learned that Westfall was in hiding, temporarily living on Sebastian Beales's ranch in Nueces County near Live Oak. Helm and a small posse rode to Beales's place and made a thorough search, but Westfall was nowhere to be found. Although *Flake's Daily Bulletin* reported that Helm's posse had captured Westfall and killed him when he tried to escape, the editor erred, for the man lived to fight on anew for the Taylor ring. Yet, *Flake's* mistake underlined a major problem that pro-Democratic newspapers had. Their editors were quick to publish false information—even if they had to make it up—that cast the Republican party and its agencies in an unfavorable light. Westfall's escape from Helm was actually simple. He hid and slept in the bush close enough to Beales's house to see who came and went. When he saw Helm's posse, he made his escape and left the area.[37]

In mid-August, another problem developed. Helm was then in Lavaca County looking for Taylor men when he learned that gang members, the four Kelly brothers—William, Eugene, Henry, and Wiley—had attended a circus at Sweet Home. Although Henry was the worst of the lot and had a long criminal record, all the brothers were in the Taylor circle. After getting drunk during the circus, at least two, Henry and William, caused pandemonium by shooting up the place and wounding some of the performers as well as some of the people in the audience. That action prompted Helm to go after them. He contacted the DeWitt County Sheriff and asked for more manpower. The sheriff responded by sending Deputy Sutton and a few other men. As well, C. C. Simmons, Deputy Sheriff of Lavaca County, joined Helm and Sutton, showing them arrest warrants for Henry and William Kelly. After interviewing enough witnesses to be certain of the identity of those whom he sought, Helm put the wheels in motion that led to a most controversial incident.[38]

The authorities, Simmons included, broke up into small groups and went to arrest the two Kelly brothers as well as Alexander Cudd, Whit Johnson, and John Criswell. The latter three were quickly found and placed in DeWitt County's porous jail. Criswell and Johnson soon escaped, but authorities found them and returned them to custody after a shoot-out wherein Johnson was severely wounded in the leg. All told, Helm, his men, and various local officers seemed to be clearing Lavaca County of crime. They made a total of fifty-four arrests, a feat that Adjutant General Davidson called "highly commendable" while telling Helm to continue his pursuit and arrest of criminals. But it was the Kelly affair that brought tremendous criticism. In part complaints arose because William and Henry Kelly were sons-in-law of Pitkin Taylor and because they often rode with the Taylor raiders. Hence, the clan's partisans became enraged when Helm's men arrested two of the brothers.[39]

Sutton arrested William Kelly at his home while other officers arrested Henry Kelly, all then joining for the ride to jail. The two Kellys tried to escape, and the posse killed them. That they tried to escape was not unusual, for they were wanted felons. They had successfully escaped from custody before and believed that they could easily do it again. Certainly, they deserved incarceration. Mentioned earlier, for example, was Henry Kelly's brutal rapes of two young black women and his attempted murder of a freedman and a Freedmen's Bureau agent. On all occasions, he managed to successfully escape the law. However, controversy followed when different parties told conflicting versions of the shooting. The lawmen claimed that the prisoners attempted to run. Relatives of the prisoners claimed that the posse wantonly murdered the brothers. The bitter controversy engendered was such that Jack Helm asked for a formal investigation, for he was not present when his men killed the Kellys. He did not have all the details he needed to understand just what had happened. When the investigation began, Adjutant General Davidson relieved Helm pending the outcome of the probe.[40]

The subsequent investigation did little to clear up the matter; the case hinged on the officers' testimony versus testimony from the hostile witness Amanda Kelly, Henry's wife, a Taylor before marriage. The jurors were suspicious of Amanda's story, for she waited several weeks before going public with her charges. She appeared to have been well coached by the Taylors' attorney, Bolivar Pridgen. Without hearing any additional witnesses for the defense, the grand jury, numbering sixteen, cleared the officers of any wrongdoing because certain aspects of Amanda Kelly's testimony were suspect, especially regarding the question of just where she was (how far away she was) when the officers shot the brothers. As it turned out, she was at the home of William

Day, who was her half brother. That house was at least four hundred yards away (four football fields) from the site of the killings, her vision obscured by a copse of trees. Moreover, it was twilight when the events occurred. She was not an eyewitness even though she claimed to be.[41]

Dist. Atty. J. A. Abner concurred with the jury finding, and Helm hoped that was the end of the matter, especially after Abner said that Helm's blows always struck at the "most desperate characters." For one, Governor Davis was pleased about the decision, for he continued to believe that a "slow Civil War" was still ongoing in Texas. Interestingly, the Taylor apologist and propagandist Jack Hays Day, without realizing it, agreed with the lawmen's assertions about exactly where Amanda Kelly was when the lawmen fired the fatal shots.[42] He said that "as she [Amanda] reached the [Day] house, she heard shots and ran back [to the grove of trees]. About four hundred yards away she found Will dead and her husband, Henry, dying."[43]

As time passed, more unfounded rumors hurt Helm's darkening reputation. A San Antonio newspaper editor reported in October of 1870 that Helm and his posse of forty-five men had visited Lavaca County's Sweet Home. Supposedly, Helm levied a special tax on the county's settlers to pay for one of the posse's meals. The pro-Republican editor of the *Austin Daily State Journal* denied that such an incident ever occurred, but the tale may have had a basis in fact. If he "levied" a "tax," Helm's actions were legal, for law required that the counties where the State Police operated were responsible for their expenses.[44]

Nevertheless, critics added that fact to their list of grievances against the police. Staunch, vitriolic Democrat A. H. Longley of the *Weekly Austin Republican* cast dispersion on Helm and held that "E. J. Davis is responsible before God and man for the murder[s] . . . of Henry and William Kelly. He cannot escape this responsibility, because he knew the character of Helm and his gang when he commissioned them to do this murder most foul." Longley continued, saying that more than "thirty men have been butchered in cold blood in DeWitt and adjoining counties by the State Police."[45]

Longley, however, did not divulge the source of information about the supposed butchering, most likely because it never happened. Like most Democratic editors, Longley had a lively imagination and used it when falsifying supposed "facts" if such facts hurt the Republican party and thereby helped the Democrats. In "fact," legal authorities were engaged in the work of finding and arresting felons like the Kellys.

Conversely, the good that Helm did often went unappreciated. For instance, in Matagorda County he and his men broke up the Lum gang that had been killing stolen cattle at the rate of one hundred per day just for their hides; Helm counted more than one thousand carcasses on the day he

Jack Hays Day was the chief apologist for the Taylor ring; his vitriol knew few bounds.
Courtesy Sharon Barnes, Director, Regional History Center, the Victoria College/University of Houston at Victoria Library

investigated. He and some of his men tracked the gang. When the lawmen found W. W. Lum and his men, they asked for surrender; instead, a desperate shoot-out began as Lum and his men drew their guns. Firing shotguns and handguns became the order of the day, after which several of Lum's men lay dead, whereupon the rest finally surrendered. Upon questioning, the badly wounded Lum admitted to the slaughter of the cattle and acknowledged that he had murdered three men and robbed several others. Helm thus put an end to one crime ring.[46] Despite Helm's positive accomplishments, the Kelly matter would not go away. The *Austin Daily Republican* printed Amanda Kelly's testimony along with that of others as well as a scorching letter from

State Senator Pridgen, who had once started a fist-fight with Helm, that castigated the captain even though he was not present when the shooting occurred and even though he had been the officer who called for the investigation. The senator demanded another immediate investigation of the incident. He also wanted proof that Stapp, Moore, Jim Bell, the Choates, the Kellys, Dobe Poole, and any other men killed by Helm's posses were indeed Taylor men guilty of crimes.[47]

The senator held that the whole sorry lot were fine, upstanding citizens who never committed any wrongs, this assertion despite the legion of indictments pending against every one of them. Pridgen's statement was dismissed out of hand by those who knew of the Pridgen and Kelly families' connections with the Taylor ring. It was known that Pridgen and his brother Wiley made a pile of money off cattle rustling. Moreover, Pridgen was still collecting his legal fees for keeping the law off the members of the ring. Helm further disturbed the senator by finding and arresting his brother, the murderer Wiley who had various indictments against him. And, as mentioned, the DeWitt grand jury who examined the Kelly killings unanimously agreed that the evidence did not justify an indictment. That only made Senator Pridgen more determined.[48]

Writing to Adjutant General Davidson, Pridgen said Helm violated the "laws of civilization" and "good morals." In turn, Davidson informed Governor Davis who asked Pridgen for proof of his assertions. Although the only "proof" was still that of a prejudiced witness, the Davis administration faced so much criticism that Davidson finally dismissed Helm from the State Police, a sacrifice to the passions of the moment. However, the hard-pressed lawman continued to play an important role in the authorities' attempts to bring members of the Taylor gang to justice, for he remained Sheriff of Lavaca County. But Pridgen still would not go away. He wrote Governor Davis on behalf of ring members Jim Taylor and William Day who faced indictments in DeWitt County but who were on the run. Posturing as a defender of justice, Pridgen virtually accused Helm, Sutton, and "Doc" White of wanting to murder the two outlaws. Pridgen asked the governor to personally guarantee the safety of all the brigands close to the Taylors.[49]

Despite controversies, Helm had his supporters, one being state legislator F. E. Grothaus who wrote the *Austin Daily State Journal*. He averred that "law-abiding Republicans" were "highly pleased" about Helm's work in bringing in felons. Grothaus criticized Republican Senator Pridgen for deserting his party and his constituents and voting with Democrats. Grothaus appeared not to know that the Taylors had retained Pridgen, paying him a handsome fee for representing the ring's interests and keeping Taylor men out of jail. Had Grothaus known of Pridgen's role in helping the Taylors, he would have understood the wayward Republican's voting record. About Helm, Grothaus reminded the editor and the reading public that grand jurors had investigated the death of the Kellys and ruled no bill.[50]

In another development, Billy Taylor and a few of the other crime band members popped up in Bastrop County in early September. Billy caused some mayhem in Bastrop town for which state policemen arrested him, the charge being disturbing the peace. He made bond and left the area. Local lawmen apparently did not know that there were indictments against him in several other area counties.[51]

Somewhat later, Taylor man John Davis of Spekesville in Lavaca County surfaced in Columbus, Colorado County. On arriving, Davis took his horse to Finucan's Livery Stable. He stuck up a conversation with freedman Edward Jackson. Davis asked him whom he had voted for in the late election. Jackson answered "Davis," obviously meaning the Republican E. J. Davis. The freedman then walked away but did not get far. John Davis pulled a sixgun and shot the ex-slave in the back, killing him. Witnesses got a good look at Davis, who was about five feet, eight inches tall and about twenty-five years old. He had dark hair and dark eyes and wore a brown suit. Of course, the murderer quickly fled, but State Policeman Fayette Yancy and Allen Naill of the State Guards immediately pursued. On the fastest horse, Yancy got close enough to Davis to begin firing at him, getting off about eight shots, all off target. At one point Davis's horse stumbled in a ravine and fell, but so did Yancy's. Davis was quicker to get up than the policeman. He remounted and made his escape, leaving behind his saddlebags, a revolver, and a hat. The person who reported the murder and the chase said that "this is not the first murder, by many, which he [John Davis] has committed."[52] Yet, he was free to continue adding muscle to the Taylor ring.

Meanwhile, Helm continued to experience travail. The State Police arrested him in April 1871. The cause: "miscellaneous offenses."[53] Later, the exact charge was listed as assault and battery. However, authorities dropped such charges once they made a full investigation.[54]

Shortly a wing of the Taylor bunch moved into Walker County where the men began stealing cattle and horses. In area towns they committed devilry that included public drunkenness, assault and battery, and other offenses. Brave county lawmen arrested several members of the crime ring, but its leaders quickly assembled about twenty heavily armed men. All rode into Huntsville to liberate their comrades. The raiders surrounded the jail and attacked it. Amid rifle bullets flying and shotgun blasts erupting, the sheriff and a few deputies were no match for the raiders. To save their own lives, the lawmen fought their way out a back door, leaving the jail open. The renegades freed their friends, all then running to their horses. Called "desperate young fellows," the entire group then made good their escape.[55]

Others in the crime ring were operating in Kimball County by February 1871. Capt. John W. Sansom reported that the Taylors were cow thieves who were "stealing, killing, and branding unlawfully." While moving from Kerr County into Kimball on a scout, one of Sansom's sergeants accidentally stumbled upon one hundred hidden cattle hides. After hearing the sergeant's report, Sansom sent a fifteen-man squad to find and to arrest the rustlers. Writing Adjutant General Davidson, the captain said he hoped to "report to you the arrest of the Taylors and the gang who run with them" within a few days. However, Sansom admitted that "the thieves work carefully and . . . they have their friends to let them know when danger approaches." Sansom believed that Governor Davis should declare martial law in all counties between Kimball and the Rio Grande to stop the thievery. He called for military trials for any members of the crime ring found and arrested because civil courts usually refused to convict them. "I think," he concluded, "they would have a wholesome fear of a military court that they do not have for the civil."[56]

Shortly, Doughboy experienced trouble. In mid-April 1871 at Sutherland Springs in Wilson County, a state guardsman named Black saw and recognized him. Assisted by a number of men in Capt. A. McCluny's company of the State Guards, Black arrested Taylor for the murders of Major Thompson and John Littleton and for three other crimes as well. Doughboy secured the legal services of T. T. Teel, made bond, and went free. Captain McCluny soon wrote Governor Davis inquiring about a reward for "Doughboy Taylor." Davis responded, telling the captain that there was no reward for a "Doughboy Taylor." The governor added that there was a $500 reward for "P. G. Taylor" for the 1867 murder of Major Thompson.[57]

Apparently, the governor—and probably many lawmen and soldiers—were confused, for "P. G. Taylor" was indeed Doughboy. Once freed, he quickly left Wilson County, moved further south, and made Kerrville his headquarters. Father Creed moved his operations to Kimble County and continued to use Doughboy and others. Now, with the military gone and with detectives like Bell no longer a factor, the pickings became easier as long as the Taylor gang stayed away from Sutton, Helm, and Tumlinson of DeWitt County.[58]

Meanwhile, Doughboy, his Arkansas wife long forgotten, tried to settle down with his Texas wife and become "respectable." He sought employment as Texas agent for a cattle-buying company in New York. Such a job would give the Taylor ring a bigger market and further enrich the gang. He was most disappointed and bitter when the firm hired Sim Holstein. Accustomed to having his way, accustomed to assaulting and often to murdering men who stood in his way, Doughboy made the biggest blunder of all his young lifetime of mistakes. One afternoon, he sought out Holstein, who was staying in Kerrville's hotel. In the street near the hotel, Taylor engaged him in some light conversation but then suddenly drew a gun after he deduced that his quarry was unarmed and would be an easy kill. Doughboy got off an errant shot before Holstein took the gun away from him, clubbed him to the ground with it, and then shot him. When Taylor got up, Holstein shot him a second time. Rising again, the felon stumbled toward his house, yelling for help. Holstein ended that possibility by shooting him yet again. Doughboy lived on for about six hours, all the while cursing the unarmed man whom he had just tried to murder. Finally, the youngest of Creed's sons, one of a terrible twosome, had gone to embrace the Grim Reaper. Ironically, Holstein shot him with his own gun, a weapon that had killed so many others.[59]

By the time that Holstein ridded the world of the murderous Doughboy, John Wesley Hardin had made what was his second appearance in South Texas, and this time he was going to stay. Originally known by the alias, Wesley Clements, he would soon command the Taylor raiders.

CHAPTER SEVEN

Enter John Wesley Hardin

BY the time John Wesley Hardin became a coleader of the Taylor gang, he had developed a criminal career that could match or exceed the deeds of the most infamous of the Texas desperadoes. He committed most of his crimes before he reached twenty-one years of age.

The second child of the Methodist preacher James Gibson Hardin and Mary Elizabeth Dixon Hardin, John Wesley Hardin—named for the Englishman John Wesley who founded Methodism—was born on a farm about ten miles southwest of Bonham, Fannin County, Texas, on May 26, 1853, at a place called Blair's Springs on Bois d'Arc Creek. The Hardins had ten children, nine of whom survived infancy. James Hardin had once been a circuit-riding preacher, but he had his own church by the time John was born. According to Hardin legend and lore, an elderly midwife predicted John's future, or, more correctly, his possible futures. The woman supposedly told his father that John was "destined to be one of the greatest men of his age, or one of the worst. He will either be [your] staff . . . or he will bring your gray hairs in sorrow to your grave"[1]

Although he was born in Fannin County, Johnny, as his mother called him, had no memory of the area. While he was just a toddler, his father moved the family, first to Moscow in Polk County and later to Sumpter in Trinity County, which was adjacent to and just north of Polk. Moscow was a tiny hamlet with a population of about 250, but by the 1850s it had become a trading center for area farmers, complete with general stores, sawmills, and cotton gins. By 1857, it boasted the Mason's Male and Female Academy, a quality school. But soon the Hardin family moved to Sumpter where Johnny's father established a school and preached part-time. Now a ghost town, Sumpter was the first seat of Trinity County. By the 1850s the town had but a tiny population of less than two hundred souls. Heavily forested like Polk, Trinity by the 1850s was a thriving place that profited from the steamboat traffic on the Trinity River. Like Polk, Trinity evolved into an agricultural area, where planters and yeoman farmers grew great amounts of cotton and corn. Still, slavery was slow to take hold in Trinity County. In 1860, only 791 slaves lived within a total population of 4,392.[2]

Larger Polk County, on the east bank of the Trinity River, was once the home of the Hasinai Indians, a Caddo tribe. Later came the Alabama-Coushatta Indians. Some Muskogees also originally settled the area. Rapidly settled by white and black Americans from 1835 to 1860, the county evolved into a plantation-slave region, producing 9,307 bales of cotton in 1859. By 1860, slaves made up the majority of the population, 4,198, out of a total count of 8,300.[3]

In his largely rural setting, John Wesley came to understand both the plantation South and the yeoman farmer South. He grew up much like a typical frontiersman. Early on, he became proficient in riding and training horses. He learned how to wield a knife and how to use firearms, be they shotguns, rifles, or handguns. As soon as he was old enough, he took to the forests and the streams, hunting, fishing, and learning about self-reliance. Although he was not well educated by modern standards, he attended schools taught by his father. He learned at least the rudiments of reading and writing, and he mastered his numbers.[4]

As Johnny matured, he had many of the same experiences that other boys in the area had. The lush farmland, adequate rainfall, and a long growing season attracted settlers. They grew great stands of corn; hills of potatoes, Irish and Sweet; several varieties of beans; squash; tomatoes; onions; pumpkins; some wheat; and a few other eatables. Small orchards bore different kinds of fruit, and pioneers could pick wild berries in their season. Almost all farmers had chickens for meat and eggs; dairy cows for milk and butter along with a few beef cattle; and the ever-present pigs, pork being the mainstay of the Old South. Men supplemented the diet of their families by hunting the white-tailed deer, squirrels, rabbits, and other small game. They fished in rivers and creeks. Most farmers and the smaller group of planters strove for self-sufficiency.

Since the great majority of whites in both Polk and Trinity counties were from the Deep South, young Johnny grew up among people who believed in white supremacy and in the mental inferiority of blacks. Apparently, he never questioned such "truths"; rather, he internalized them. As he matured, he expected total deference on the part of slaves and free blacks. In his later life, whenever blacks did not show John Wesley the deference he believed was his due, trouble usually followed. Indeed, as an adult, he became known as a "nigger killer." But, then, Johnny was an all-around bigot; he hated Hispanics and Native Americans, too.[5]

Although he lived through the Civil War, John Wesley Hardin was too young to understand the complex causes that led Dixie to make war. He was only eight years old when Confederates attacked Fort Sumter. Indeed, many adults did not fully understand the explosive issues that rocked their world from 1846 to 1860. However, a consensus developed, even if that consensus had questionable views. According to many secessionists, Northern aggression caused the sectional problems, along with the refusal of the Yankee majority to accept the states' rights theory of constitutional law, which, according to Southerners, had been the intention of the Founding Fathers in 1789.[6]

The majority of Southerners refused to give up slavery or the right to carry slaves into the common territories of the United States. Indeed, so many crises from 1846 to 1861 involved slavery that many historians believe that Dixie's system of human bondage caused the war. Some white Southerners even believed that "all" Northerners were like the abolitionist John Brown and obviously hoped that slaves would rise up and kill their masters. These views John Wesley Hardin soaked up, just as he internalized the view of black inferiority. As he once announced: "I grew up a rebel[. I] saw Abraham Lincoln burned and shot to pieces in effigy so often that I looked upon him as a very devil incarnate."[7] Interestingly, John's father was a Unionist before the war, but his son clearly did not embrace those views. Indeed, in 1863, ten-year-old Johnny and a cousin tried to run away. They wanted to join the Confederate army so that they could whip the Yankees and save old Dixie. Johnny's father learned of the scheme and nixed it, afterward giving his boy a sound thrashing.[8]

After the war, Trinity County became a most violent place, and as John Wesley began to mature, he learned that violent men who were willing to kill virtually controlled his county. For example, the Freedmen's Bureau's records reveal that fifty-five violent crimes occurred in Trinity County between January 1867 and December 1868; the number represents a tremendous undercount, for scores of crimes against blacks were either unreported or simply never investigated. Much of the discord was racially and politically motivated. Former Confederates and their sympathizers intended to dominate the black population while awaiting the Democrats' return to power. By 1868, John Wesley's vicinity had at least one Klan group whose members terrorized the freedpeople and their white Unionist allies. Many county officials belonged to the Klan and cooperated with the forces of suppression. Sumpter's Justices of the Peace John W. Hamilton and Samuel Rich as well as several lawyers, including S. I. Robb and J. R. Stevenson, led the local terrorists. They managed to drive many Unionists and loyal attorneys from the county.[9]

As well, the local Freedmen's Bureau Agent Lt. Charles Schmidt came under attack. In early 1868, the merchant E. B. Robb went to Schmidt's office in Sumpter and assaulted him. In the process, Robb spied the United States Flag, grabbed it, and tore it to pieces. Civil authorities, said Schmidt, were either afraid to act against felons or refused to act. Robb remained free. On April 30, 1868, the bureau agent reported that former Rebels who controlled most county offices in 1866 were still in power, adding that "their services are worth little or nothing." Schmidt believed that the founding of the Klan had rekindled the "spirit of Rebellion." Continuing, he said the county's men were now going heavily armed in public and were "threatening a war of extermination against [white Unionists and freedmen]."[10]

John Wesley spent time in neighboring Polk County, where he had relatives. He visited them often. He observed similar trends relating to both the suppression of freedpeople and crime. Like Trinity County, Polk went out of control just after the Civil War. According to one report, bands of armed men infested both counties. Slaveholders refused to free their chattels. Jefferson Davis was still a hero, and former Confederates persecuted loyal Union men who lived in constant fear that ex-Rebels would kill them. By 1866, folks in Polk, Trinity, and Jasper counties were requesting military protection from desperadoes, a request the high command granted by sending a company of cavalry to the area.[11]

The Polk County Freedmen's Bureau Agent James P. Butler reported in 1867 that the county was a "hell hole of crime, a cesspool of iniquity" and added that the county was "infested with a band of desperadoes and robbers whose highest aim was to murder and plunder." The notorious Benjamin F. Prior was apparently the leader of the band. Later, he and his men often rode with the Taylor gang. Writing from his headquarters in Huntsville, Butler said he would be wasting time to go after the felons in Polk, for he only had a personal guard of three enlisted men to help him, and the raiders could easily overcome such a small force. Race relations had deteriorated to such an extent that the area's freedpeople were so afraid that they had stopped even complaining about the desperadoes. Blacks had ample reason to be afraid. From August 1866 to August 1867, "unknown parties" lynched at least ten of Polk County's freedmen. Such murders continued into and beyond 1868. Even the towns of Moscow and Livingston remained out of control, much the same as the countryside. As late as March 1870, conditions had not improved. A. J. Harrison reported that Rebels still controlled the most important county offices, the same Rebels who had controlled the county before the war. As well, Harrison confirmed that the county had a Ku Klux

Klan organization whose members joined common criminals in terrorizing all people loyal to the Union.[12]

Such was his environment while Johnny was coming of age. He became accustomed to fear, to violence, and to terror before he even reached his teenage years. Meanwhile, in school Johnny frequently caused friction, apparently establishing a reputation as a bully. He had a quick temper, was willing to fight at the drop of the hat, and demonstrated a particular hatred of black people. That his father was the headmaster may have led to Johnny's habit of demanding to be the supervisor of the other children, especially his friends. On one occasion while wielding an open pocket knife, John threatened to kill one of his teachers because the instructor was preparing to spank one of his friends. On another occasion Charles Sloter was one youngster who challenged Hardin. John responded by almost killing the boy, stabbing him in the back and chest. Johnny justified his act by claiming that the boy had used vulgarity in speaking about a girl, but school board members were horrified nevertheless. John's behavior would likely have gotten him expelled had his father not been head of the school; as well, he could have faced criminal charges.[13]

However, Johnny avoided any other serious problems until November 1868 when he visited his Uncle Claiborne Holshousen, a local judge who lived near Moscow in Polk County. Many members of John's extended family also came to the Holshouen place for a day of socializing. During the day, the younger set engaged in various sorts of horseplay before John Wesley's Uncle Barnett Hardin arranged a wrestling match that pitted Hardin and a young friend against the ex-slave, Mage Holshousen, who had belonged to the judge before emancipation. The match was intended to be all in fun, just a little extra entertainment. Bigger and stronger than the boys, Mage won the first match. Then, he won a second match. The two white teenagers had not been much competition for the mature, hard-muscled freedman. John Wesley took his defeats hard, both as a boy and as a man. In this case, he determined to get even. Of course, the situation was all the more galling because Mage was black and supposedly "inferior" to Johnny.[14]

The day after the wrestling matches, John Wesley took Judge Holshousen's Colt .44, hunted for Mage, and found him on a pathway in a wooded area. The youngster emptied all the rounds from the Colt into the freedman, leaving him mortally wounded but alive. Only after the crime did the boy think that he might have acted rashly. Now believing that he might be in trouble that he could not handle, he went to his Uncle Holshousen and spun a tale. He claimed that Mage had a stick and tried to hit him. The boy said the ex-slave's aggression justified firing all the rounds of a handgun into him.[15]

The boy and his uncle, joined by one of the judge's neighbors, went to the scene of the shooting where they found Mage clinging to life even as his blood continued to soak the ground where he lay. Mage managed to tell his version of the altercation, one that differed greatly from what John told his uncle. Enraged, the boy wanted to shoot Mage again, but his uncle prevented that. Still, they watched as Mage suffered while Judge Holshousen tried to gauge the trouble that his nephew had brought upon himself. In murdering Mage, Hardin crossed the line from being a neighborhood bully to being a cold-blooded killer. Judge Holshousen gave his nephew a $20 gold piece and told him to flee, advising that he talk to his father before anything else happened. The teenager did so, and the good reverend became an accessory after the fact by advising his son to run. The preacher gave his son a loaded shotgun and extra shells just in case he had to fight the authorities.[16]

Some of Hardin's apologists have blamed Gov. E. J. Davis and his State Police for John Wesley's errant ways. Such views have no validity. Davis did not come to power until 1869, and the State Police force was not organized until 1870. Yet John Wesley killed Mage in 1868 as well as killing several other men prior to 1870. It is erroneous to blame his outlaw career on the governor, his police, or his Reconstruction policies.[17]

During Reconstruction, whites frequently murdered blacks and seldom faced punishment, but at times the authorities took meaningful action. The Freedmen's Bureau entered the state in 1865 shortly after the war. The Fifth Military District was created in 1867. The personnel of both tried in the face of much hostility to secure justice for the new freedpeople. In the case of Mage's death, Agent Schmidt investigated the shooting and interviewed the dying Mage after his family took him home. Later, the agent reported that Hardin had shot the freedman five times and had done so without cause other than being bested in a supposed friendly wrestling match.[18]

That Johnny had no cause to murder the freedman did not surprise Trinity County's Sheriff Thomas H. Kenley. Already, the sheriff had described John Wesley as a "very quarrelsome boy." Mage lingered for a time but soon died, whereupon authorities charged John Wesley with murder, but even before the freedman expired, Schmidt and other authorities took to the field and scouted for the boy. They did not know John Wesley had earlier talked with his father, who advised him to leave the immediate vicinity and go into hiding.[19]

Polk County Sheriff G. W. Barfield also scouted for Johnny but could not find him. The boy had fled to Logallis Prairie, a small place about twenty-five miles north of Sumpter. His brother Jo was teaching school there. Although John contacted his brother, he stayed with a family friend, a man named Morgan who had established a farm in a remote area. He stayed with Morgan because he and his brother both knew that the military and civilian authorities would likely be watching Jo's place. Living free and unmolested on the Morgan place for about six weeks, John spent his time fishing and hunting small game and wild cattle. According to some sources, including Hardin's *Autobiography,* in December 1868, Jo told him that three federals stationed in Livingston, members of the Sixth Cavalry, were quizzing area people about him.[20] That raised a question. Would the young fugitive flee again and wait to be found, or would he take the initiative?

Johnny answered by taking the fight to his perceived enemies. He supposedly set up an ambush on the Hickory Creek crossing where the troopers would negotiate the creek. Because the trail meandered through a virtual thicket, John Wesley slipped into the mass of Mother Nature where his quarry could not see him. He had a shotgun and a Colt .44 handgun. When the men were at point blank range, Hardin opened up with the shotgun, its blasts knocked first one and then another of the men off their horses. Each died on their way to the ground. The third man, a black trooper, got off a shot that gave Hardin a flesh wound on his left arm. He then tried to flee, but Johnny caught him and demanded surrender in the name of the "Southern Confederacy." The trooper got off an errant shot, but Hardin's aim was better. Using the Colt, he shot the black man to the ground.[21]

The problem with Hardin's account is that there is no evidence that three troopers died in the area during December 1868. Nor did any three disappear together. Military records in the National Archives reflect no such facts; therefore, Hardin's tale, or part of it, might be fanciful. It is possible, however, that three lawmen were tracking him and that the boy ambushed and killed them, later embellishing his account by making it appear that instead of killing Texas officers, he had only killed the hated Yankees because they deserved it. Hardin's autobiography makes most clear that he identified with the old Confederacy and its causes; he believed that Yankee occupation and their rule of old Dixie was heinous. Like many of the members of terrorists groups and like many raiders, he was willing to do battle with the Northerners to hasten the day when ex-Confederates Democrats could regain power. And by the end of 1868, it was possible for him to believe that the day of reckoning was near because pro-Democrat terrorist Klan organizations were flourishing, adding members daily. Over time, at least seventy-seven Texas counties had at least one such group that joined common criminals in meting out death and destruction to white Unionists and their black allies.[22]

The people that renegades and terror groups targeted hoped the military and the Freedmen's Bureau would help them, but by 1868 federal forces in Texas had been reduced to 3,770 men, and they were scattered about in thirty-seven posts. The army placed most on the Indian frontier. Only 1,291 manned the nineteen interior garrisons of the state. Most posts did not even have company strength. Further, many were manned only by infantrymen who were of little use because the more mobile Klansmen and raiders usually had good mounts. As well, the Freedmen's Bureau could not reach all areas of the state because it was so undermanned and underfunded. The agency had only fifty-seven local posts and sixty-nine sub-assistant commissioners at its peak in 1867.[23] Men like Hardin took advantage of such manpower problems.

After killing his three pursuers at Hickory Creek, John Wesley had to run again. He went to the home of his widowed Aunt Susanna Dixon Anderson who lived in Navarro County at Pisgah Ridge, a small farm community south of Corsicana. When she opened a one-room log cabin school (the old Nash School) in January 1869, Hardin joined her and taught a class of about twenty-five. Amanda Tramel was one of them, and she never forgot the experience of having a desperado as a teacher, a fact she learned later. Forever after, many of his pupils always remembered him. He schooled them in the basic "3 Rs" after beginning each teaching day with a prayer. Other than his teaching, Hardin practiced his shooting skills, handguns being his preferred weapons. He began to drink more, frequently to the point of drunkenness. He became a mean drunk who often went looking for trouble.[24]

After the three-month school term, Hardin went to live with his Uncle Alex Dixon, a brother of Hardin's mother who lived in Navarro County in the Richland bottoms near Corsicana. There, he came under the influence of Alex and William Barakman, his older cousins. They were contractors who drove area cattlemen's herds to market. Studying their work and helping them, he learned the cowboy's trade. He continued to drink, and he took up gambling, usually with cards, playing poker and seven-up. He wagered on horse and dog races and on cockfights. He practiced frequently with handguns and became a more proficient shooter. He also began getting in to more trouble, each incident worse than the last.[25]

For example, after the turn of 1869, he met the desperado Frank Polk and briefly ran with him. They were together long enough to jointly murder Tom Brady, but details of the shooting are unknown. Federal soldiers eventually came looking for Polk and Hardin. Although John Wesley escaped the dragnet, the troopers found and arrested Polk, who soon escaped and went into hiding in Freestone County. Polk cashed his ticket to the underworld when he and Wortham City Marshal Charles Powers got into a gunfight wherein the two men killed each other. Teaming with Polk only temporarily, Hardin next took up with Simpson "Simp" Dixon, a relative. From Northeast Texas, Simp had earlier been involved with what some historians called the "Lee-Peacock Feud." Young Dixon had become a member of the area Ku Klux

Klan and had announced that he intended to kill Yankees and freedpeople for as long as he lived. But authorities finally managed to drive him from his home territory. Simp rode south to Navarro County where he had relatives. The new team of Hardin-Dixon soon attracted trouble. The county had a functioning Klan terrorist group; both Simp and John Wesley joined it and began deviling the freedpeople in the area. A squad of troopers came into the area looking for Dixon and eventually found him when he and John Wesley were riding in the countryside. Although a gun battle occurred, both young hotspurs escaped. In his *Autobiography*, Hardin claimed that he and Simp killed one federal apiece and that the rest of the patrol fled. Afterward, the deathly duo lost themselves in the countryside.[26]

The end of summer 1869 found Hardin again on the move. With his older brother Jo, he went to Hillsboro to live with their Aunt Ann Hardin. Roaming Hill County, John Wesley often went to Towash, twenty miles west of Hillsboro to gamble at cards. He frequented the Boles racetrack near Towash to wager on horse races. He was there with friend James Collins on January 4, 1870. After he picked several winning horses and put $325 in his pocket, Hardin joined a poker game with players Collins, Benjamin Bradley, and Hamp Davis. As they played their cards in a small dilapidated one-room cabin, a "Judge" Moore joined the game. While playing, John became drunk and started cheating; he often did both. His manipulation of the cards led to hard words between him and Bradley, who drew a knife when he tired of talk. Too drunk to defend himself (and temporarily unarmed), Hardin backed away, turned, and ran outside while Collins grappled with Bradley to give John Wesley his chance to escape. Safely outside, Hardin remembered that he had left his pistol and his boots inside against a wall. Collins came outside to check on Hardin and gave in to John's request when he demanded the loan of Collins's handgun. When Bradley came outside, Hardin shot him to death before going to find Judge Moore whom he also killed. After robbing the pockets of the two dead bodies, Hardin left the Towash area decidedly drunk but richer for the experience. A Hill County grand jury later indicted Hardin for the Bradley murder in October 1872, but lack of witnesses led a judge to dismiss the case. Yet, Texas Ranger George W. Baylor said in an affidavit made in 1872 that John Wesley had admitted to him that he had killed both Bradley and Moore.[27]

After the murders, Hardin fled when he learned that the authorities were looking for him. With Alex Barekman, he rode toward his Uncle Robert E. "Bob" Hardin's place near Brenham. They stopped at Horn Hill in central Limestone County on January 20, 1870, where they found encamped the personnel of a traveling circus. After joining the group around a campfire, John had an altercation with a circus employee, whereupon he fired a .45 slug

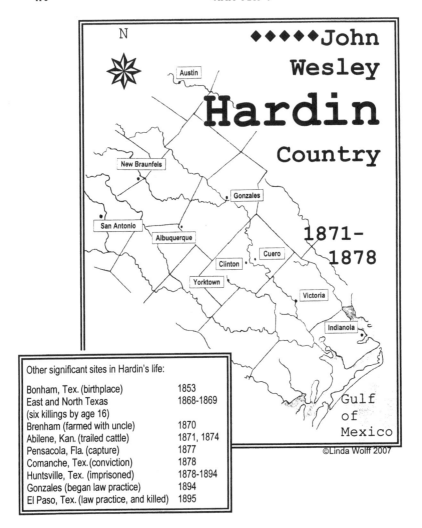

N

♦♦♦♦♦♦John
Wesley
Hardin
Country

Austin

New Braunfels

Gonzales

San Antonio

Albuquerque

Clinton

Cuero

Yorktown

Victoria

1871–
1878

Indianola

Gulf
of
Mexico

©Linda Wolff 2007

Other significant sites in Hardin's life:	
Bonham, Tex. (birthplace)	1853
East and North Texas	1868-1869
(six killings by age 16)	
Brenham (farmed with uncle)	1870
Abilene, Kan. (trailed cattle)	1871, 1874
Pensacola, Fla. (capture)	1877
Comanche, Tex. (conviction)	1878
Huntsville, Tex. (imprisoned)	1878-1894
Gonzales (began law practice)	1894
El Paso, Tex. (law practice, and killed)	1895

into the man's head. In his autobiography, Hardin claimed that the man had struck him and thus earned the retaliation. However, other accounts question Hardin's explanation. Military historian Charles Askins asserted that, yes, John Wesley indeed went to the circus but chose not the pay the admission ticket. He simply slipped in under the tent. A security guard saw him and caught him, intending to toss him out.

Responding, the young killer pulled his concealed revolver and murdered the guard. The true details of the incident will likely never be known, for Hardin always justified all his killings by blaming the victims.[28]

Forced to run from Horn Hill, Hardin and Barekman split up, Barekman riding for Pisgah and John Wesley racing toward Brenham by way of Kosse, a railroad town in southwestern Limestone County. After taking a room at the local hotel, he dallied for several days. One day Hardin struck up a conversation with a local girl who was working as a prostitute in the Three Star Saloon, her manager being Alan Comstock. Quite taken with the girl, Hardin enjoyed her company for several nights in and around the saloon. But trouble with Comstock came soon. The pimp may have been jealous, or there might have been a dispute about money that the young hotspur did or did not pay for the girl's services. In any event, after hard words, Hardin shot the man in the head.[29]

Now forced to flee from Kosse, Hardin rode to his Uncle Bob Hardin's place near Brenham, arriving there either in late January or early February 1870. He remained there for a few months. Sometimes helping with farm chores, Hardin spent most of his time in town drinking and gambling. Now in an area where local authorities did not know him, he adopted the alias John Wilson and created an innocent past. Occasionally, "Wilson" went to Evergreen, about forty miles to the west where he spent time at the racetrack, wagering on horse races. He frequented a local saloon, playing poker and getting drunk. He encountered "Wild Bill" Longley, just a year older than he, at the race track. A killer much like John Wesley, Longley was born in 1851 in Austin County, but in 1853 his family moved to a new farm near Evergreen in Lee County. Like Hardin, Longley had a long criminal record that included multiple murders and sundry robberies. According to some sources, "Wild Bill" had killed six men before he even reached the age of twenty.[30]

Longley studied Hardin and decided to be most careful around him. Reportedly, he told a friend that John Wesley had the "eyes of a gunman," eyes no doubt like Longley's own. Being somewhat testy with each other, the two joined a poker game. Although the two were wary of each other, they came away from their game with mutual grudging respect. Indeed, the two joined forces and started stealing horses from farmers and ranchers in the region, who made repeated complaints to civil and military authorities. Responding, Capt. John Whitney came out of his headquarters in Brenham with a squad of troopers and made a six-day scout, but the troopers failed to find either of the robbers, after which Whitney asked his superiors to offer a re-ward for their capture. Later, Longley at times rode with the Taylor gang although he did not appear to be a leader like Hardin became once he joined the unholy band.[31]

The military's pursuit of him frightened Hardin, as did the fact that Texas Rangers under Capt. Leander McNelly were on his trail. Leaving the Evergreen area, he traveled northeastwardly until he reached the Louisiana border, where he adopted a new alias and invented a new past. Although he likely stayed in Louisiana for several months, it is possible that he sought and found the desperado Cullen Montgomery Baker, the "Swamp Fox of the Sulphur," whose raiders roamed both northeastern Texas and southwestern Arkansas. If so, he probably renewed acquaintances with Bill Longley, who was known to ride with Baker during the time Hardin was in hiding.[32]

John Wesley returned to Hill County in the fall of 1870 and temporarily resided there before roaming into McLennan and finding more trouble in Waco. As was his habit, he fell in with the wrong crowd. By November, he was running with Kinch West and his band of about a dozen lawless men. They deviled so many people that a local judge complained to Gov. E. J. Davis, saying that the county was virtually out-of-control and that many men were not obeying new gun laws. The judge had recently attended "Robinson's Circus" and loosely counted the number of armed men, putting the tally at about 150, some of whom may have been West and Hardin men. Shortly before the turn of the new year, John Wesley killed another man, L. J. Hoffman, who had been a state policeman before securing the position of United States deputy marshal. Hoffman went to the wrong barber shop at the wrong time. As he entered the shop, John Wesley was there. Hoffman recognized him, and a shoot-out followed. It ended with Hoffman lying dead on the floor while Hardin made a break for freedom. He fled and went into hiding, for lawmen were again on his trail.[33]

Hoping that the authorities would expect him to move south, he instead moved northeastwardly and popped up in Longview, an East Texas hamlet, on January 9, 1871, only to be arrested by State Policeman E. T. Stakes. The officer read the charges: four acts of murder and one count of horse theft. The authorities' plan was to take Hardin to Waco to stand trial for Hoffman's murder. After some confusion that included releasing Hardin and then arresting him again, the young killer warmed to his cell mates, sharing his tobacco and whiskey with them. One of those cell mates, thanks to the smuggling of a friend, had a Colt .45 with four rounds in the chambers. John Wesley bought the gun and secreted it. He tried to talk his cell mates into a jail break, but they declined.[34]

Quickly came the transfer, and when State Policemen Stakes and Jim Smalley took Hardin from the jail and started the trek to Waco, they did not search him. That was a deadly mistake. By the evening of January 22 after being joined by L. B. Anderson, John Wesley's party make camp for the last time, for they were close to Waco and would reach it the next day. After setting up camp, Stakes and Anderson left to search for a farmhouse where they could get fodder for the party's horses. With Smalley left alone to guard him, Hardin grasped an opportunity when his guard was temporarily distracted. John Wesley pulled the secreted gun and shot his guard to death, after which he commandeered the policeman's horse and rode hard for Mount Calm in southern Hill County, where his parents now lived.[35]

John's father listened to his son's woebegone tale and advised him to head south and lose himself in Mexico, for prison or death might be the only other alternatives. Apparently willing to accept the advice, the killer loaded his guns, saddled up, and headed for the Rio Grande. But before he even reached Belton, state officers, three in number, found and arrested him. The lawmen planned to take him to Austin, but when night closed in, they camped for the first night about ten miles south of Belton. The guards rotated watch through the night so that one would guard the prisoner at all times. But they failed to chain him down, a big mistake. On one shift, the guard fell asleep while Hardin was yet awake. The young killer grabbed a doubled-barreled shotgun and killed two officers. Then he grabbed a sixgun and killed the third.[36]

Taking the best horse, Hardin rode back to his parents' place at Mount Calm. He told his father of his newest troubles and newest murders while, of course, spinning the story to make himself appear blameless. Although his father did not believe his son was telling the truth, he again advised John to go south and this time not to stop until he reached Mexico. He must go, said his father, if he hoped to escape a rope. No doubt trying to pressure his son to take his advice, the elder Hardin accompanied John Wesley back to Belton, where they parted when the man of God turned back toward home. John then rode on through Waco and Austin, but proving unreasonable and stubborn, the younger Hardin refused to heed his father's advice. Just south of Austin, his horse veered to the southeast and loped toward Gonzales County where Hardin had relatives, the Clements clan. John Wesley was first cousin to the Clement brothers—Emanuel Jr. (called "Mannen"), James (called "Jim"), Joe, and John (called "Gyp"). Their mother was the sister of Hardin's father. All the brothers were contractors who drove herds to Kansas or other markets. Because all were members of the Taylor cabal, almost immediately Hardin became involved with Creed Taylor's ring, for a great number of cattle that the Clements brothers took up the trail were stolen.[37]

As he talked to his cousins, John Wesley learned much about the doings in the area. He decided that he could make much money if he joined them and the Taylors. Soon Hardin was on the Taylor payroll, making $150 a month while "real" cowboys earned only about $20 to $30 a month. His first chore for the Taylor ring was to help gather a cattle herd and push the beeves up the Chisholm Trail with the railhead at Abilene, Kansas, as the destination. The herd that Hardin helped round up included stolen cattle mixed among legally acquired beeves. Contractors Carroll and Jake Johnson took to the trail first, moving a herd of sixteen hundred. With Hardin and Jim

Clements as trail bosses, a second herd of about fourteen hundred closely followed the first. On the trail, John Wesley and Jim Clements were more than simple cowboys. They served as gunmen and enforcers when necessary. During the drive, Hardin met Taylor man and a future benefactor Fred Duderstadt, a German born in 1850 who accompanied his parents in a move to Texas in 1855. By 1870 Fred had established a ranch in Gonzales County and became close to the Taylor gang. He married Henrietta Tennille, whose brother George was also a member of the ring. Duderstadt went up the trail with Hardin, and the two became good friends.[38]

During the drive and the return to Texas, Hardin killed several men, from eight to twelve depending on the source of one's information.[39] Clearly, during the drive he killed so many men that he proved to be a psychotic, a pathological sociopath, a professional killing machine. As always, he blamed others for his deeds while he killed methodically and remorselessly. He may well have been the most dangerous man to ever go up the Chisholm Trail. Cowboy Babe Moye went up the trail with Hardin and the Clements brothers and, later, had little good to report about any of them, saying that they were "loud, boisterous, bull-dozing braggadocios and [that] when together usually carried things with a high hand." Along the trail, they even bragged that they were going to kill James "Wild Bill" Hickok, Abilene's city marshal. Then, they intended to run off the other town officials and "tree" the place. Moye lived long enough to read Hardin's autobiography and averred that there was little truth about what he said occurred in Abilene. Around Hickok, the rowdies were most careful not to incur his wrath. Moye said the marshal did not take Hardin very seriously. Rather, he treated John Wesley much like a child while still watching him closely.

Hickok called Hardin "Little Arkansas" because he was so young and so "green." Only one incident occurred that might have caused trouble. In a saloon one evening, the young hotspur got drunk and took his pistol in his hand and began playing with it or, perhaps, threatening someone with it. Hickok came in and simply told him to put the gun away before he "let it go off and hurt somebody." Babe said the young killer complied with the marshal's order without saying a single word. But, Hickok did not try to take the gun despite a town ordinance banning carrying weapons in public. Whether Hickok acted out of friendship or out of fear will never be known. In all, Moye had little respect for Hardin and the men who ran with him; yet, he knew how dangerous that they were and clearly considered them as unrepentant criminals.[40]

About Hardin's motives and justifications for his murders, the writer Waldo E. Koop made an interesting point. Hardin blamed his evil ways on the excesses of Reconstruction under Radical rule; he blamed the State Police; he blamed E. J. Davis; and he blamed white Unionists and freedpeople; he blamed just about everyone else. Yet, he rode across the Red River on his trip to Kansas, and that trail became a killing field. According to Koop, Hardin killed at least six men, maybe more, on the cattle drive. Even though he had temporarily left the radicals and police behind, he did not stop killing.[41] Instead, as Koop said, "when removed from the conditions [of Texas,] he went from bad to worse."[42] Clearly, Hardin had only himself to blame for his murderous career.

John Wesley spent some time in Kansas before he returned to Texas. He took a quick trip to Missouri, possibly to see his old friend Dick Johnson. Johnson was one of three shooters who ambushed and killed the Unionist Lewis Peacock in North Texas in 1871. Hardin was in the area at the time (helping with the cattle drive mentioned previously) and was suspected of being one of the other assassins. Even if not, Hardin was close to Johnson and probably knew that he had fled to Missouri after murdering Peacock. Hardin made the trek to Missouri to see his old cohort. He got into trouble there, for state authorities put a $1,000 reward out for him. Such a high bounty meant that Hardin had committed a capital crime, probably yet another murder.[43]

Returning to Texas by August 1871, Hardin and cousin Gyp Clements spent some time in Hill County hiding out at Barnett Hardin's place, who was another cousin, before returning to Gonzales County. There, they stayed at the Clements family home, a place built like a fortress, complete with several firing port-holes along all walls. As one observer said, it was a "haven" for fugitives like Hardin and Gyp Clements.[44]

Destined to become the coleader of the Taylor ring, young John Wesley had clearly lived an event-filled, violence-prone, murderous life. He was a professional killer, a hired gunman, just the type of fellow the Taylors needed to fight the law and to continue building their criminal empire. In a very short time, the "Taylor gang" would become known as the "Hardin-Taylor gang" or the "Taylor-Hardin gang."

A Matter of Attrition

AFTER John Wesley Hardin returned to Texas, he became one of the two leaders of the Taylor raiders, the other being Jim Taylor. With Hardin involved, the murder rate attributed to the ring went up precipitously. In September 1871, a posse from Austin rode into Gonzales County looking for John Wesley, intending to arrest him and any other renegades they could find. Warned of the posse's movements by friends, Hardin and his men set up an "ambushcade." After a wild shoot-out, John Wesley lost not a man, but three black officers lay dead. Because they could not penetrate the raiders' position and because their men were falling, the lawmen broke off the fight and returned to Austin empty-handed.[1] Afterward, John Wesley wrapped himself in the Confederate flag and used the "Lost Cause" and Southern honor to justify himself, saying that he "declared openly against negro or Yankee mob rule and misrule in general."[2]

While Hardin was proclaiming his Confederate loyalty, Jack Helm faced more scrutiny. Grand juries of several counties indicted him for various crimes, the most serious coming from Hopkins County in North Texas, where Helm had led lynchers who hanged several innocent men during the Civil War. He also faced at least one charge of assault and battery. About the charges, one trial jury acquitted him, another deadlocked, and a judge therefore freed him. About the Hopkins County indictment, Helm was later found not guilty for lack of conclusive proof.[3] The lawman, then, remained free to pursue members of the Hardin-Taylor ring.

On October 19, 1871, more of Hardin's mayhem erupted at a country store owned by Neill Bowen, a Floridian who came to Texas in 1850 and who would soon be Hardin's father-in-law. Bowen's store was in the small community of Smiley in Gonzales County near Pilgrim Lake. There, freedmen

Green Paramore and John Lacky found John Wesley and several of his men. Both black men were Special Policemen who acted as auxiliaries of the State Police. Most specific, Adjutant General Davidson ordered them to look for Hardin, who was known to be in the area. The twenty-eight-year-old Paramore was originally from Georgia, a farmer whose part-time service with the police made him extra money from time to time. John Lackey was a thirty-five-year-old blacksmith by trade. Although the two men proved successful in their quest, tragedy struck them. Hardin was in Bowen's store, saw the policemen when they entered, and became enraged. Not only did the black men have guns, but they were also peace officers. Backed by the guns of several of his men, John Wesley shot and killed Paramore, firing a ball into his head at close range, and wounded Lackey, whom he shot through the mouth and tongue. The latter saved himself by running from the store, sprinting through a field, and diving into nearby Pilgrim Lake. Except for surfacing amid reeds to breathe, Lackey stayed submerged until Hardin and his men thought he had drowned.[4]

Almost immediately after Paramore's death, area freedmen collected at Lackey's blacksmith shop. They wanted to retrieve Paramore's body and give the man a proper burial. They talked with the local black leader Henry Maney, asking if they could take guns with them. They were afraid to go unarmed because Hardin and his men might still be in the vicinity. Maney told them that they had the right to take arms, especially if they feared for their lives. Those who owned guns went to their homes to get them, be they revolvers, shotguns, or rifles. The young killer learned about the blacks' plan to bring weapons when they came to collect Paramore's body. Out in the countryside, he recruited about twenty-five Taylor men who prepared a major ambush; John Wesley, however, only wasted his time because his "ambushcade" proved unnecessary. Gonzales Sheriff James T. Matthieu and the town mayor, one Keyser, backed by three white men who had shotguns, convinced the blacks to stay put, Keyser threatening to arrest them if they did not lay down their arms. Under duress, they obeyed. They dissolved their would-be posse and went to their homes as lawmen lost a real chance to corral Hardin and other Taylor men, for the blacks could have been deputized and gotten on with the chase. A massive blood-letting would likely have been the result, but the Hardin-Taylor men might have seen their numbers reduced drastically.[5]

Governor Davis considered declaring martial law in Gonzales County because local authorities did not even try to find Paramore's murderer. As for the legal system working, on October 24, 1871, the Gonzales County grand jury indicted Hardin for the murder of Paramore, the witnesses including Lackey, Daniel T. Price, and John Connelly, the latter two having been in

Bowen's store when the shooting began. The jury charged no other Taylor men because the witnesses did not know them. Moreover, Hardin was the only one who fired a weapon. But indicting John Wesley and bringing him to justice were two very different propositions. Realizing that, Governor Davis on November 5, 1871, offered a $4,000 reward for "Wesley Clements" (one of Hardin's aliases) wanted for "the murder of Green Paramore." Despite the lure of a reward to bounty hunters, Hardin never served a day in jail or in prison for the murder of Paramore and the attempted murder of Lackey.[6]

Shortly, a development in Brazos County may have involved a member of the ring. There, Josh Butler killed an "Alf" Taylor after accusing him of horse theft. Taylor drew a gun, but Butler was faster. The latter's gun blew Alf off the horse, after which Butler reclaimed his property. However, there is no mention of an "Alf Taylor" being involved with the Hardin-Taylor raiders.[7]

Meanwhile, bounty hunters were combing the region looking for John Wesley. He realized that Taylor Country was getting increasingly hazardous for him. He packed some belongings, saddled up, and rode for his parents home near Mount Calm in Limestone County where he could hide, for local officers there did not want him for any offense. He stayed through Christmas of 1871, after which he took a quick trip to the Indian Nations, possibly to check on a herd going to Kansas, even though it was the wrong time of year to move beeves. Then he returned to Mount Calm for a night's rest before getting back to Gonzales in early January 1872. He reached there in time to help celebrate the marriage of Gyp Clements to Annie Tennille—whose father George Tennille was a Taylor man—with dinner and dancing. The eighteen-year-old Hardin enjoyed the party even more because his recently acquired sweetheart, the fourteen-year-old Jane Bowen was present. She was a pretty girl, born in Karnes County in 1857.[8]

Soon, Wesley and Jane decided to make their relationship permanent. On February 27, 1872, they picked up a marriage license, and the two wed on March 18.[9] Called "one of the prettiest and sweetest girls in the country" by admirers, Jane had met John Wesley earlier when he was on his way to visit the Clements family. He passed through a place called Coon Hollow, near Smiley. As mentioned, her father Neill Bowen had a general store there. Immediately after the couple married, they lived with Jane's parents in a small upstairs apartment with an outside staircase. Soon, however, they moved out to be on their own. They settled just south of Smiley in Gonzales County near the lines where Gonzales, Karnes, and DeWitt meet. They lived on a ranch owned by Fred Duderstadt, long a friend of the Hardins and the Bowens. As mentioned earlier, Duderstadt was in the Taylor ring. He had met John Wesley on the trail to Kansas in 1871 and had watched him murder several men. Even when the young killer was on the run, Jane always kept the home and eventually raised three children (the first born when Jane was but fifteen years old) there with the help of the Duderstadts. After she died in 1892, she was buried in the old Asher Cemetery, near "Old Davy" at Mount Creek.[10]

Hardin was never a good family man, for he was running from lawmen a majority of the time. He was an absentee husband and father and seldom gave any money for his family's support. Usually he was never around long enough to fulfill the duties of husband and father. He spent more time sleeping on the ground while hiding from the law than he spent in Jane's bed. For what little his wife and children had, they could only thank the Duderstadts. When John Wesley visited his wife and the children, the time spent with them were usually of short duration and filled with tension because lawmen or bounty hunters might appear at any time. When not forced to run, Hardin spent most of his days in sundry towns in the area, gambling at cards and drinking his life away. He went to many a bawdy house. Generally, he preferred the company of young men like himself rather than a home life with his family. Hardin's *Autobiography* is indicative of the kind of husband and father he was: He almost never mentioned Jane or their children. Instead, he proudly focused on his own life, all the while making excuses for his murderous ways. Why Jane remained his wife is a mystery.[11]

Soon after he married, Hardin was once again in trouble with local law enforcers in Gonzales County, who cited him for carrying a pistol in public. In a later incident, county authorities arrested him for the more serious crime of assault with intent to murder, but some of the ring posted bond, and he went free. The Gonzales city marshal was apparently the only local law enforcer who was willing to confront John Wesley. Indeed, the new County Sheriff Dick Glover supported the Hardin-Taylor band, likely because his brothers Ed and John were members of the ring. The sheriff even offered his home as a safe haven for John Wesley whenever he was on the run from other authorities. The killer frequently slept at Glover's home, for he knew that he was safe there. Yet, wanted for a legion of crimes, Hardin was always on guard. More than once, he told the sheriff's wife that if she got up at night to care for her young children to call out to him; otherwise, he might accidentally shoot her.[12]

Shortly, John Wesley was again on the move, this time gathering horses to take to Louisiana for sale. He left Gonzales in late May or early June and began his trip with the herd, some of which he had stolen. While his loyal Taylor men took care of the movement of the herd, John rode on ahead and visited his Uncle Barnett in Livingston, Polk County, close to the area where he had grown up. Next, he set up horse races with some men in San Augustine County. He won about $250 in prize money. After the races, Hardin and

Billy Harper, one of his men, rode on to Hemphill to await the arrival of the horse herd. Once in town, John Wesley passed time gambling and drinking day by day. But, he could not avoid trouble because he was becoming too well known by too many people.[13]

After Harper left to join the men with the herd, John Wesley had an altercation with the son of white State Policeman William Speights. The young man, John "Sonny" Speights, was a peace officer in Livingston. He caught Hardin illegally wearing a gun in public. He tried to arrest John Wesley who had one gun in his belt and two more concealed. Hardin quickly drew and fired a derringer, the shot disabling Sonny, who took the bullet in his right shoulder. After he was hit, he half-ran and half-staggered to the courthouse looking for both protection and assistance while Hardin jumped atop a horse belonging to someone else and quickly rode it to the town stables to get his own mount. Alerted by the wounded Speights, the county sheriff and his men sprang into action. They opened fire on the felon just as he was climbing onto his horse Joe. Spurring the steed, the desperado escaped unharmed, but Joe took two balls in his neck. With the authorities looking for him, Hardin had to move fast. He learned that his stolen horse herd had almost reached Hemphill, and he rode out to meet it, whereupon he sold every head to brothers Jess, John, and Billy Harper, who could take the herd on to Louisiana and make a tidy profit.[14]

Hardin rode away, seeking a new place to hide. He went back to Livingston to stay with his uncle, but he was soon in trouble again. He arranged another horse race with two local men and asked Dick Hudson, later a DeWitt County lawman, to hold the stakes ($250 total, including forfeit money). When the locals tried to get out of the race after first agreeing to it, John Wesley appealed to Hudson, who had been one of his childhood friends while he was growing up in Polk and Trinity counties. Hudson ruled for Hardin, who took the money and rode back to his Uncle Barnett's place. There he hid for several days and passed his time by hunting and fishing. However, he could not stay away from drink for too long; nor could he stay away from the gambling tables. With yet another cousin, Barnett Jones, on August 10, 1872, he went to John Gates saloon in Trinity city (in Trinity County) to spend a day drinking and playing "ten pins."[15]

According to Hardin's later account, after playing with others for a time and losing—something uncommon for him—he played with Phil Sublett and won about $50 that Sublett tried to avoid paying. After hard words by both men, Hardin slapped the man and put a gun in his face. In the end, Sublett decided not to make a fight of it and likely be killed. Instead, both men went back to the bar to drink their fill, with Hardin being richer by $50. Shortly, however, John noted that the young man had slipped away. Thinking that the man might have gone to get a weapon, Wesley, as he reported in his autobiography, retrieved his two handguns from the saddle bags he had stored behind the bar. Indeed Sublett came back armed, and just as a drunken third man approached Hardin and distracted him, Sublett fired a shotgun blast that struck and severely wounded his target in his side to the left of his navel.[16]

Although his wound was severe, John Wesley got off one good shot that hit Sublett in the shoulder, whereupon the Trinity County man turned and ran away. However, some of the details Hardin gave are not necessarily true. Hardin's account did not match the action of a later Trinity County grand jury. After hearing various witnesses testify, the jury indicted John for attempted murder, the verdict revealing that he had been the aggressor rather than Sublett. After the shooting, Hardin's kinsman Barnett helped him. The young killer thought he was dying, but Barnett got him to the local physician's office with hopes that the youngster might cheat death. The doctor told John Wesley his wound was likely fatal but there was a little hope if he would do what he, the physician, asked of him. Wesley agreed, afterward telling his cousin to cut the telegraph wires into town so that no messages about him could go in or out of Trinity City. Next, the physician and Barnett helped him get to a room in the hotel where he settled in, accepting the doctor's treatment and trying to heal.[17]

After about fifteen days, area authorities finally learned of Hardin's identity and his whereabouts. Forced to move, John Wesley, again helped by Barnett and the doctor, managed to get out of town. He made his way to his old hometown of Sumpter where he sought treatment from the physician Orwin Teagarden, originally a Virginian who became a friend of the Hardin family once all had moved to Texas. Teagarden not only treated the young hotspur, but he also opened his home to him. He minded harboring, aiding, and abetting a murderer not at all. John could not stay long with his savior, however. The authorities were now tracking him. For some time, his friends moved him frequently, first to one temporary safe place, then to another. Two Special Policemen finally tracked him to a spot near Lufkin in the Angelina County home of Dave Harrell and family. A gun battle quickly ensued. Firing both barrels of a shotgun, Hardin killed one and wounded the other, while taking a ball that burrowed into his thigh. Although he survived the shoot-out, John Wesley could not remain free forever. Soon, Cherokee County Sheriff Dick Reagan, originally from Tennessee, and his posse found and arrested him. A moment of high drama occurred when one of Reagan's deputies thought that John Wesley was reaching for a gun; the deputy shot him in the knee.[18]

After being held in Rusk for a time at the home of Reagan, whose family nursed him back to health, Hardin soon found himself being taken to Austin to be incarcerated. Sheriff Reagan and a deputy escorted him to the Travis County jail, where County Sheriff George B. Zimpleman took charge and tossed him into a cell in one of the worst jails in Texas. Down by the Colorado River, it was old and rotting. Lawmen held him there prior to another transfer, this time to Gonzales to stand trial for murder. In early October 1872, State Police Captain Thomas Williams led the four-man squad that escorted Hardin to Gonzales where he was put in another rather porous jail. Williams complained to local authorities that they might as well let the desperado go, for the jail would never hold him.[19]

Williams was correct about the inadequacy of the lock-up, but Hardin could not break out. Yet, he was in a better place than Austin because many of members of the Taylor ring were near and were willing to help. Indeed, the new Gonzales County Sheriff William E. Jones was close to several members of the Taylor band. When removing Hardin's shackles, Jones told the youngster to be patient because ring members would rescue him shortly. With Jones's approval, John's men smuggled a saw to him. He used it to cut the bars on his cell window, the sheriff later explaining that all six of Hardin's guards must have fallen asleep at exactly the same time. After he slipped through the hole in the window, Hardin met Jones, Mannen Clements, and another Taylor man, Bud McFadden, who furnished him a horse to ride. McFadden helped the jailbird get back to his home on Duderstadt's ranch, while Clements honored a promise he made to the sheriff.[20]

In return for helping John Wesley, the sheriff demanded that the Hardin-Taylor bunch help him murder a freedman who had supposedly killed one of Jones's relatives. Mannen honored that promise by committing another murder. Concurrently, Hardin reached Duderstadt's ranch and had a reunion with his wife, Jane. He stayed about a month while recuperating from his wounds. Why the authorities could not find him is almost a mystery, but one in part explicable because Sheriff Jones continued to protect him.[21] Had he been in DeWitt County, likely Tumlinson and Deputy Sutton would have learned his whereabouts and come after him. But, apparently, he was safe as long as he remained in Gonzales County.

While John continued to recover from his wounds, one of his men, John Gorman, was meting out chaos in Bastrop County. He was living at Serbin and temporarily keeping company with Turk Turner while leading a wing of the Hardin-Taylor ring that numbered about fourteen men. After donning Klan disguises, Gorman, Turner, and their band generally tormented the black community of Hog Eye before murdering one of the freedmen there. At Bastrop town Gorman and Turner shot down a man named Tyley before they fled. Quickly, lawmen went in pursuit while Governor Davis placed a

Pitkin Taylor and his wife Susan. With his brother Creed, he was a founder of the Taylor ring. An unidentified assassin shot him in October of 1872. He died in March of 1873 from the wound that the killer gave him. No one ever learned the identity of the murderer.
Courtesy Sharon Barnes, Director, Regional History Center at the Victoria College/University of Houston at Victoria Library

$500 bounty on both the desperadoes. Shortly, however, Marshal Thomas F. Purnell and his posse managed to arrest the two miscreants and most of men riding with them. A federal judge set bail so high that the murderous marauders remained in jail. However, all escaped before their trial date.[22]

In October 1872, an unidentified party dealt a blow to the Taylor clan. One night, an assassin caught Pitkin Taylor in a vulnerable position without bodyguards and shot him. Although he was still alive after the incident, his wounds proved fatal. His family took him to Sweet Home in Lavaca County where he could best be protected. He lingered until March 1873, when he went to meet his Maker. His assailant had obvious reasons for shooting him. First, he was a cofounder and a member of the Taylor ring, even though he had lately remained in the background. Second, he refused to let the Kelly matter die. Indeed, he kept pressuring the Taylors' lawyer Bolivar Pridgen for more legal action against the lawmen who killed the two brothers. No one ever learned the identity of Pitkin's murderer. His daughter Amanda Kelly saw one of the killers, but she could not identify him, a fact suggesting that the stranger was not a local leader, for she knew most of the area lawmen. The killer may have been acting independently, perhaps seeking revenge for sundry acts committed by the Taylor ring.[23]

By the time the assassin shot Pitkin Taylor, Hardin had recovered from his wounds. Naturally, he found trouble again.

After he married Jane, he became close to her brother Brown Bowen, Florida-born on September 27, 1849. The family moved to Texas, and the brother and sister grew up in Karnes, Gonzales, and DeWitt counties, the heart of Taylor Country. Once in the crime ring, Brown made his living like the others: rustling cattle and stealing horses. But, the friendship that developed between Brown and Hardin led to disaster. One of them murdered Thomas Holderman on December 15, 1872, at the Billings Country Grocery (saloon) in Gonzales County at Nopal, a store belonging to George Tennille's father-in-law William Billings.

Gang members Jim and Gyp Clements, Tennille, Rockwood Birtsell, Holderman, Bowen, and Hardin spent the day around the store, drinking, racing horses, and target shooting. Some sources say that John Wesley or Brown, or possibly both, believed that Holderman was a spy for Deputy Sutton and other DeWitt County authorities. Other accounts identified him as an informant for the State Police. Although there was no proof of such assertions, Holderman quickly became a marked man. After drinking with the others, he had his fill, went outside, made a pallet under a tree, wrapped himself with a blanket, and went to sleep.[24]

He never woke up. Hardin or Bowen crept up on him at approximately 6 P.M. and fired a round into the back of his head, one that traveled far enough to exit his head through its left eye socket. The lethal round killed the victim instantly. Learning of the murder and believing that Bowen had done the shooting, area authorities, including the new sheriff, Green DeWitt, and Deputy Sheriff Richard B. Hudson, found and arrested him, holding him briefly in Yorktown before transferring him to the Gonzales jail.[25] Later, Sheriff DeWitt told the Texas attorney general that Bowen belonged to "a strong band of thieves and murderers headed by John Hardin, alias Wesley Hardin, alias Wesley Clements, who is reported to have committed sixteen different murders." However, DeWitt said he had not made an effort to arrest "these parties [the Hardin-Taylor raiders] because the citizens would not answer my summons."[26] DeWitt concluded that even if he could arrest members of the cabal, a jury would probably find them not guilty, regardless of the offense.[27]

In February 1873, a grand jury surprised the sheriff. Its members indicted Bowen for Holderman's murder. Bowen remained locked up until March 22. That day, John Wesley and some Taylor men decided that he had spent enough time behind bars. Hardin and about a dozen others rode into Gonzales heavily armed, each man having either a Winchester or a shotgun and at least one handgun. They outnumbered lawmen at the scene and managed to get into the jail. They threatened the guards with death if they raised any alarm. The renegades liberated all the prisoners incarcerated there and helped Bowen escape—all without firing a shot. Reporting the incident to Adj. Gen. Frank Britton, the sheriff admitted his impotence. The adjutant general told Governor Davis that he accepted some of the responsibility. Britton said he should have intervened personally, but he had not sent in the State Police because the Democrat legislature had withheld their pay and their morale was low. In any case, Britton doubted that he could send enough of them to Gonzales County to even make a difference.[28]

Within two months, Bowen proved to many observers that he should have remained behind bars. He rejoined the raiders and helped steal more cattle and horses. Worse, in May, he murdered a DeWitt County freedman and raped a freedgirl during the same incident. After remaining in the region until August, Bowen finally decided that the authorities were closing in on him. He immediately left Texas for Louisiana and apparent safety. Later, he moved to Florida, the state of his birth. But years later, Texas authorities caught up with him and returned him to Texas. He eventually stood trial for murder of Tom Holderman. Convicted by a jury, sentenced to hang by a judge, Bowen steadfastly denied that he had shot the man, arguing instead that Hardin had committed the offense. The inquest held after Holderman's death provided a little support for Bowen's assertions. The uncertain inquisitors held that either John Wesley or Bowen had killed the man. However, John "Mack" Billings, son of the store owner, was near his father's store when the killing took place. Hardin quickly took the twelve-year-old inside and told him to hide, saying that Bowen might kill him because he was an eyewitness who could identify the shooter. And witness Mack did in Bowen's later trial. Bowen's pleas notwithstanding, he had to face the hangman.[29]

Meanwhile, others in the crime ring remained busy. Operating in Lavaca County, gang members committed a most heinous triple murder. The teenaged Thomas Fowler and the Wyatt brothers Itha (age fourteen) and W. B. (age thirteen) stumbled upon the Lavaca County wing of the ring. They were killing cattle for their hides and leaving the carcasses to rot. Although the boys tried to flee, the thieves caught all three. After a quick discussion, the renegades decided to kill the teenaged trio who, if left alive, would likely inform the county sheriff about their doings and their location. As well, the three children could not identify them in court if they were dead. With no remorse, the gunmen then executed the boys, shooting them down even though not a one was armed and not a one was of legal age.[30]

Concurrently, several Hardin men were operating in Hamilton County, stealing horses and rustling cattle. Led by Asa Langford Sr. and his son Asa Jr., the small band soon had trouble with area ranchers. Collectively trying to save their herds, some cattlemen confronted the Taylor thieves. Ranchers G. W. Hughes and Richard Payne died in the effort, both being slain by the father and son team and one other shooter. Afterward, the remaining cattlemen scattered to save their own lives. Authorities caught Langford Sr., but he was soon out of jail on bond, free to continue his depredations. Along with his son and others, he returned to the spread of Hughes's widow where, in broad daylight, they rustled the rest of the herd in front of witnesses. G. W. Hughes's brother Marion went after the malefactors but could not catch them.[31]

Yet another wing of the ring was operating in Coleman County. Although they killed no one, the force, which numbered about twenty to twenty-five men, had enough manpower and fire power to intimidate local officials and other civilians. Having no fear, the renegades rounded up a herd of stolen beeves and drove them out of the county. Others of the ring were operating in Refugio County. Ranchers there told Britton that armed bands of men were killing their cattle and skinning them, leaving the carcasses where they fell. The Refugio cattlemen asked for a unit of the State Police, but Britton could not send anyone to help.[32]

Meanwhile, John Wesley was busy corralling a cattle herd although he had scant regard for the owners of the beeves. He planned to drive them twenty-five miles to the new town of Cuero, a place that would thrive, for it was on the railroad route from Indianola that cut through Taylor Country. As the drive was getting underway, Hardin let his men handle the herd while he rode into Cuero, where he immediately went to the saloon and had a few drinks before going into a back room and joining a poker game. DeWitt Deputy Sheriff John B. Morgan happened to be in town and learned of John's arrival. Although the young gun was now using the alias "Fred Johnson," the messenger who reported the news gave a description of the suspect, and the deputy knew that the description matched John Wesley perfectly. Morgan immediately went to the saloon to arrest the desperado, but the lawman died in the effort. After a tense confrontation, both men drew their revolvers, Hardin being the faster. The murderer fired at Morgan, the ball striking him just above the left eye and entering his brain; obviously, the shot killed the deputy instantly. In his killings, John Wesley often tried for a head shot as with the deputy, because many men wore iron plates over their chests, thereby hoping to gain the advantage in any gunplay. After the shooting, Hardin quickly fled. Although some time passed, eventually a DeWitt County grand jury indicted him for murder. Years later, a jury convicted him of manslaughter after plea bargaining had taken place.[33]

Now using the alias "Jack Slade," Hardin popped up in Hamilton County in February 1873 to help the ring members who were already there stealing cattle. For inexplicable reasons, he murdered a woman named J. Carpenter before riding back to DeWitt County, where he shot an unidentified stranger in early March. About the woman Carpenter, a lawman reported that "it was a very bad murder," and he asked the adjutant general to offer a reward before the lawman gave a description of the murderer that exactly fit John Wesley. Next, the young hotspur, still calling himself Jack Slade, shot a man named Cooper to death on March 30, 1873. As more time passed, Hardin acquired yet more aliases trying to hide his identity. Shortly, the authorities in Gonzales County reported that an unidentified assailant murdered a stranger and that John Wesley, by whatever alias, was the suspected killer. Near the end of May, Sheriff Helm, Deputy Sutton, and a posse of about fifty men ventured from DeWitt to Gonzales County, looking for members of the Hardin-Taylor gang and hoping to arrest at least the leaders. While Helm's scout was unproductive, it did spur a meeting between John Wesley and his top lieutenants. At Mustang Mott, he met with Mannen Clements, George Tennille, and Jim, John, and R. P. "Scrap" Taylor. All agreed to continue their war on the authorities and marked a number of their quarry for death. Supposedly, the names of Sheriff Helm and Deputy Sutton topped the list as did a well known local political leader, F. S. Robb.[34]

Earlier, in his April crime report to Governor Davis, Adjutant General Britton singled out the work of the Hardin-Taylor ring. "In Gonzales County," Britton wrote, "there is a strong band of thieves and murderers headed by John Hardin, alias Wesley Hardin, alias Wesley Clements who is reported to have committed sixteen different murders and has threatened to kill a member of the legislature, Hon. F. S. Robb." Continuing, the adjutant general reminded the governor that John had a price on his head in Texas as well as "a one thousand [dollar reward] by the state of Missouri."[35] Britton also reported that the ring had spread into Refugio County. Ranchers there said that "armed bands" were "killing and skinning their cattle." Because the criminal band included so many men, local authorities could not even challenge them. As well, in Guadalupe County where the ring sometimes worked, "unknown parties" got into the courthouse and destroyed the "cattle record."[36]

Even though they were increasingly hunted, on April 1, 1873, three of the Taylors' desperadoes went after Deputy Sutton. They caught him in Cuero

Alf Day, a Taylor partisan and Taylor relative by marriage, was with Scrap and Jim Taylor when they tried to assassinate Bill Sutton in a Cuero saloon.
Courtesy Sharon Barnes, Director, Regional History Center at the Victoria College/University of Houston at Victoria Library

while the deputy was relaxing in the Banks Saloon and Billiard Hall, not knowing that trouble was afoot. Scrap and Jim Taylor and Alf Day ambushed him there. From the saloon porch, Scrap fired a shotgun blast through an open window that stuck the deputy on his left side and left arm, almost shattering that arm. A second blast hit the victim in the left breast. Miraculously, Sutton got to his feet and escaped through a back door before the marauders could finish him. During his two-month convalescence, lawmen and other friends guarded Sutton's home around the clock to prevent another assassination attempt. On June 13, the deputy was well enough to travel but not to ride. He set out from home in a buggy with several bodyguards, including Deputy Sheriff John Meador, Horace French, Ad Patterson, and "Doc" White.

The men were going to Clinton to attend the pretrial hearing of Scrap Taylor, whom authorities had arrested for the attempted murder. But seven men of the Taylor gang ambushed the Sutton party on the road to Clinton. The raiders intended to finish the job on the deputy and therefore to stop him from testifying against Scrap and others at the scheduled hearing. The attackers included Bill, Scrap, and Jim Taylor; Alf Day; Patrick "Bud" Dowlearn; and two other men. The guerrillas shot French's horse out from under him, wounded two more horses, and left Meador with a slightly wounded leg; but the killers could not get to Sutton.[37]

By the time of the latest incident, the Texas Legislature had dealt law and order in the state a tremendous setback. On April 22, 1873, the resurgent Democrats repealed the State Police Law and, in effect, reversed the progress that the police had been making. Once again, justice came county by county or did not come at all. All manner of jurisdictional problems arose again as in days of yore. Moreover, views about "law and order" seemed to change. Briefly, in the time of uncertainty that followed "redemption," the "good guys" (lawmen who cooperated with the Republican government) became the "bad guys." Conversely, to a degree, some of the "bad guys" (ex-Confederate raiders and outlaws like Hardin and the Taylors who attacked Republican rule) now became the "good guys," especially those people who wrapped themselves in the Confederate Flag and postured as upholders of the "Lost Cause." For a brief time, all was confusion. Even the Texas Rangers who, in part, replaced the police were often uncertain of who were friends or foes in any given South Texas county. As regarding the Taylor gang and the old authorities, Texas Rangers temporarily seemed free to pick and choose whom to believe. Many of them believed the Taylors, the group always insisting to a man that they had been persecuted by the evil forces of Yankee Republican rule. Although rangers in the field would soon learn the truth about the crime ring, the time was ripe for more murder and mayhem.[38]

The day after the legislature repealed the police law, Sheriff Helm and his DeWitt County posse rode to Gonzales County to Fred Duderstadt's ranch. Long a member of the Taylor-Hardin gang, he had participated in many of their crimes; but, having no warrant for Duderstadt, the posse only questioned Jane Hardin about her husband's whereabouts. Although she told them nothing, the lawmen would have been most disturbed if she had told them what her husband planned, for she knew about the earlier meeting at Mustang Mott where leaders of the ring agreed to continue their operations, including cattle rustling, and to exterminate lawmen if challenged. The band apparently believed that the abolition of the State Police gave them the upper hand. They were correct.[39]

Despite repeal of the police act, State Police Lt. J. Redmon, then on the trail of John Wesley, refused to give up. He made one last report of his actions to the adjutant general before Britton was replaced by Democrat William Steele. Hardin and many of the Taylor men were off with a herd of cattle, moving north, generally heading for Denton County. From the town of Denton, Redmon and one lonely private began a pursuit on April 19 as Britton had ordered. The policemen moved south as far as Bosque County. Thenceforth, they chased the equivalent of ghosts up the Brazos River and through Hood County. Turning up nothing, Redmon then headed for Red River Station, the main crossing on the trail to Kansas, while Pvt. J. Foreman made a thorough search of Montague County. But, again, fate foiled Redmon. He later learned that the suspicious Hardin had moved his herd westward from the main trail after he crossed the Colorado River and thence moved north into Indian Territory. The murderer and cattle rustler had once again slipped away.[40]

In his last report, Lieutenant Redmon commented on the recent change of government as well as the demise of the police. In Denton, Redmon said, there was "great rejoicing over the repeal of the Police Law by the Ku Klucks murderers and thieves." Redmon added that when the town folk received the news, the people "fired anvils from 2 o'clock [until 4 o'clock] . . . I do believe that there are men in this county if they had the power and it would be not found out on them would murder every Republican in it, but thank God they are afraid to do the crime they so much desire."[41] Redmon added that the citizens of Denton threatened to mob the commander of the federals in their county but could not find him because he happened to be on a trip to Austin.[42]

Further south, as if to validate Redmon's concern, the Hardin-Taylor raiders stuck again in mid-May 1873 after John Wesley returned from his cattle drive. In the DeWitt County countryside not far from the Karnes County line, Hardin and Jim Taylor assembled about forty of their men and ambushed a small sheriff's posse that included Joe Tumlinson, James W. Cox, J. L. Griffin, Henry Ragland, and John W. S. Christman. Shooters included Jim, Tom, and Scrap Taylor; Patrick Hays; Alf Day; Bud Dowlearn; Gyp and Mannen Clements; George Tennille; and the Nickles brothers. Hardin was likely one of the killers, too, according to a report later filed by L. B. Wright, a Republican political leader. Even if John Wesley was not present, he planned the assault and later admitted that the Taylor renegades definitely made the attack. Shooting from an ambush, the desperadoes had the upper hand in the fight, having their quarry almost surrounded before giving their positions away. In the attack, the raiders killed Christman outright while a shotgun blast severely wounded and knocked Cox off his horse. The onslaught caused the small posse to scatter, after which one of the Taylor-Hardin guerrillas rode up to Cox, lying on the ground but still alive. The murderer dismounted, approached him, produced a knife, and cut the lawman's throat from ear to ear.[43]

Next, Hardin and Jim Taylor targeted Helm for assassination. The two men, possibly accompanied by others of their gang, sought Helm out in Albuquerque, a hamlet that no longer exists, in western Gonzales County (one source said the town was in Wilson County). Although different accounts disagree on the exact details, it appears clear that John Wesley and Taylor came into town at different times from different directions. Hardin got there first and began a polite conversation with a Mr. McCracken, who doubtless wondered why John Wesley not only wore a side arm but also took his shotgun from his saddle horn and carried it about. Taylor came in later and rode to John Bland's blacksmith shop, where Helm was working to improve a farm implement, a type of cotton worm eradicator for which he already held a patent. Neither was he wearing a gun, nor was he close to one, a fatal mistake. Taylor walked up to him and tried to back shoot him, aiming his sixgun at the lawman's head and pulling the trigger. When the gun misfired, Helm spun around and grappled with Taylor, but the assassin got of an effective round that buried itself in the target's breast.[44]

Staggered but remaining on his feet, Helm prepared to charge Taylor. Military science applies: Run away from a knife because it cannot hurt you unless you are close; charge a gun because that is your only chance to stay alive. As he tried to charge, Hardin, who had left McCracken and walked to the shop, saw the action and quickly fired a shotgun round at Helm, the blast shattering one of the lawman's arms. As Helm retreated, John trained his shotgun on spectators while Jim Taylor shot Helm, who may have grabbed a knife, in the head repeatedly, the knife being rendered useless. The controversial lawman died as five balls destroyed his head and at least twelve buckshot hit an arm and his chest. Despite Helm's cloudy reputation, the peaceful folks would miss him; he had been effective in hunting down members of the ring and other lawbreakers.[45]

Continuing his war, Hardin had more run-ins with the law. For example, authorities in DeWitt County arrested him again for carrying a pistol in public. Released on bond of $100, he failed to appear in court at the appointed time. The judge issued a warrant for his arrest, but he continued to walk the streets of Clinton and other area towns with scant regard for gun laws; no authority brought him in. Back in command, former Confederate authorities apparently excused his crimes and preferred not to trouble him.

However, cases of mistaken identity may have confused the authorities. Earlier, as mentioned, Hardin murdered one Cooper in Cuero on March 30, 1873, but he was using the alias Jack Slade.[46]

Far more serious than flaunting gun laws, the Hardin-Taylor raiders continued their murderous ways. After killing Helm, their next target was Joe Tumlinson. In early August, John Wesley and about forty of the Taylor men, soon to grow to a force of about seventy-five, surrounded the Tumlinson home on his ranch just west of Yorktown. The leaders of the group were the same men who had fired the shots that had killed Cox and Cristman. At the time, about a dozen of Tumlinson's loyal men were there. For two nights and a day, the tense confrontation threatened to escalate into bloody war as John Wesley's men stayed formed in a battle line. But, both groups, armed to the teeth, managed to stalemate each other. While Hardin's gang had the Tumlinson forces far outnumbered, some men in the house pulled off a successful ruse. They allowed their enemies to see them briefly through a window, then changed shirts and allowed themselves to be seen again. They convinced the wild bunch outside that there were more men in the house than there actually were. John Wesley originally planned to have a number of his men sneak up to Tumlinson's porch where several of his men slept and murder them, but barking dogs foiled that plan. According to the Unionist *San Antonio Daily Express,* the Hardin-Taylor desperadoes had been engaged in guerilla warfare ever since the resurgent Democratic party had abolished the State Police. The siege at the ranch was one example.[47]

As the stalemate continued, Jim Taylor went into Cuero to buy turpentine balls with which the raiders intended to burn Tumlinson's place and force the men inside to abandon the house, after which all would be exposed and vulnerable. While Taylor was away, a Tumlinson courier got past the renegades and rode into Clinton seeking help. Republican L. B. Wright was on the scene when the messenger arrived. Wright later informed the governor of what had transpired. The Hardin-Taylor forces wanted kill Tumlinson and several others who had either belonged to the State Police or who had helped the police in their pursuit of the gang. Wright said, "I was in Clinton in attendance at the District Court. When the news arrived I reported it to Judge D. D. Claiborne, and he ordered the deputy sheriff to summon a posse to relieve Tumlinson."[48]

DeWitt County Deputy Sheriff D. J. Blair obeyed the judge and formed a posse, but he could come up with only nine men willing to serve. After galloping their horses to the Tumlinson place, the lawmen found the guerrillas still laying siege to the house. Temporarily in command of the desperadoes, Lazarus Nickles refused to let the deputy and his men through to the house, but negotiations began. The situation became even more tense when, as

Wright later reported, six of the posse members revealed themselves as Taylor men; they went over to the enemy. Deputy Blair then was hopelessly outnumbered; however, when Tumlinson's courier found the sheriff and told him of the difficulty, he organized a bigger posse. He drew approximately fifty loyal men from Cuero and Clinton who rode to Tumlinson's ranch to learn exactly what was happening. Just before the posse arrived, the brigands agreed to a compromise that ended the siege.[49]

The stalemate ended in a most bizarre way, even by the standards of fighting Texans. Deputy Blair negotiated a cease-fire and persuaded both groups to sign a "treaty." He then herded what was left of his posse, the Taylor men, and Tumlinson's forces back to Clinton. Hardin and his men headed the column while Tumlinson's men trailed behind with the deputy sheriff's men in the middle. The sheriff and his larger posse met the strange assortment of folks on the road and joined the convoy to town. In Clinton, the Taylor forces halted on one side of town while Blair escorted Tumlinson's smaller force to the other side. Then, the county clerk drew up a "proper document" that was readily signed by forty-one men on August 12. They promised to refrain from "hostile acts" and to allow community peace to return. Although Tumlinson and Hardin signed the document, one leader's name was absent: Deputy William E. Sutton who might not have been present at the time. More likely, he knew that murderers like John Wesley and the Taylors would never keep such a pledge. That was also the belief of the county clerk who said that men like Hardin, George Tennille, the Taylors, and the Clements brothers would never remain peaceful. They were too accustomed to taking what they wanted and shooting anyone who interfered, all the while claiming to be fighting for the old Confederacy. About John Wesley, specifically, contemporary sources gave varied accounts of the number of people he had killed, but one held that the total was now at least twenty-six. No one who signed the "treaty" really believed that Hardin would obey its terms.[50]

The county clerk explained that the problem was regional. Most of the Hardin gang lived in Gonzales County, not DeWitt, and cooperation between the counties was difficult as was coordination when different authorities acted together. About the arrangement, Wright wrote Davis expressing much disgust at the goings-on. Wright said Judge Claiborne knew that Hardin and others with him were fugitives from justice, some facing charges as serious as murder. But the judge negotiated with John as an equal and dared not attempt to arrest any of his men because they were too numerous and, if angered, might start a bloodbath in Clinton.[51]

As events proved, the "treaty" lasted only three months or so. In late December a DeWitt posse of eight men finally tracked down the fugitive Wiley W. Pridgen, a Taylor man who lived in Thompson Station (now Thomaston) just south of Cuero. Pridgen had a murder indictment against him. He had earlier led the men who ventured to Victoria and took two men out of the county jail and executed them. He had also killed two other men. The lawmen found him at his kinsman Jim Pridgen's country store a few miles south of Cuero. Standing in the doorway of the store when the posse rode up, Pridgen immediately grabbed his gun and fired a few misdirected rounds, whereupon the posse used their shotguns and sixguns to kill him. Shot in one arm and in the heart, he died lying in a pool of his own blood. The new Democratic authorities arrested several men for killing Pridgen: Deputy Sheriff William Meador, who led the posse; James E. Smith; John Guyens; Jim Mason; Doc and Jeff White; Edward Parkinson; and A. Patterson. How-ever, all went free because Pridgen was a known murderer, a wanted man. The reason for the killing of Pridgen was, perhaps, as bizarre as the earlier "treaty." It may have been, in part, revenge-driven. In Victoria, on September 20, 1867, Pridgen had words with Neil Brown about a horse, one that Pridgen had stolen from Brown. Pridgen took exception to something Brown said, pulled a revolver, and shot him down. More than one account of Wiley Prid-gen's death asserted that Brown's teenaged son James was among his killers and may well have fired the first shot.[52]

Almost immediately, the Hardin-Taylor leaders learned of Pridgen's death. John Wesley and Jim Taylor assembled some men and rode for Cuero. Simultaneously, Sutton and some other lawmen started riding toward the town. Learning that Sutton's posse was near, the desperadoes dismounted and set up an ambush on the upper Clinton-Cuero Road. After being fired upon, the posse retreated and took the lower Clinton-Cuero Road. The Hardin-Taylor bunch raced to Cuero and set up another ambush near town. But the posse stayed out of gun range and rode on into town in a roundabout way. Several posse members intended to file more charges against Scrap Taylor, one of the men who had earlier shot Sutton.[53]

The Hardin-Taylor men intended to stop any court proceedings that would involve Scrap. Just after the New Year holiday, the two groups occu-pied Cuero, with Sutton and other deputies taking over the Gulf Hotel and the Hardin men taking over buildings on Main and Evans streets in addition to the lumberyard downtown. The townspeople readied for a war. All men on both sides were heavily armed. A battle appeared imminent, so much so that some of the urban folks hurriedly left their homes and businesses and rode to more peaceful environs. At one point, the two groups had at each other near the lumberyard, but neither group suffered casualties. Meanwhile, the sheriff became most upset, as did other officials, because John Wesley had brought too many men for the authorities to corral. But, the next day Tum-linson arrived, heading a party of about twenty men. Thus reinforced, the posse now almost had parity with the marauders. Another stalemate developed and gave the town's residents a chance to settle matters without bloodshed. Negotiators framed another "treaty," despite the ludicrous nature of lawmen bargaining with known felons. Eighty-seven men signed the "Treaty of Cuero," another agreement that did not last.[54]

Despite the "treaty," DeWitt County authorities shortly charged at least twenty-four men of the Taylor-Hardin band with rioting. The list included two of the Clements brothers; the crime ring's lawyer Bolivar J. Pridgen; Fred Duderstadt, upon whose land in Gonzales County that the Hardins lived; George Tennille; Jim, Billy, and Scrap Taylor; Alf Day; and John W. Glover. As well, authorities charged other men in the ring with other crimes: Asa Langford Jr., for a murder in Coryell County, and Buck and J. Roland, Fred Pell, and James and Isaac Wright for horse thefts in DeWitt County. Apparently, local lawmen were becoming more willing to confront members of the crime ring.[55]

CHAPTER NINE

Lawmen Begin Taking Control

I N the winter of 1873–74, after the standoff with the authorities, the
Taylor-Hardin gang defiantly remained active in DeWitt County. They
committed robbery and murder, and they continued to rustle cattle and
steal horses. Although the guerrillas continued to bawl about the "Lost
Cause" and Confederate honor, Gov. Richard Coke and Adj. Gen. William
Steele now understood the menace of the crime ring and determined to break
its hold. Statewide, many Democrats tolerated the abuses of terrorist groups
and desperadoes because the action of the violent men furthered the aims
of the Democratic party, but once the party regained political power, leaders wanted to end the hostilities. New Texas Ranger forces came into Taylor
Country planning to end the reign of chaos. Unfortunately, the lawmen only
succeeded in driving the raiders from the Cuero-Yorktown-Clinton area into
Comanche and Brown counties. There leaders John Wesley and Jim Taylor
could hide with Hardin's father, who was now a preacher and a teacher in
Comanche town, or with Wesley's brother Jo, who was now practicing law
there while also engaging in fraudulent land schemes in both counties. Jo
had long provided phony bills of sale for stolen cattle that Hardin and Jim
Taylor supposedly bought. In sum, Jo had become a master swindler who
used legal tools to allow all manner of shady business deals, many of which
benefitted the Taylor clan. Knowing that John Wesley's kinsmen were among
their supporters, the gang set up a headquarters near Logan's Gap, where stolen stock could be held prior to disposal. According to one source, stockmen
in the region of Blanket Creek in Comanche County suffered the biggest
losses. However, the ranchers of Brown County had copious losses, too. In
addition to their thievery, Hardin and Taylor set up horse races but seldom
paid when they lost.[1]

The gang's new operations soon led to trouble. One of Hardin's men named Davis came into Comanche, got drunk, became loud and boisterous, and quickly came to Marshal Jeff Green's attention after he threatened to kill several local men. Green found the man in a saloon and warned him that he must be orderly.

Green left and went back to his office after Davis agreed to calm down. That did not happen. The man kept drinking and abusing others. After learning that his town still had trouble, Green returned to confront the malefactor, who quickly drew a gun on him. Given the threat, Green backed out of the saloon into the street, but Davis followed with gun in hand. Suddenly, from the other side of the street, resident Henry Ware yelled: "Davis, don't shoot." When the gunman glanced toward Ware to see who was calling him, Green had the opportunity to save his life; he took it. He quickly drew his gun and fired. The one bullet was true, and Davis collapsed backward, instantly dead with a hole in his heart. Only then did the marshal notice that the main street was full of witnesses; there was no question that Green shot in self-defense.[2] Now, the Taylor ring was reduced by one more.

Shortly, Hardin gave the Comanche marshal more headaches. In town with Ham Anderson, Gyp Clements, Stephen Cowan, and John Denton, the murderer passed a day in January in a saloon gambling and drinking. John Wesley became so loud and rowdy that someone alerted Marshal Green, who went to the scene and tried to arrest the young hotspur for a misdemeanor, probably public drunkenness. But Hardin's men interfered, allowing him to escape and to ride out of town. Green then arrested all four, charging them with "resisting a peace officer." However, the men soon paid their fines and went free. Curiously, no one in Comanche knew of the desperadoes' past records and did not know that they had criminal charges pending elsewhere, for Governor Davis was no longer in power, and Democrats had disbanded the State Police.[3]

By early 1874, the Taylor-Hardin gang's rustling finally exhausted the patience of area ranchers, especially those in Brown County. In March, sixteen of them, all irate, complained to Brown County Sheriff J. H. Gideon and demanded that he confront the rustlers and bring the guilty to justice. Gideon contacted Deputy Charles "Charlie" Webb, a former Texas Ranger, and gave him the job of breaking up the outlaw band by whatever means necessary. Almost simultaneously, Comanche County citizen complaints finally forced Marshal Green and a posse to respond to the lawlessness. They tracked and killed Charlie Davis, probably the brother of the Davis earlier killed by Green. The posse ran Jim Beard out of town; both Davis and Beard were members of the ring. Deputy Webb suspected that Hardin himself was involved in the recent troubles. Indeed he was; moreover, the young hotspur bragged that he would not cease his activities nor would he submit to any arrest by county or state authorities. Brown County historian T. R. Havins later described Hardin as a "most despicable character" who was "cruel, heartless, and a calculating killer" and "engaged in all types of lawlessness."[4]

Despite other concerns, both Hardin and Jim Taylor still focused on Sutton, considering him their number one enemy, but he was a hard man to kill. Not only had he recovered from the shotgun blast that Scrap Taylor gave him in Cuero, but he also survived a fight south of the town where he had a horse shot out from under him. Just a bit later, members of the ring attacked him again, and he had another mount go down; yet, he survived. A short time later, Hardin personally rode into Victoria County and camped out near Sutton's home, hoping to assassinate him. One night the renegade even used an old trick trying to lure Sutton outside. Hardin got into Sutton's garden and rang an old cow bell, hoping that the lawman would think that one of his cows was guilty of trespass and come out to correct the situation. The lawman refused to take the bait. Hardin had no success and gave up on his plan, but Sutton's good luck was about to end. Perhaps he knew it. Even though he had never been involved with law enforcement and therefore had dealt no harm to the Taylor ring, Sutton's brother James had already sold his land and stock and moved to escape the Taylors and thereby save his life and those of his family. He did not go far, settling anew in Wilson County, still part of Taylor Country, but the move got him away from DeWitt County, always the epicenter of trouble.[5] But Bill Sutton had grit; he refused to go into exile.

In March 1874, Sutton's cowboys started a herd north toward Kansas. With his wife Laura, young, beautiful, and pregnant, Sutton intended to go to Indianola, board a ship going to New Orleans, and then reach Kansas by rail. Still in Comanche with most of his gang, Hardin learned of Sutton's general plans but needed more specific information if he were to plan an assassination. Sutton knew John Wesley but did not know his brother Jo or his cousin Alex Barekman. Barekman originally lived near Corsicana in Navarro County, but he fled southward to elude authorities after murdering Colonel William Love by shooting him in the back. John Wesley asked the two to find Sutton and determine his exact plans; Hardin intended to have Jim Taylor kill him. Jo and Barekman met Sutton in Victoria, supposedly by chance, engaged in unimportant talk, and in the course of the conversation, learned the definite date, March 11, 1874, that Sutton would sail for New Orleans. According to at least one source, ex-State Senator Bolivar Pridgen also learned about the date from a Victoria banker and gave his information to Hardin. If so, he was acting out of revenge for the earlier killing of his kinsman, the murderer Wiley Pridgen.

Yet another source held that an unnamed Victoria banker directly relayed Sutton's plans to the Taylors. If so, it appears that there was a grand conspiracy to rid the world of the pesky deputy sheriff. After Jo gave the news to his brother, the latter talked with Jim and Bill Taylor, telling them to target Sutton for death. The two eagerly took the assignment because both held Sutton responsible for bedeviling their cattle rustling schemes and for Pitkin Taylor's death, along with the demise of their cohorts, including their kinsmen Buck and Charlie Taylor. Hardin arranged for some of his boys, from six to eight of them, to reach Indianola before the two assassins. Their real intent to protect the shooters, they seemed harmless, just branding cattle in a local pen when the Taylors reached town. The Sutton party had already arrived, having come to Indianola by carriage.[6] After they reached town, Jim and Billy Taylor bought fresh horses for their escape and tethered them near the ship that the Suttons were boarding. After that, they struck while Sutton, his wife, and their employee Gabriel W. Slaughter were buying tickets for their trip. Slaughter was to have been Sutton's trail boss on the Kansas drive, but he became ill, and the Suttons decided that he should accompany them. As the killers approached, Slaughter recognized at least one of the Taylors and asked Sutton if they should draw their guns and get ready for a fight, whereupon Sutton waved him off, saying that there were too many people around for the brigands to "pull anything." He was wrong.[7]

As Sutton was buying tickets, Jim Taylor filled both his hands with six-guns and, without warning, shot Sutton and Slaughter repeatedly. He shot his victims in their backs several times, thereby giving them no chance defend themselves. Sutton took several balls, including one to his back, one to his brain, another to his heart. While Jim Taylor was murdering Sutton, Billy Taylor finished Slaughter. Billy fired only once, close up, his ball hitting Slaughter in the face and going to his brain. As Laura Sutton began screaming, blood, gore, and brain matter seemed to have splattered everywhere, her dress included. Jim quickly picked up Sutton's holstered, unfired handgun, an ivory-handled Smith and Wesson American model, then the most accurate handgun in the world. The two murderers quickly fled, reached their horses, and rode away heading for Boliver Pridgen's place in Thomaston.[8]

The two killers left behind a scene of utter chaos in Indianola, including a beautiful young pregnant widow's mournful wails. As soon as she recovered, Laura Sutton offered a $1,000 reward, to be added to Governor Coke's $500 bounty, to anyone who could deliver Jim Taylor inside the jailhouse door of DeWitt County. She offered no reward for Billy Taylor because the Cuero town marshal had already detained him. She made her offer on May 21 and described Jim Taylor so that any bounty hunter could recognize him.[9]

After the two shooters reached Pridgen's place and informed him of their success, the ex-senator became euphoric. He prepared a celebration that included much drink and a meal with two turkeys as a main course. He also barbecued a calf. After the feast, the men partied much of the night away. The next day, a smiling Pridgen watched the Taylors leave, going toward John Wesley's stronghold in Gonzales County. There, Hardin's men were branding stolen cattle that they had rustled in DeWitt County. His hands included Alf Day, Scrap Taylor, Kute Tuggle, Jim White, "Pleas" Johnson, and "Pink" Burns. The stolen beeves were mixed with some cattle that Fred and John Duderstadt had legitimately sold to Hardin, a move that provided a little cover for the stolen stock should lawmen inspect the growing herd. When Jim Taylor arrived, Hardin's men were ready for a drive to Kansas although DeWitt County authorities held up the herd, after which Hardin's men started pushing the beeves toward Comanche. Hardin and Taylor went on ahead to visit the Hardin family and to hatch a plot to murder Deputy Webb, who had earlier troubled them.[10]

Once Sutton was out of the way, Hardin and Jim Taylor made Brown County Deputy Webb their next target. He met the rustlers for the first time in April 1874 when he investigated the lynching of a Mexican bandit on the Williams ranch. While pursuing that investigation, Webb rode into Comanche County and, at one point, met some of the raiders: Hardin, Jim Taylor, and Alex Barekman, along with the Dixon brothers, Bud and Tom. All were working to gather a stolen herd for a drive to Kansas. A confrontation followed when Webb wanted to inspect the beeves. The gang members refused to allow an inspection and cursed Webb as a meddler. They warned him to stay out of their business and to stay out of Comanche County. Although they were hostile to lawmen generally, the renegades were especially brutal toward Webb because he would have discovered that most of their herd was purloined if they had allowed him to inspect it. Such hard feelings later led to Webb's murder.[11]

The Hardin-Taylor bunch stayed in Comanche County through the month of April, continuing to build their stolen herd, one that Jo Hardin made certain had a long, convoluted paper trail that might take legal experts weeks to sort out. Hardin's men were ranging over both Brown and Comanche counties and legitimate ranchers and farmers in both continued to suffer heavy losses. To ensure that they would have no trouble as the herd was leaving the area, John Wesley and Jim Taylor took the corrupt Comanche County Sheriff John Carnes with them, along with Deputies Jim Millican and Bill Cunningham. Those lawmen had been bought the same way that Creed Taylor bought his gunmen. John Wesley reasoned that before anyone could sort out the status of his stolen beeves, the cattle would be well on the way to Kansas, and the Hardins, Jim and "Buck" Waldrip, the Clements brother, Sheriff Carnes, and others would become richer when buyers bought the herd. However, Deputy Webb threatened to upset the plans. He finally deduced that Hardin's herd was stolen, but it was now moving, and he could not find it. Nevertheless, he found and arrested Buck Waldrip and cohort James Beard. He tossed both felons in the Brown County jail and charged them with cattle rustling. When a number of furious Brown County cattlemen showed up in Brownwood with twin lynchings on their mind, Webb protected the prisoners, ultimately transferring them to the jail in Georgetown, Williamson County, where Sheriff Sam M. Strayhorn promised to protect them. Soon, the two rustlers made bond, went free, and rejoined the Hardin-Taylor men.[12]

Even as Webb was investigating, Jim and Billy Taylor, fresh off their murders of Sutton and Slaughter, worked the herd without undue trouble. They helped finish the job of rounding up stolen cattle until they had created a large herd, one worthy enough for the Chisholm Trail. After the herd moved north toward Wichita with Joe Clements acting as trail boss, Jim and Bill Taylor again ventured into DeWitt County. On April 3, they rode into Cuero where they brazenly spent a day and evening celebrating their misspent lives by becoming drunk and rowdy. They openly wore their guns, thereby violating the gun laws. That was a mistake, for they came to the attention of a new lawman, Reuben "Rube" Brown, the recently installed town marshal. He became a major defender of law and order, and that made him anathema to the Hardin-Taylor forces.[13]

Little is known about Reuben Brown, but according to the 1870 census he was Texas-born, lived on the Brown family farm, and was eighteen years old. Earlier, he had been in posses on scouts for malefactors, but his first real action against the Taylor-Hardin ring came that April day when the two terrible Taylors were in town. Brown arrested Bill Taylor for carrying a gun, the Smith and Wesson that originally belonged to Sutton. A resident quickly alerted the lawman that Taylor had a price on his head and was wanted for first degree murder in addition to other felonies. The resident showed Brown a copy of Governor Coke's proclamation putting a reward on Taylor's head for the murder. In capturing Billy Taylor, the marshal had the help of the Cuero "Home Protection Club," a group of plucky townsmen who had finally had enough of the violence that beset their area. However, Jim Taylor managed to sneak out of town without a confrontation.[14]

Once Brown had Billy Taylor in custody, he did not keep him long. The authorities decided to send him to Indianola from whence he would be carried to Galveston, that town having one of the most secure jails in Texas. But, first, Brown had to get Taylor from Cuero to Indianola. Under heavy guard, the prisoner boarded the train and began the trip, but before the iron horse reached the coast, Hardin and his guerrillas tried to liberate him. From out of nowhere, they burst through the bush and spurred their horses until they were parallel to the iron beast. The raiders fired shot after shot at the windows of the train, still riding along beside it; however, the posse guarding Taylor returned fire and finally drove the raiders away. Thus, Hardin and the others could not rescue their man. And they could not even contemplate breaking into the heavily manned Indianola jail to free the murderer whom lawmen later transferred to Galveston. Although they could not free Billy Taylor, the gang could go after Rube Brown, the marshal who had arrested him.[15]

Before getting revenge, however, Hardin and his men rounded up another cattle herd, one that eventually numbered about one thousand head, mostly stolen, and prepared to drive them up the trail. Leaving the cattle with trail boss J. B. "Doc" Bockius, Hardin and Jim Taylor rode to Comanche town because John Wesley wanted to visit his parents. Then, during the first week of May 1874, Hardin and some of his men—including Jim and Ham Anderson; Bud and Tom Dixon; Alex Barekman; Jim Milligan; and Bill Cunningham, who later turned state's evidence against Hardin for the murder of Deputy Webb—rode to Brown County to steal more cattle. They drove their new purloined herd to Buck Waldrip's place to pen the animals. Already wanted for several felonies, including cattle rustling and horse stealing, Waldrip was in jail at the time, for Webb had found him at home and arrested him. Only Waldrip's wife was home. She related a woeful tale. Deputy Charles Webb had just recently arrested her husband, she said, and she made much of the situation, claiming that Webb and his posse had "abused her" and used insulting language. Now riding with his brother, Jo Hardin told the woman not to worry because the gang would "take care" of Webb at the proper time.[16]

Although they wanted Webb dead, the Hardin-Taylor bunch first went after Marshal Green. Leaving their headquarters on the Guadalupe River, Hardin and Jim Taylor came to Comanche, as did the Dixon boys, Bud and Tom; the Andersons, Ham and Jim; and Alex Barekman. The group's goal remained as it had been: to kill Marshal Green and Deputy Webb, both of whom, by enforcing the law, interfered with the designs of the desperadoes. As well, the raiders wanted revenge for the capture and incarceration of their friends in crime, including Billy Taylor and Buck Waldrip. Green's friends learned that the renegades were after him and convinced him to take reasonable precautions, such as traveling outside of town as little as possible. He also allowed bodyguards to attend him and to help him do his job.[17]

Deputy Sheriff Webb was not so lucky. As mentioned in the introduction, Hardin, Jim Taylor, and Bud Dixon murdered him on the main street of Comanche on May 26, 1874. As Webb's bloody body was falling, the murderers turned their thoughts to escape. Immediately after killing the law-man, Hardin, Taylor, Dixon, and other gang members controlled the imme-diate area around the saloon. Even if Sheriff Carnes had wanted to arrest the shooters—and he did not—he could not take effective action because there were too many desperadoes. Carnes later said he had sent for the Texas Rang-ers with the hope that they could restore order. However, he had been in-volved with some of the gang's rustling and had made a tidy sum of money; he had no desire to arrest the killers even if he had a reasonable chance. As the standoff was continuing, Hardin's father and brother Jo rushed to the scene. Both carried loaded shotguns. They intended to save John Wesley, but a crowd of men, trying to control the situation, disarmed them.[18]

John Wesley and his men, their guns still trained on the crowd, backed into the saloon. Someone gave the sheriff a loaded shotgun, and he used it to protect the criminals who had given him so much money. He went to the front door of the saloon as Hardin and his men were retreating and tempo-rarily held back the crowd, threatening to kill anyone who rushed him. Given the chaos outside, John Wesley, Taylor, and Barekman slipped out a side door and ran to some horses on the opposite side of the street. Bud Dixon and Anderson hung back long enough to fire several shots at the crowd, blasts designed to buy a few moments of time because the local men in the street had to duck for cover. Then, Dixon and Anderson ran to catch up with their cohorts. Getting out of town alive was anything but easy. About ten men fired at the killers as they were escaping. Taylor, Barekman, and Bud Dixon returned fire to keep the armed townsmen away. The murderers were then able to make their hurried escape just as Henry Ware ran down the street behind them, firing his revolver repeatedly but to no effect.[19]

As fast as their horses could run, the malefactors rode to the Leon River just east of Comanche and hid in the thick brush there. But authorities caught Bud Dixon easily and arrested several other Hardin men later, the list including Alex Barekman, Jim Anderson, and Tom Dixon. However, Barekman escaped on the night of his capture. Almost immediately after the violence, a group of men from Comanche County, twenty-three in number, petitioned Governor Coke. On May 28, 1874, they asked for protection and relief from the Hardin-Taylor guerrillas. They said a band of murderers and thieves "headed by the Notorious John Wesley Hardin and Jim Taylor" in-fested their county. The petitioners added that the renegades were in such great numbers that they "invariably escape before a sufficient number of citizens can be armed and brought together."[20]

Interestingly, not one of the petitioners was a lawman; they were simple, peaceful men—ranchers and farmers, along with businessmen and other ur-ban folk from Comanche. They were afraid and sick of the outrages. They complained that, at great expense, they had to keep an armed posse on full-time duty just to protect their lives, their families, their stock, and their other property. They demanded help. They wanted Coke to send in at least twenty-five Texas Rangers charged with the specific duty of bringing in John Wesley Hardin and Jim Taylor. The governor intended to take more action because now that the Democrats were back in power, they wanted all the state's turmoil to end. They no longer needed violent men, no longer tolerated terrorists and outlaws.[21]

Meanwhile, Ham Anderson joined Barekman in the countryside, and the two went into hiding as did Hardin and Taylor and other gang members who had been in Comanche. Winding up together, Hardin, Taylor, Barekman, and Anderson went into a thicket, called the Devil's Truck Patch, near the Leon River. When close to being discovered, they moved on to Round Mountain, the two hiding places being only about five or six miles apart. Concurrently, because of the serious nature of events, Governor Coke quickly answered the pleas of the Comanche petitioners. In fact, he had heard of the murder and had acted before he received the petition. He ordered Ranger Maj. John B. Jones, commander of the Frontier Battalion, to send men into Comanche County. On May 27, 1874, a squad of fifty-five, commanded by Capt. John R. Waller, arrived in the area and immediately went in pursuit of Hardin and his men, as did posses from several counties. A Civil War veteran and once the sheriff of Erath County, the no-nonsense Waller had broad powers. He was to arrest all marauders and thieves who had violated the criminal laws of Texas.[22]

Waller's first targets were members of the ring, whom he described as murderous desperadoes who "preyed on the lives of the citizens." He added that the Hardin-Taylor marauders were far more dangerous than the hostile Indians. However, Waller voiced one complaint when reporting to Jones. Many of the captain's men had inferior arms and needed replacements; as well, they needed more ammunition to engage in a manhunt that could end in a massive gun battle. Even so, Waller kept men scouting for the desperadoes twenty-four hours a day. Despite their lack of good equipment and supplies, one of Waller's squads found Hardin, Taylor, and a few of their men just three days after the rangers arrived in the county. There was a brisk skirmish on horseback with a number of volleys exchanged, but the gunfight was not decisive. Later, on a drizzling, rainy day, rangers on another scout found Hardin, Taylor, and about six of their men on the Brownwood–Comanche Road. The lawman gave chase, but the renegades had better horses and outran them—only to run headlong into another scout led by Waller himself. A wild shoot-out began. Hardin's bunch was between the two ranger squads. The raiders profited by their position, for the lawmen had to be most careful lest they fire wildly and shoot each other. Although the lawmen numbered about forty, in all the confusion, little was accomplished. The marauders managed to ride through Waller's line of men, the only casualty of the day being Hardin's horse Frank, who took a slug in one of his hind legs.[23]

Even as the rangers were trying to corral the raiders, the Hardin family, still headed by the good reverend, John Wesley's father, did everything possible to aid the villains. They brought food for man and horse, fresh water, more weapons, more ammunition, and good information on the rangers' whereabouts. Reverend Hardin also supplied good saddle horses for the fugitives. Waller finally deduced that the desperadoes' families were helping them. Because Wesley's big brother Jo and younger brother Jeff were doing so much to aid the murderers, Waller arrested them along with some members of the Barekman family. A little later, he arrested Reverend Hardin, who had done so much to further his sons' criminal careers; John Wesley's mother; Jane Hardin; Jo Hardin's wife; Barekman's wife; Mattie Hardin; Tom Dixon; Jim Anderson; William Green; J. B. "Doc" Brockius; and a few others. Waller kept them under guard for about two weeks while his men continued pursuit in the field.[24]

In that two weeks, John Wesley and Jim Taylor became more desperate. They had but few friends in the area who were not incarcerated; they were running out of cohorts who could help them in their attempts to escape. At one point, Hardin and Taylor were hiding in the root cellar of a friend's cabin, the owner having pulled a rug and a bed over the trap door to the basement. The Brown County posse tracked the malefactors to the cabin and went in to search it. As the search was taking place, the posse from Comanche arrived, mistook the Brown County posse's horses for those of the gang, and starting firing into the house. When the Brown County men fired back, a general shoot-out occurred before the leaders of both posses discovered their mistakes. Those errors resulted in the wounding of several men, but there were no fatalities.[25]

Although neither posse discovered Hardin and Taylor, who cowered in the cellar until it was safe to come out, the two fugitives decided that Comanche County was now too dangerous for them. However, before they could escape, a posse cornered them in the Leon River bottoms about ten miles from Comanche. With seven of their men, Hardin and Taylor fought back in a sporadic gun battle that lasted a full day. Both factions made it rain bullets. Rifle fire and shotgun blasts shattered the quietness of the countryside. Although Hardin had his horse shot out from under him, the lawmen still could not capture or kill their quarry. At another point, Waller and his men were in hot pursuit on horseback, and between his men and their targets, bullets were flying pell-mell. Still, Hardin and Taylor were not about to surrender. One news correspondent commented, calling Hardin a "fearless man" who would likely "kill some more before he is taken."[26]

Still, the law enforcers had hope, for they had Hardin's father and mother, his brothers, his wife, and his children. They believed that John Wesley would try to rescue them, but that was not to be. Hardin put his own safety first, just as he always had done in the past. He planned his escape regardless of what might happen to his kin. However, a problem developed when most of the malefactors slipped away, leaving only Hardin, Taylor, Barekman, and Anderson. When the last four left on the trail that led out of Comanche County, Barekman and Anderson had second thoughts. They decided that they did not want to leave their homes, their decision being much to the surprise of Hardin and Taylor. Although John Wesley warned them both of their impending deaths, the two held firm, in part because Barekman was married and had a ten-month-old baby. Anderson, too, had many relatives and friends in the area and did not want to leave them. Although Hardin and Taylor were about ready to desert the area, they first rode to Bill Stone's ranch near the Leon River bottoms between Walnut and Bucksnort creeks about fifteen miles from Comanche and about four miles from the Devil's Truck Patch. Stone fed the raiders and gave them ammunition and other supplies. In mid-afternoon, the Hardin men left the ranch house and found a spot on the perimeter of Stone's place to spend the night. Before sundown, a squad of Waller's Texas Rangers, acting on an informant's tip, arrived at Stone's place and searched it, a task that yielded no fruit. Not realizing that Sheriff Carnes was a Hardin man, the rangers almost allowed him to steer the group away from the area, but Waller's men decided to spend the night near Stone's place.[27]

On June 1, their final night together, the four desperadoes bedded down after Hardin told Barekman and Anderson to stake their horses, something they did not do. Awakening early, Hardin scouted and saw lawmen who were entirely too close. After returning to camp and packing, he and Taylor rode south to escape into oblivion while Barekman and Anderson went back to Bill Stone's ranch. Again, Stone hid and fed them. An informant talked with the rangers, who learned that the pair might be at Stone's place, but the two left just ahead of the lawmen. Going into hiding again in the Devil's Truck Patch, Barekman and Anderson were soon spotted by a teenager who was hunting for wild cattle; the boy quickly informed Sheriff Carnes and other lawmen. Other intelligence assembled by the sheriff indicated that Stone was providing the two raiders with food and water and as much intelligence as he could gather. Carnes was in a big fix. Now he had to turn on two of the men he had used to line his pockets with cash and coin. His job was definitely at stake and perhaps his freedom, too. After recruiting a posse, Carnes went to

Stone's place. Arriving after sundown, the sheriff questioned Stone, who said Barekman and Anderson had decided to go to Mexico when the opportunity presented itself. After spending the night at Stone's, the posse split up. Some men rode into the thicket for a search; others followed Carnes to Bucksnort Crossing where the fugitives would likely try to cross the Leon River.[28]

After waiting for what felt like eternity, the sheriff left the creek and climbed a hill for a look about. He saw two horses grazing in a nearby pasture. The two outlaws had again failed to stake their horses. That was a costly mistake because the horses wandered and unwelcome eyes saw them. When Carnes spotted the horses, he knew that Barekman and Anderson could not be far away. However, before the sheriff could spot the desperadoes, the members of the posse who went into the thicket saw them first and opened fire. From their hiding place in the bush that the lawmen had finally discovered, Barekman and Anderson fought back gamely rather than surrender to face serious legal charges, some of which carried the death penalty. They continued to return fire for a time, but the posse finally shot them down. Near the end, several shots hit Anderson simultaneously, causing his immediate death, while another blast mortally wounded Barekman who shortly died at the scene. After pitching the dead bodies into a wagon, the posse went back to Comanche town. Later, Sheriff Carnes, who was always after gold, tried to claim the reward for killing Anderson and Barekman but was stymied by ranger commander John Jones who learned that the sheriff was not at the scene when posse members killed the perilous pair. The reward went to the men who had actually discovered and killed the two desperadoes.[29] In addition to the killing of Barekman and Anderson, Waller and his men arrested twenty-two members of the Taylor ring between May 28 and June 12. The rangers sent seven of them to the DeWitt County jail. They sent the other fifteen to various county jails, depending on charges against each. Meanwhile, after they heard the news of Webb's death, about twenty Brown County ranchers mustered at the courthouse in Brownwood; they came heavily armed, most with pistols and shotguns, some with rifles. Brownwood's town folk knew that major events were about to take place, as the men mounted their horses and left town riding eastwardly toward Comanche. Joined en route by another twenty men, including a few stalwarts from Coleman County, the Brown County vigilant committee learned that the Comanche sheriff had lodged Jo Hardin and the Dixon brothers on the second floor in a building on the square whose security was almost nonexistent. It was the best that the sheriff could do, for workers had torn down the old jail and still had the new one under construction. About midnight on June 7, the forty-man posse, all wearing masks, marched on the temporary jail. They entered the building and disarmed the guards without a firing shot. The posse did not trifle with Taylor men James Anderson, Buck Waldrip, William Green, or Doc Bockius who were in the jail at the time. The Brown County men did not know that the four men were members of the Taylor ring. The posse's targets, then, were Jo Hardin and the Dixon boys.[30]

Leaders of the Brown County bunch did not waste time. They tied and gagged the three men, drug them outside, put them on horses, and led the steeds to a copse of live-oak trees about one mile out of Comanche. There, posse leaders put three ropes around three necks and tied the other ends to tree branches. By then, a rather nice crowd of town folk had assembled to watch the spectacle. The posse allowed each doomed man a last word, but the Dixon boys, who were chained together, declined to speak. Jo Hardin, however, begged for his life and pleaded innocence, saying that he had not been a party to illegal acts. Only if observers ignored his real estate fraud and his aiding and abetting multiple murders could that statement be true. With Jo Hardin still whining, three men—standing close to the horses upon which the victims sat—used rawhide quirts to spur three horses onward, leaving three bodies swinging from the ropes on the live-oak tree.[31]

Even as the three Taylor men were swinging to their deaths in Comanche, the authorities in DeWitt County and members of the ring staged a small scale war on the town streets of Cuero on Sunday, June 7, 1874. Skirmishes continued as day became night, but on Monday morn, witnesses observed that six dead horses were apparently the only mortalities; or, if men on either side had been killed or wounded, their friends had taken them away. That Monday was Marshal Brown's last day as a lawman. He resigned, citing personal reasons. Most likely, he probably blamed himself for not being able to stop the gun-fest that had occurred the day and night before. Still, Brown was not out of harm's way, for the Taylors had long memories. After escaping jail in Indianola during a freak storm, Bill Taylor threatened to kill him, a promise actually fulfilled by Jim Taylor and four other men much later. The five assassins caught Brown, who was in a Cuero billiard hall-saloon engaged in a card game, and shot him to death, primarily for his role in the law-and-order campaign and for his earlier arrest of Bill Taylor.[32]

Meanwhile, the Texas Rangers investigated the war in Cuero and held the authorities blameless. The rangers secured warrants for the arrest of many of the Taylor gang for rioting, the second time such charges had been brought against some of them. The list included two of the Clements brothers; Bolivar J. Pridgen, the ex-state senator and Taylor family attorney; two of the Duderstadt men; Alf Day; and three of the Taylors. The rangers were also after several other Hardin-Taylor men for assorted crimes. The lawmen were looking for James and Isaac Wright and Buck and James Roland, all four wanted for horse theft. Of course, the rangers were still after Hardin and Jim Taylor but could not find them.[33]

While the woebegone authorities searched for a way to restore peace, Hardin and Jim Taylor slipped away from Comanche County despite all attempts to corral them. However, they did not go far. They rode into Brown County and stayed there temporarily. In early June observers spotted them close to Brownwood. According to Ranger Capt. W. J. Maltby, now commanding forces in the area, John Wesley and Taylor threatened to kill a number of people, principally the ones who had been part of the posse that hanged Jo Hardin and the Dixons. However, since the men who took Hardin and the Dixons out of the Comanche jail wore disguises, Taylor and Hardin had trouble identifying their would-be targets. Trying to run the two desperadoes to ground, Ranger Major Jones personally led reinforcements and joined Captain Matlby's men in late June. Jones found the men on Clear Creek, about fifteen miles west of Brownwood. But scouts of the area turned up nothing.

After spending the last night in the county with Bud Tatum, the two raiders left the area. Alerted to the presence of the rangers, Hardin, Taylor, and several of their men moved into Coleman County from whence they scattered. Hardin and Taylor rode to the cedar breaks about six miles northwest of Austin where "Fancy Jim" Taylor, also called "Little Jim," had a place. They hid there for a time, Taylor trying to get over dysentery and Hardin trying to heal from the wound caused by Webb. While they were there, two of their men, the brothers Charles ("Charlie") and Alf Day, arrived and gave the bad news that the last cattle herd was now in Hamilton County and in danger of being seized by the local lawmen, for the authorities there suspected that the Taylor bunch had stolen most of the beeves in DeWitt County. After they delivered their report to Hardin, the Day brothers rode back to Hamilton County to rejoin the men moving the herd.[34]

While the aftermath of Webb's murder was playing itself out, the ring ridded itself of a spy in DeWitt County. Bill Buchanan, apparently a man loyal to the law, attempted to get close to the gang in the hopes of bringing its members to justice. He rode to see his cousin Tom Brown, who was married to Bolivar Pridgen's sister. Through Brown, Buchanan gave the Taylor forces inaccurate information about area lawmen and attempted to lead several of the raiders into an ambush. However, Bill Buchanan's uncle, Thompson Brown, had also married into the Pridgen family. It may have been that Bill confided in his uncle and that Thompson Brown gave the plot away. The result was Bill Buchanan's death. Pridgen ambushed him near Cuero and shot him to death.[35]

Scrap Taylor was but a young soldier in the Taylor ring. He was lynched for his crimes on behalf of the ring.
Courtesy Sharon Barnes, Director, Regional History Center of the Victoria College/University of Houston at Victoria Library

Shortly, the sheriff of Hamilton County staged a coup. In June 1874, he captured seven members of the crime ring and the 2,500 cattle herd they had stolen. Earlier, the Day brothers had started the cattle moving with Doc Bockius serving as trail boss. The drive went well, and the herd went undetected until it reached a point near Hamilton. The sheriff joined a band of thirteen rangers commanded by Sgt. J. V. Atkinson. The posse discovered the beeves, knew they were stolen, and confiscated the entire herd. They arrested Bockius and as many of his cowboys as they could find, the list including various Taylor gang members: Scrap Taylor, "Kute" Tuggle, Jim White, "Pleas" Johnson, "Pink" Burns, Thomas Bass, G. W. Parkes, J. Elder, and the Day brothers. The ranger detachment then drove the herd and the arrested men back to Comanche County, from whence another detachment was to take some of the prisoners to Austin while taking others to Clinton.[36]

Writing his friend Governor Coke, the Comanche attorney J. D. Stephens predicted more trouble. He told the governor that the prisoners were in Hardin's gang and that they were murderers and robbers whom Hamilton County authorities had caught moving cattle without "legal authority." He named all the men that the sergeant named, saying that all were crime ring members. Stephens asked Coke to help Sergeant Atkinson in any way possible to ensure the prisoners received the justice they deserved. But he warned the governor to expect that Hardin and Taylor would want revenge and would therefore be even more deadly than before.[37]

Almost concurrent with Stephens's warning to Coke, the Day brothers, along with others, broke out of the Clinton jail, stole horses, and galloped away. They rejoined Hardin and gave him a full report of what had happened in Hamilton County, but there was nothing Hardin and Jim Taylor could do to save their scheme to sell the stolen herd. Further, a judge issued a warrant for the arrest of Hardin, Taylor, and all their hands, for some of the stolen cattle belonged to Deputy Sheriff Dick Hudson. As well, the rangers continued to look for Hardin, Taylor, and Jim White, who were of particular concern to the rangers. They were regarded as the worst of the lot, especially the thirty-year-old White, whom one ranger called a "man-killing type." De-Witt County authorities took some of the Clinton prisoners to Austin, but Taylor, White, Bockius, and Tuggle remained in the jail. Sheriff Weisiger and Deputy George Boston tried to protect the prisoners, but rumors had it that vigilantes intended to have them; either that, or they would burn down the courthouse and perhaps most of the town along with it. On the night of June 21, a posse of irate men, all wearing disguises, indeed rode to the jail. Lawmen could do nothing because they were heavily outnumbered. Some of the vigilantes got into the jail, took the prisoners, marched them to the nearest tree (another live oak), and unceremoniously hanged Scrap Taylor, White, and Tuggle. Bockius managed to escape, thanks to the valor of Taylor man Joe Sunday who rode into the posse and hoisted Bockius upon his horse and galloped away.[38]

As many of the Taylor men were now either killed or jailed, in early July Adjutant General Steele visited Taylor Country to learn more about the ring's continued activity. He immediately began gathering intelligence. He visited Cuero, Clinton, Victoria, and Indianola as well as ranches and farms in the countryside. After talking with dozens of people, he reported to Governor Coke, giving him a summary of what he had learned. Saying that he had nothing but condemnation for the Hardin-Taylor ring, Steele told the governor that during the spring and summer John Wesley and a group of Taylor men had been gathering cattle without reference to ownership and shipping them to New Orleans. Hardin and Jim Taylor had also sent several herds north to Kansas. Steele said many ranchers whom the ring had victimized were afraid to interfere or even to complain because Hardin was such a "desperate character" who was always backed by "an armed party." The adjutant general warned the governor that the entire area was like a powder keg that could blow at any time. Whenever threatened, the renegades went into hiding, only waiting for the right time to get back to their "business" of robbing others. Focusing on DeWitt County, the adjutant general reported that a majority of the town folk and people in the hinterland had finally stood behind authorities like Tumlinson and others because they were trying to help the people cope with the Taylor crime wave. Conversely, Steele reported that when the Taylor band members came into town, they were given to rowdiness, drunkenness, and outright riotous behavior—wearing weapons openly, shooting their guns in town, and threatening the local authorities, indeed actually shooting one of them. Clearly, most of the people in Cuero knew right from wrong and were now sick of the whole sorry lot of the Taylor-Hardin raiders.[39]

All things considered, the crime ring seemed to be collapsing.

CHAPTER TEN

Exterminating the Taylor Crime Ring

VEN as the Taylor ring's manpower seemed to be dwindling, more trouble developed, this time in Austin. After learning that rangers would soon take some prisoners (Taylor men) to Clinton to stand trial, a number of the relatives and friends of the incarcerated men came to see them. A sergeant allowed private conversations over the objection of his men, who feared possible escape plots. When Governor Coke learned of the secret talks, he addressed the rangers, telling them that if trouble developed, to kill all the prisoners first and then to protect themselves as best they could, for the Democrats no longer needed violent men and chaos. Still, according to one officer, Hardin and Taylor could easily raise a company of about forty renegades, a number of men that might well overwhelm the ranger party of thirteen that guarded the Austin jail. But no attack came, possibly because would-be rescuers learned of Coke's directive. On the first night's camp on the way to Clinton, an oversight by a lawman allowed two Taylor men to grab one gun apiece, but the guards retook the weapons before the prisoners could use them.[1]

As the group approached the Guadalupe River, the prisoners began educating their escort about the best crossing. The captives held that the best route was to go down the west side of the river for about seven miles and then cross. After making camp and planning to find the crossing the next morning, rangers talked with two freedmen who saw their fires and came into their midst. A lawman told the blacks what the prisoners had recommended and asked for the advice of the older freedman. He told the rangers that the planned route would take them into an area that was one of the best hiding places of the Hardin-Taylor guerrillas. Consequently, the group crossed directly at Clinton the next evening, whereupon they rode straight into two hundred armed men. After backing out of their range and sight, Ranger W. M. Green called for Sheriff Weisiger and spoke to him privately, telling him who the prisoners were.[2]

Fearing a multiple lynching, the sheriff pulled the felons off their horses and had his own men mount them. After loudly telling the rangers to take the "prisoners" to the hotel for supper, Weisiger quickly assembled a small posse of trustworthy men to hide and to protect the real prisoners. Temporarily the posse and the rangers had the upper hand, but after the rangers left two days later, a disguised armed group that greatly outnumbered the sheriff's men took control of the captives and hanged them. The perpetrators were no doubt happy to cut into the numeral strength of what was left of the old ring.[3]

However, for a time the marauders continued to flourish even though the ring had lost many men. Writing from his post in Brownwood, Captain Maltby informed his superior, Major Jones, that the situation in Brown County was still critical and that he, Maltby, needed to stay at his present post because the "lives of the responsible citizens" were still at risk. Unaware that Hardin had left the area, the captain said that "the notorious outlaw John Hardin and a band of desperadoes" threatened all the peaceful folk. Maltby again complained that his men were poorly armed. He needed a good sixgun, as did most of his men. The squad also needed ammunition for their rifles. Clearly, the men wanted to go after Hardin, but they needed the firepower necessary to do it. Maltby was heartened when new pistols arrived. Yet, as he tested them using Smith and Wesson cartridges, he found them unreliable. He asked headquarters for different ammunition. The captain said his men were ready to do battle as soon as they received the new munitions.[4]

Soon, Maltby took the field with part of his command. Although his unit neither captured nor killed any brigands, he apparently drove them from Brown County. Major Jones made that judgment when he reinforced the captain as his command camped along Clear Creek, about fifteen miles from Brownwood. New scouts continued to turn up nothing, which prompted Jones to transfer Maltby's forces, some men going to Caldwell County and others to Eastland County.[5]

Shortly, in yet another county, another Taylor man fell. Called a trusted friend by John Wesley Hardin, George Tennille was much like Creed Taylor; that is, he aided and abetted the crime ring but usually stayed in the background and was not present during most of the killings. Tennille was more the advisor, less the gunman. However, as mentioned earlier, he did establish a horse thief operation, probably acting independently of the Taylors. He had been a signer of the "Cuero Treaty," had been indicted for rioting, and was a shooter in various other incidents, including a few murders. He ran

afoul of authorities for the last time in July 1874. He committed devilry
in Bexar County. Contacted by authorities there, Sheriff Green DeWitt of
Gonzales County, where Tennille resided, agreed to find and to arrest him.
Gathering a posse of nine men, the sheriff left Gonzales town on July 8.
Moving in the direction of Salt Creek, the posse rode to John Runnel's house
about fourteen miles from town.[6]

The sheriff correctly believed that Runnel had been harboring the felon.
Indeed, Tennille was there. He had hidden his horse in a thicket near the
house. DeWitt found the horse and left some men to guard it. Then, he
divided his men, having them form two wings, one of which rode up to one
side of the house, while the second wing approached from the other side.
When the posse was still about 150 yards from the house, Tennille spotted
the lawmen. He burst from the house and sprinted to his horse only to find
the men the sheriff had left there. They demanded surrender. Instead, he ran
into a cornfield to hide. The sheriff's men surrounded the field, and at least
one saw Tennille lying behind a brush fence with a gun in his hand. Several
times the sheriff entreated the wanted man to surrender, but Tennille refused. Instead, he tried to shoot at his adversaries, but he had trouble either
with his gun or with its ammunition because his weapon would not fire. He
was in the process of reloading when one of the possemen shot and killed
him, thus reducing the outlaw population by one more. According to one of
the sheriff's men, Tennille was saying a prayer as he died, the lawman adding
that it was a very good prayer.[7]

In mid-1874, Captain McNelly and his men again moved directly into
Taylor Country. After making a number of scouts to gain information and
look for the gang, McNelly reported to the adjutant general that "a perfect
reign of terror" had now engulfed DeWitt and adjoining counties and that
civil authorities could not or would not establish law and order. Moreover,
some of the desperadoes continued to devil the freedpeople. McNelly reported that the crime ring of South Texas, still led by Creed Taylor, still had
about one hundred well-armed men on the payroll. They were scattered in
such counties as Washington, Lavaca, Gonzales, DeWitt, Karnes, and other
fringe areas, but they could concentrate rapidly when necessary to cow civil
authorities.[8]

The captain acknowledged that Joe Tumlinson still rode for the authorities, but McNelly originally regarded him with suspicion. Taylor propaganda
apparently convinced the ranger that the Tumlinson forces were the worse
of two evils even though he and most of his men were sworn deputy sheriffs.
Further, Creed Taylor had once been a ranger, a fact that McNelly appreciated. Misdirected respect for Creed might have colored McNelly's judgment.
As well, McNelly realized that the state was now in the hands of the ex-Rebel

redeemers and that the Taylors had sided with those rebels from the beginning. McNelly did admit, however, that if he and his men could defeat the Taylor ring, many of the desperadoes who worked for pay would be out of a job. They had a self-interest in keeping the struggle with Tumlinson ongoing because they were accustomed to their lucrative monthly wages.[9]

Within a week of arriving in DeWitt County, Captain McNelly had all the action he wanted. Because John M. Taylor was to appear as a witness in Bill Taylor's murder trial for killing Sutton and Slaughter, the captain detailed a sergeant and three privates to escort the witness from Yorktown to Clinton. Some distance from Yorktown, the men had an encounter with Joe Tumlinson and his posse of about a dozen men, all still working with the sheriff's office. In a case of apparent mistaken identity, Tumlinson's men opened fire on the rangers, believing that the rangers were part of the Taylor bunch. The mistake was explicable, for Tumlinson and his men recognized Taylor and thought that any people with him had to be part of the ring. During the brief gun battle, two horses suffered mortal wounds, a ball wounded Pvt. John W. Chalk, and the witness escaped, only to be caught the next day. After about a fifteen-minute skirmish, Tumlinson discovered his error and called off his men (perhaps the rangers made it known who they were and produced proof). "Old Joe" apologized to McNelly and offered to replace the dead horses. Despite that, McNelly came away from the incident with a greater dislike for the man, telling Steele that "old Joe" believed that he must kill off the entire Taylor ring before the region could see peace again. Tumlinson was essentially correct.[10]

Once McNelly and his men arrived in Cuero with John Taylor in tow, McNelly assigned a few of his men to board the train for Indinaola and make sure that Taylor reached the place still alive. Rube Brown, the ex-marshal, and several other men also boarded the iron horse for the purpose of killing Taylor, but the guards foiled that plan and ejected Brown and his men from the train. Once in Indianola, Taylor was safe, for Governor Coke had earlier ordered Steele and some other rangers to not only bring Bill Taylor from Galveston to Indianola, but also to protect John Taylor once he was in the latter town.[11]

Shortly, McNelly had new headaches, for he received intelligence that Hardin and Jim Taylor had returned to the area. As he told Steele, he believed that their capture would create new circumstances that might lead to the end of the troubles wrought by the Hardin-Taylor bunch. Then, incredibly, a number of the Taylor men sought out McNelly, came into his camp, and begged for protection from Tumlinson, who, McNelly believed, could raise one hundred men if necessary. Yet, McNelly's views were changing every time he received new intelligence. He soon saw that the crime ring was the major problem in the region. He reported that most of the desperadoes were now scattered through Gonzales, Lavaca, and other counties, but they could still rapidly converge and put about one hundred men into the field.[12]

Tumlinson remained a complication for McNelly because "Old Joe" did not trust outside authorities, the rangers included. He preferred that the state lawmen leave the Taylors for the local authorities to manage. He certainly did not believe that the rangers should be helping the Taylors by allowing them into camp and protecting them there, especially not after all the murders and the stolen cattle and horses. Tumlinson still had the support of the local judge and district attorney, and he was now focusing on Hardin, Jim Taylor, and former state senator Pridgen who continued to help the ring. McNelly believed that, particularly, Pridgen's life was not worth straw because Tumlinson held him responsible for his actions as a leader and protector of the Taylor desperadoes. Pridgen was so afraid of retribution that he started sleeping in the woods at night for fear that lawmen might raid his home. To get Bolivar Pridgen, at least one source alleged that the lawmen may have committed an atrocity. Supposedly, Tumlinson and others went after Bolivar, who was not at home. But the posse may have found Bolivar's former slave Abraham, who continued to work for his ex-master. Questioned, Abraham refused to reveal his employer's whereabouts, after which the posse may have killed him. However, the tale of Abraham comes from Pridgen himself and other Taylor partisans. The story is hard to accept because of a lack of any real documentation and because known felons made the charge.[13]

In August 1874, Adjutant General Steele once again toured the DeWitt County area and reported that a small scale war still ongoing. The continuing bloodshed was such that, after hearing from Steele, Governor Coke ordered McNelly to organize a volunteer force of fifty men from Washington County, where he had been transferred, and to ride back into DeWitt County. McNelly made his headquarters in Clinton, while the volunteers from Washington County readied to help local lawmen like Tumlinson exterminate the Hardin-Taylor renegades, for one wing of the ring was still operating in their county, stealing horses and rustling cattle. Elements of the ring also tried to get into Victoria County, but its officials quickly organized their own volunteer company, one with enough strength to put the renegades on the run. But, according to Steele, the raiders could still outnumber lawmen whenever they chose to converge at any certain site. Steele believed that more regular state or federal forces should be transferred to the DeWitt region to effectively stop the Taylor horde.[14]

The presence of the rangers and their determination to disperse the felonious band had a profound effect on John Wesley. He learned that the state forces were still looking for him and apparently would not rest until they caught him. In essence, South Texas was becoming too unsafe for Hardin. As well, county or state authorities seemed to be eliminating gang members daily, and he believed that it was only a matter of time until lawmen corralled him. On the move, he first made his way to Gonzales County where for a time he hid with friends. He visited his wife several times. Then, he slipped away and rode for Polk County where he still had other relatives. But he could not stay out of trouble. In August 1874, after a dispute with another man, Hardin murdered him, whereupon a Polk County grand jury indicted him for murder. By the time the jury acted, Hardin had moved into Trinity County where he tried to kill yet again. That led a Trinity County grand jury to indict him for assault with intent to kill. In early September, a Hill County grand jury indicted Hardin and his man S. W. McKee for murder. By then, Hardin was back in Gonzales County, where, in September 1874, a judge issued a warrant for his arrest on a new murder charge, a fact that made his situation worse. After riding back to Hill County, he murdered yet another man.[15] He was totally out of control.

Forced to flee with a posse at his heels, Hardin went to the farm of his uncle who lived near Brenham. After a few days, he made an important decision. Seeing no better options, he finally decided to take his family and clear out of Texas.[16] Simply stated, with a crackdown coming, Hardin believed that prudence demanded he make a getaway. He went home to Gonzales to see his family. He and about twenty of his men camped at the place of Neil Bowen, his father-in-law. He spoke with some other members of the ring. Though he did not see Jim Taylor, he did receive a message from him. He learned that Tumlinson now rode at the head of a posse of about seventy-five men who were ranging the countryside looking for him. John Wesley quickly collected money for selling a cattle herd and sent his wife and children to New Orleans by way of Indianola. Although he had a few more harrowing experiences as he prepared to leave, Hardin soon rode overland to join his family.[17] Near the end of 1874, John, his wife, and his children relocated to the Florida Panhandle where he took the alias John H. Swain. Likely, he chose Florida because his wife's brother had already located there. Thus did the killer leave Texas and run out on what was left of the Taylor band. Now the ever-depleted ring would have to deal with the law without Hardin's guns to protect them.[18]

Even as the authorities were having some success, the forces of law and order in Taylor Country suffered a major blow when Joe Tumlinson died late in 1874. He was one of the few men in the Taylor struggle to die of natural causes. He was the last major leader of the old lawmen, for Sutton, Cox, and Helm had preceded him in death. Although the peaceful folks lost a valued leader, many members of the Taylor gang were dead, in jail, in prison, or in self-imposed exile—and Tumlinson helped make all that happen. John Wesley Hardin and Jim Taylor were yet alive, but authorities were combing the region looking for them, unaware that Hardin had already fled the state. As for Jim Taylor, he rode south, crossed the Rio Grande, and temporarily escaped his pursuers. Afterward, affairs seemed so quite relative to what had gone before that Steele transferred the ranger force out of DeWitt County.[19]

More developments were on the way. On January 20, 1875, the legislature renewed its $4,000 bounty on the head of Hardin, calling him a "notorious murderer." To collect the reward, his captor only had to deliver him dead or alive to the Travis County jail.[20] In late January or early February 1875, Bell County Deputy Sheriff William M. York received intelligence that Hardin and Jim Taylor were south of the Rio Grade, information that was true about Taylor but false about Hardin, who was already in Louisiana. York asked Governor Coke for the appropriate letters of introduction and authority to find the felons, arrest them, and bring them back to Texas.[21]

On February 5, 1875, the murderer and ex-state senator Pridgen returned to the fray, determined to attack the legal authorities who were trying to break up ring. Because he could not get his version of "justice" in Texas, he wrote the attorney general of the United States. Referring to the summer of 1874, Pridgen alleged that Ku Klux Klansmen wearing masks had terrorized everyone in DeWitt County, including both black and white citizens. Supposedly, the masked gang even fired into a camp of rangers then assigned to the area. The civil authorities, he charged, were paralyzed and "completely overpowered." Continuing, Pridgen said Governor Coke had sent in a company of state troops to help the local authorities. But the governor had hampered them with strict instructions. They would not act, Pridgen maintained, against a "Ku Klux confederation."[22]

Instead, the masked gang were exploiting county resources, including food, asserted the ex-senator. Neither the county sheriff nor the state troops did anything to break a "conclave of midnight assassins [that] have been permitted to assemble for unlawful purposes in open day light armed with their paraphernalia [in] McNelly's camp. Innocent people [the Taylor band] sought protection for their lives in Capt. McNelly's camp; they should have been protected . . . but such was not done." Pridgen next asserted that a "Democratic grand jury had indicted 29 parties for various offences," including the torture and death of one of Pridgen's ex-slaves. Yet, the former state senator maintained that despite all of the lawlessness, the United States marshal whose district included DeWitt County would not act, nor would the state troops. Pridgen announced that he was a marked man and could "not return to my family in safety." The ex-state senator demanded a federal investigation. However, all Pridgen's self-serving words could not hide the

The lawyer Bolivar J. Pridgen became a murderer on behalf of the Taylors. He represented them in court and allowed the ring to flourish for years.
Courtesy Sharon Barnes, Director, Regional History Center of the Victoria College/University of Houston at Victoria Library

fact that he had been associated with the crime ring for years, that he had committed crimes himself, and that many people now knew it.[23]

About the time that Pridgen was writing the attorney-general, U.S. Marshal for the Eastern District of Texas L. D. Evans ordered Deputy Marshal Fred M. Reinhardt into action. In February he ordered Reinhardt to arrest Joe Tumlinson's brother Gus and a number of other men in DeWitt County. Upon arriving in DeWitt, the deputy immediately made contact with McNelly and his men, Steele having ordered them back into the area. Knowing that the Tumlinson group included the lawmen of the county, McNelly declined to cooperate with the deputy without written orders from Governor Coke. Reinhardt left, immediately rode to Austin, and received an audience with the governor. Coke then called a meeting of the state senator and the house members who represented DeWitt County. To a man, they all refused to override county authorities because they knew that Pridgen and others had told slanted stories about affairs in the area, making local lawmen appear to be law breakers when in fact they represented the law.[24]

In a new development involving the fringe of the ring, on March 23, 1875, W. R. French wrote Governor Coke on behalf of Tom Holderman's mother who lived in Yorktown. She had heard that Brown Bowen, accused of murdering her son, was in or near Pollard, Florida. She asked Coke to file the appropriate extradition papers to secure Bowen's arrest and return to Texas. Later, lawmen indeed caught Bowen and returned him to Texas, where he soon met the hangman.[25]

Meanwhile, Pridgen's actions in trying to turn lawmen into villains and the real villains into choirboys were parts of patterns that were occurring in all the settled areas of Texas. A. C. Hill of Gonzales County was one man who protested those trends by taking his complaint straight to President U. S. Grant in April 1875. A Unionist before, during, and after the war, Hill told Grant that because he would not support the War of the Rebellion, he lost all his property to area Confederates. Then, Southern partisans shot him repeatedly in one encounter; next, they imprisoned him for six months. He had a firm belief, he told Grant, that the Rebels would have executed him had it not been for his serious wounds and other health problems. His growing number of afflictions apparently convinced the local Confederates that he had ceased to be a serious threat to their rule.[26]

By the end of the war, Hill had regained his health, had joined the State Police once it was organized, and had risen to the position of captain after serving the state on its frontier while working out of forts Griffin and Richardson. As a state policeman, he arrested all manner of "desperadoes, horse thieves, Ku Kluxers," and others. After the legislature abolished the State Police, Hill became a Deputy U.S. Marshal for the Western District of Texas. Then, once the Democrats were firmly back in control of Texas, he suffered ongoing harassment by the new state "authorities." That harassment included several assassination attempts. The ex-Rebels also brought false charges against him and forced him to waste time and money on ridiculous legal proceedings that he always won—until early 1875 when new Rebel authorities arrested him in Gonzales for openly carrying a weapon. When he refused to pay a $50 fine, the judge tossed him back in jail and held him indefinitely. Hill argued that as a deputy U.S. marshal, he had every right to wear a gun when going about his duties. About his opponents, Hill averred that "these prejudiced set of mad men whose motto is 'rule or ruin'" intended to erase Republicanism from Texas. Hill concluded by saying that "unless speedy relief is given, Republicans must seek a better country for safety than Texas. There does prevail today a worse spirit than in [1861]."[27]

As if to prove Hill right, Pridgen wrote the U.S. Attorney General again on April 26, 1875, and continued to spread tales of evils that did not exist. Now he argued that the United States Marshal had abused his office. He would not act against the "Ku Klux Murderers in DeWitt County." The marshal would arrest no one, Pridgen said: "The criminal parties have indulged in a high carnival of bloody deeds unparalleled in the annals of human infamy . . . the people . . . have been . . . intimidated into submission." Pridgen further complained that he was still a marked man. His opposition had raided his house, he said. They had "outraged" his "little children." At about "ten o'clock at night . . . [they] completely riddled his home with buckshot and Winchester rifle balls." Pridgen demanded relief and protection for his family and for himself (Pridgen died of old age in 1903 after a pleasant retirement).[28]

As was Pridgen's first letter to the attorney general, his second was, of course, slanted. A murderer in addition to being the brother of a murderer who was already dead, Pridgen had been firmly in the Taylor camp for years. He had made much money as the legal representative of the Taylor ring. But, while little of what he said could be believed, he managed to turn the tables on his enemies, the enemies being the legal authorities of DeWitt County. He came up with a number of witnesses who testified before United States Commissioner Sandford Mason of Galveston who believed the testimony. Pridgen managed to have twenty-two men indicted under the Ku Klux Klan Act, that development bedeviling the legitimate officers of the law. But nothing came of the case despite the pressure that Pridgen put on federal authorities. A trial judge threw the cases out of court.[29]

More dangerous than Pridgen's campaign against area lawmen, Billy Taylor took action. After escaping from the Indianola jail because of the severe hurricane that slammed into the coast on September 15, 1874, he hid for a time and committed no new depredations. But he could not stay out of trouble indefinitely. With six members of the gang, he soon popped up in Clinton. Heavily armed with shotguns and sixguns, they rode up to the Kilgore Drug Store. They were looking for Deputy Sheriff Add Kilgore, intending to kill him because in the past he had arrested a number of the Hardin-Taylor ring. Taylor and four of the men dismounted and looked about the main street, while two men held the horses. Kilgore was nearby, saw the men, and knew that they were after him. With a sixgun in each hand, he ran into Sam Webb's general store and quickly told the young clerk Lewis Delony, a part-time deputy sheriff destined to become a full-time lawman, that "They are after me. I want you to close up the store and help me fight them."[30]

Delony was otherwise minded. He believed that two against seven represented terrible odds. So did store owner Sam Webb and his son Larry. They had been in the store but immediately fled when they realized that gunplay was in the offing. The instant after Delony walked back to the store counter, he knew the Webbs had fled, leaving him to cope with the situation alone. Instead of agreeing to fight, Delony hid Kilgore in a storeroom and covered him up with corn shucks. Moments later two men came into the store by a side entrance, and three came through the front door. All five had Winchesters and looked prepared to use them. Bill Taylor questioned Delony who told the would-be assassins that Kilgore had run through the store and left by the back door, whereupon all five men ran out the back door in pursuit. Of course, they did not find their quarry and returned to the store. Taylor drew his revolver and put it in Delony's face while saying, "Lewis, you are lying[.] He is hid in this store. And if you don't tell me where he is, I will blow your damned head off." Lewis responded calmly, saying "Bill, take that pistol down[.] It might go off."[31]

Just as Taylor lowered his gun, he noticed that the storeroom was padlocked. He asked for the key, and Delony complied. As Taylor was unlocking that door, Delony moved behind another, a place where he had earlier placed a loaded shotgun. He was ready to fight if the renegades found Kilgore. Delony hoped that the deputy with his two guns could take down at least three and thereby leave Lewis and his double-barreled shotgun with only two targets. The two men in the street tending the horses? Delony thought he could deal with them later if he survived. However, as fate apparently decreed, the renegades looked around the storeroom, but their search was sloppy. They did not find Kilgore. They gave up the hunt, went to the saloon next door, and drank the rest of the day away, after which they left town. Still, Kilgore remained hidden, for the Taylor bunch might return.[32]

Late that night, Delony helped the deputy by bringing his horse to the back of the store and tethering it. Kilgore crawled out of the store until he reached his mount after which he bounced atop and rode directly to Sheriff Weisiger's place about eight miles down the Guadalupe. Both men then returned to Clinton where they put together a small posse. They tracked the desperadoes, led by Billy Taylor and his close second Joe Bennett, one of his relatives. The posse followed the trail that left Clinton and led to Yorktown. But, despite the lawmen's efforts, all but one of the Taylor men had gotten away, the officers losing their trail. They managed to find and to arrest ring member Killensworth, whom they took back to Clinton and pitched in jail. Just one night after the authorities incarcerated Killensworth, disguised vigilantes walked into the jail, overpowered jailor Bigham White, and shot the prisoner to death.[33]

Even though he lost Killensworth, Bill Taylor remained active. Earlier, he had sent word to Rube Brown that he intended to kill him. He turned the threat into action on November 17, 1875. Along with three of their men—two being Mace "Winchester Smith" Arnold and Joseph Bennett—Bill and Jim Taylor, who had returned from Mexico, accosted the one-time lawman in a local saloon and shot him to death, along with Thomas Freeman, a black man who was a harmless bystander. Some sources credited Arnold with firing the first shot at Brown. However, the coroner's jury did not connect Bill or Jim Taylor or any of their men to the crime. The jury listed the assassins as "unknown parties."[34]

The killings made national news; even the *New York Times* carried an account of the incident on the front page of its issue of November 19. The *Times* summary and other sources painted a picture of what likely happened. Brown was in a card game at Ryan's Saloon. He may have been dealing monte in the crowded watering hole when a lone man, nondescript, came in, went to the bar, and had a drink while looking around. Of course, he spotted Brown and on leaving the saloon informed his fellows in crime that Brown was indeed inside. Thence came Bill Taylor and the rest who shot the ex-marshal to death. Within hours of the murder, lawmen organized a posse and pursued the killers. After officers correctly guessed where the raiders were going, the posse managed to get ahead of the murderers and cut them off. The lawmen found a defensive position and set up an ambush, but they only wounded Bill Taylor and Joseph Bennett, both of whom were destined to live.[35]

Although the Taylor gang could apparently claim another victory in their war with the old Unionist authorities, Bill Taylor had to go into hiding while Jim Taylor considered his options. He was still a wanted man with a $1,500 reward on his head. Lawmen and bounty hunters sought him. He may have decided to use the law in his behalf after discussing his situation with the eminent attorney T. T. Teel of Clinton. He may have voiced a willingness to surrender if his life could be guaranteed. However, his actions may have been a ruse meant to throw his enemies off guard. And the local lawmen were indeed fooled. Sheriff Weisiger asked for and received help in keeping the county quiet and allowing the Taylor men to come into town unmolested. Deputy Sheriff Dick Hudson and the new Cuero Marshal John Meador wanted the entire Taylor party incarcerated immediately, but after the sheriff and Dist. Atty. S. F. Grimes spoke with them, they agreed to maintain the peace so that the court could convene.[36] However, matters quickly went awry.

The Collapse of the Taylor Ring

WHEN Jim Taylor rode into Clinton in late December 1875, he was not alone. Approximately forty desperadoes served as his escort, including his cousin Bill Taylor, who had come out of hiding. District court was soon to convene, and some of the Taylor bunch were due to appear to be tried for various offenses, ranging from murder to cattle rustling. Basically, the brigands took control of the town, making their headquarters in John Wofford's store where they confiscated all the weapons and ammunition. Soon, however, most of the wild bunch left town for lack of lodging; they made camp on the Guadalupe River near the Clinton crossing. Jim Taylor remained in town, as did some of his men: Mason Arnold, A. R. Hendricks, Mark King, Edd Davis, and "Hun" Tuggle. In clear violation of the law, all wore their guns in plain view.[1]

When he learned of their arrival, DeWitt County Sheriff William Weisiger believed that the men had come into town to burn the courthouse in the hopes of erasing any proceedings against them, including indictments for various crimes and notices of delinquent land taxes. The sheriff quickly went about town from house to house summoning men, only a few of whom cooperated. The posse that he put together included lawyer William Fried; Dist. Atty. S. F. Grimes; District Judge Clay Pleasants; Lawyer Sam C. Lacky; John and Jim Wofford; Deputy Sheriff Kilgore and his father, who was the local druggist; Jim and Clate Summers; and the youngster Lewis Delony. The men guarded the courthouse through the rest of the day. However, Weisiger did not try to arrest Taylor and his small band. They were professional killers, and the sheriff did not want any of the posse shot. Rather, he sent a runner to Cuero to find Deputy Dick Hudson, to tell him to organize a posse and get to Clinton as fast as possible. However, the black messenger ran afoul of the Taylor men encamped on the river near the main ferry. When the man tried to cross, the raiders captured him, and without much thought at all, hanged him from a limb of a nearby tree. An informant apparently saw the lynching and relayed word to the sheriff. When he learned that his runner was dead, the woebegone Weisiger tried to recruit another courier, but no one volunteered. For a time Clinton was isolated.[2]

According to some accounts, the bunch led by Jim Taylor roamed around town for several days, looking menacing, each having at least two sixguns in his belt. While the sheriff pondered his problems, he searched for another courier to go to Cuero for help. He finally found a fifteen-year-old volunteer, Charles "Charlie" Page, whose father the Taylor guerrillas had earlier murdered. The youngster slipped out of Clinton at night and rode several miles beyond the main Guadalupe crossing that the gang controlled. He forded safely farther upriver and continued his mission.[3]

The next day Weisiger grew tired of waiting for help. He feared the worst—that the renegades had caught and killed young Page. Desperately wanting to take some meaningful action, the sheriff, with Clate Summers accompanying him, slipped from town through the back door of Webb's house and went to the Calhoun neighborhood looking for more help. The brigands in town continued their roaming and apparently learned that a runner had gotten past the gang. Jim Taylor sent a courier of his own to deliver a message to Deputy Hudson, who had once been a childhood friend of John Wesley Hardin. The warning was simple: Taylor told Hudson that he and his raiders would kill him if he brought a posse to Clinton. Then, almost as an afterthought, Taylor ordered Hudson to leave Texas immediately if he wanted to live.[4]

The lawman not only took his job seriously, but he also took great exception to being threatened and ordered into exile. He recruited a number of stalwarts whom he deputized, their number including Christopher "Kit" Hunter; Henry J. and J. "Jeff" White; W. C. "Curry" Wallace; John J. Meador; the McCrabb brothers, Buck and John; Jake Ryan; Frank and Bill Cox; Deputy Sheriff Bill Meador; and Joe and Ed Sitterle. Warned that the renegades controlled the Clinton crossing, Hudson and his deputies followed the teenaged Page who took them upriver and showed them the best ford. Thenceforth, the posse rode into Clinton, looking for Taylor and his band. Although the Hudson party missed seeing Weisiger, the sheriff took significant action before he left town. He and Delony met with Martin King, the town blacksmith and livery man. Weisiger made King a proposition. If the blacksmith would lock up his stable with the Taylor men's horses inside, the lawmen would spare his son Mark and his adopted son Edd Davis, both then riding with the marauders. Martin King agreed to the plan, and he kept his word.[5]

After learning from Delony that the desperadoes could not get to their horses, Hudson and his posse confronted the Taylor men. The authorities had to act swiftly, for it was almost sunset, and the cover of night would give the renegades an excellent chance to escape. Weisiger left orders to surround the Taylor men in town and to use all means necessary to stop them from joining their other men who were still encamped on the river about two miles away. Should the main body of the brigands become involved, a disaster was inevitable because the desperadoes vastly outnumbered lawmen in town. Consequently, Hudson ordered the McCrabb brothers and Curry Wallace to take control of the fields leading to the river bottom and to stop the felons from reaching the main body of their men.[6]

Just as Hudson was giving his commands, the desperadoes in town apparently realized their plight; potentially, they might be caught in a trap. They ran down the street toward the stable to get their horses and flee. After they discovered that the door to the livery was locked, they tried to beat it down, but it held. A "wild west" shoot-out then began, with the Taylor men getting the worst of it. They ran to King's house but could not break down the front door. They retreated through the town's main street, firing as they ran. They sprinted through an orchard and ran into an old dilapidated log cabin, but because the posse's bullets were penetrating the structure, they quickly burst out again. They ran into a field leading to the river bottom while the posse fired effective rounds from their weapons, peppering their targets with lead. The felons kept running, trying to get to the river, but true to the deputy sheriff's orders, the McCrabbs and Wallace blocked their way.[7]

Hunter and the rest of the posse managed to virtually surround their quarry. Almost simultaneously Jim Taylor and Kit Hunter shot at each other with Winchesters. Taylor fired at least twice, one slug only blowing Hunter's hat off, the other being more damaging: It hit bone, making Hunter stagger and leaving him with a painful broken arm. One of Hunter's bullets was effective. It shattered the right-handed Taylor's right arm, after which he had to drop his rifle and use a pistol, forced to fire with his left hand. In the throes of pain and shooting with his off-hand, he found that his aim was no good. But Hunter's aim was true, even though he, too, had to drop his rifle and fire a handgun. Jim Taylor went down. As the battle raged, Delony and others in the posse closed on Mark King and Edd Davis, both of whom quickly surrendered. When the affray was almost over, Jim Taylor and Winchester Smith (Arnold) lay dead. Hunter finished off the former, while a shotgun blast to the head killed the latter.[8]

Hiding in some weeds, Hendricks, lying prone, had mortal wounds. Yet, he hoped to stay hidden and to await a chance to escape. Such never materialized. A dog spotted him and started barking; the animal gave his position away. A member of the posse demanded his surrender. The desperado responded that he was wounded too badly to rise. On horseback, Wallace hoisted the wounded man up behind him, intending to get him to a doctor. But about the time they reached the spot where Taylor lay, Hendricks slid off the horse and fell to the ground dead. While it proved impossible to help Hendricks, the posse spared Mark King and Edd Davis as promised. As well, "Hun" Tuggle surrendered and survived. After the main body of the Taylor gang learned of the chaos in town, the forty or so men, Bill Taylor included, left the area in a column two by two, preferring not to tangle with the lawmen once their leader, Jim Taylor, was gone. They also feared that the sheriff might be leading another posse to reenforce the small one in town. No one could rally the guerrillas. The Taylor crime ring was greatly weakened.[9]

The lawmen's victory in the Battle of Clinton was most important but did not completely destroy the ring. In March 1876, Captain McNelly and a squad reappeared in DeWitt County while moving from the frontier to the interior of the state. Even though Jim Taylor and many of his raiders were now dead, McNelly reported more trouble. It began when the sheriff of faraway Henderson County came to Clinton looking for a member of the Taylor gang named Allen who lived in Gonzales County; the sheriff was armed with an arrest warrant. After locating the man in DeWitt County, the Henderson County sheriff organized a posse from among local men. The posse sought out the malefactor who had been joined by others, whom McNelly referred to as the "Gonzales County wing of the Taylor party." The renegades put up a fight when found. As a result, Allen and his men shot and killed a DeWitt County deputy before the posse fired several volleys and mortally wounded Allen while also wounding one of his cohorts who was fated to live. Although Allen escaped and fled to his Gonzales County home, shortly, a Gonzales County posse sent word to DeWitt authorities that they were holding Allen under house arrest. DeWitt lawmen went to arrest the man but found him dying when they reached his place. The officers returned home and let the man die in peace.[10]

Meanwhile, the Battle of Clinton had several other postscripts. Soon after the fight, a vigilante committee descended upon the town, apparently intending to lynch prisoners King and Davis, along with others in the jail. But Jailor White and Deputy Delony held them off with cocked Winchesters. Still, the men milled around the jail for about an hour. Then came Sheriff Weisiger and Deputy Kilgore to reinforce Delony and White, after which the vigilantes left. Soon, the authorities released Mark King and Edd Davis, for they had not taken a critical part of the fight. Moreover, officials honored their earlier promise to stable man Martin King to spare the two young men. Later, on Sunday, October 2, 1876, a crowd of disguised men led by "a stranger," whom Texas Ranger L. B. Wright identified as a "worthless vagabond," rode into town using the Yorktown-Clinton Road. They went to Martin King's house intending to kill him. However, his wife told the men that her husband was downtown. The man then asked the whereabouts of her son Mark. The woman answered that she did not know, when, in fact, her son had run out the back door and escaped. Immediately, he ran downtown to warn his father, but the raiders were right behind him.[11]

They arrived in town in time to see young King loping for the stables. When they opened fire on him, the youngster ducked into the saloon and ran for the back door. As he was running though an alley toward the stables to warn his father, he heard another volley of gunfire. He believed that they were killing his sire, as indeed they were. Round after round went into Martin King's head and body. Then came the clatter of many horse hoofs galloping from town using the Yorktown Road. The noise lured Deputies Kilgore and Lewis Delony out of church. They investigated, but it was too late to take effective action. Mark ran on to the livery and discovered the dead body of his father.[12] He must have found a weapon because he bounced atop a horse and chased the perpetrators through town while shooting at them, shouting, "They have killed my father."[13] He continued the chase for a couple of miles but finally broke off the futile pursuit and returned to town. Meanwhile, Kilgore and Delony went to the Dola Davis Saloon and found Edd Davis with a badly wounded leg. Although such cannot be proven, most likely the "vagabond" and his men were remnants of the Taylor gang targeting King for revenge. Both Dola Davis and Martin King's wife recognized some of the raiders as being Taylor men even though they were partially disguised.[14]

Another postscript to the Battle of Clinton came on June 28, 1877, when several local lawmen, including Hudson, were tried for murder, a maneuver perhaps meant to clear them legally and to leave no doubt that they acted as duly constituted authorities. Deputy Delony was an eyewitness who testified for the defense. After a farcical trial, the jury took only ten minutes to deliver not guilty verdicts for Hudson and all his men. They had acted on the sheriff's orders, and Weisiger was a legally elected official.[15]

Earlier, in March 1876 remnants of the Taylor-Hardin crime ring caused more trouble in South Texas. Nueces County Sheriff William S. Halsey reported that what was left of the gang was driving stolen cattle from the Devil's River area, destination Kansas. The cattle thieves had hired various gunmen of the old band to furnish them protection as they drove their stolen herd. Halsey admitted that he was powerless to stop the rustling without state troops. He wanted McNelly and at least twenty of his rangers to assist him. McNelly was willing to help and told Adjutant General Steele that "I am satisfied that a pursuit of the cattle thieves would lead to a meeting with the Hardin gang, a consummation devoutly to be hoped for." McNelly told Steele that he would deal with the Taylor "pests" and have no "mercy" on them should he find them.[16]

Yet despite recent events and McNelly's boast, more trouble developed in Taylor Country. On August 24, 1876, a band of men robbed the bank in Goliad and rode away with their loot. Their leaders were Billy Taylor, King Fisher, and William Brookings, all three wanted for crimes ranging from murder to horse and cattle theft. Both Captain McNelly and Lt. Lee Hall began scouring the area for the highwaymen. Following the robbers' trail, Hall tracked them and saw that they finally split up, some men going into Karnes County and others going into Gonzales County, both in the heart of Taylor Country. Although Hall verged on success, the raiders managed to elude him several times.[17]

Yet more killing occurred before the Taylor gang was brought to heel. In November 1876, the physician Phillip Brassell, close to the Taylor gang, and Dave Augustine, a DeWitt County lawman, hosted a party in a schoolhouse at Shiloh, a small hamlet about halfway between Clinton and Yorktown. Each man had a daughter who taught there, and each apparently believed that the county's troubles could be put in abeyance for one night despite their recent arguments about school policy, a conflict that Brassell won when he defeated Augustine in a school board election. Several of the old Taylor ring brazenly attended the dance, including George and James Brassell, the oldest and younger sons of the physician respectively. Both of the young men had prices on their heads due to several crimes they had committed. In addition to George Brassell's other offenses, the authorities believed that he might have been in the party that had earlier murdered several men. Further, although George had he signed the Clinton "treaty" of 1873, he did not obey its terms. But, that he signed erased any doubt that he was a member of the Taylor ring, operating as a hired gunman. He was on the Texas Rangers' list of fugitives, and a DeWitt County grand jury had indicted him for uttering a murder threat, the indictment issued on April 11, 1876. Area lawmen suspected that both of the Brassell boys had been among the trigger men who had earlier ambushed and murdered James Cox and Cristman.[18]

As the festive dance was getting underway, someone rode to Clinton and alerted DeWitt County lawmen that the Brassells were at the party. Authorities there quickly organized a posse, whose members immediately saddled their horses and rode for the schoolhouse. Just as they reached the place, gunshots rang out. William "Bill" Cox, son of the murdered James Cox, reached the dance just ahead of the posse. He saw the Brassells. He became enraged because he knew that at least one of the brothers had been in the party that cut his father's throat. Bill Cox quickly drew and fired his gun, intending to kill both George and James Brassell. When the posse arrived, its men entered the fray, each man firing several shots. A general gunfight and pandemonium broke out, but incredibly, no one was killed or wounded. The crowd became greatly excited during the fracas, and someone extinguished the lights in the room. That action allowed the Taylor men to slip away unharmed. They mounted and spurred their horses and galloped into the darkness.[19]

Soon, more trouble erupted in Yorktown when organizers staged a big ball, hoping that it would not be ruined like the earlier party at Shiloh. The occasion went swimmingly until the Brassell brothers showed up; they had grit but little common sense. Afraid of what the felons might do, the ball's sponsors did not want a repeat of the disaster that occurred at the earlier soiree. They sent a runner to Clinton to ask for help. Lewis Delony was at the courthouse when the messenger arrived. He told the runner to ride for Cuero because deputies Add Killgore and Bill Meador would be there. The messenger dutifully went to the latter place and found that most of the area lawmen were there, for Cuero was also the scene of a big celebration. Deputies Kilgore and Meador quickly organized a posse of about ten to twelve men and went directly to Yorktown.[20]

The posse made its trip in vain. The Taylor men cleared out before the posse arrived. Still, knowing that the Brassell boys were among the Taylor renegades, the posse decided to ride to the Doctor Brassell's homestead to search it. Several of the possemen experienced anxiety. They believed that they were riding into a fight to the death, for Taylor men seldom surrendered. After taking the main Yorktown road, the posse soon arrived at the forks of the road, one branch going to the Brassell house, the other going into town. Very near that fork, the posse encountered about a dozen of the Taylor men who were coming from the direction of the Brassell farm. A wild and decisive shoot-out began. Mary Ainsworth, a neighbor who lived near the Brassell place, was close enough to hear the gunfire and later recounted that the fight started about 10 P.M. and that she heard two volleys with about fifty shots fired in each volley. With handguns and shotguns, the groups had at each other, and blood flowed. The posse won the fray. When the smoke cleared, old Doctor Brassell and his son George lay dead, the recipients of multiple gunshot wounds. When he realized his party was getting the worst of the fight, James Brassell managed to spur his mount and ride away, as did the other desperadoes.[21]

Delony investigated the scene the next day and put the pieces of the puzzle together that explained what had happened. While Taylor partisans claimed that the posse had wantonly murdered the Brassells, Delony knew better, for he saw all the horse tracks and saw all the bullet holes in nearby trees. It was clear to Delony that a major gunfight had taken place.[22] Reportedly, there may have been some talk before the battle. James Brassell said he and the Taylor men had not done anything wrong, to which a posse member replied, "No, you haven't done nothing but rob your neighbors."[23] Later to achieve fame as a lawman, Delony confirmed that there had been hell to pay the night before. In effect, he verified that Ainsworth was telling the truth. He saw enough horse tracks to indicate roughly the number of men who fought. He put the number at ten to twelve on each side.[24]

Despite reality as expressed by Delony, Taylor partisans concocted another story that early historians sympathetic to the Confederacy and the Taylors spread as truth, a story that has been accepted uncritically by many later historians. Supposedly, a masked band of outlaws descended upon the Brassells' home, took Phillip and George about 250 yards from the house, and executed them. The masked men shot Phillip in the chest and leg and shot his son directly between his eyes. Even Ranger Hall bought into the facts that never were. Calling the Brassell men "the most respectable people," who were "shot down in cold blood," Hall apparently ignored the fact that both of the doctor's sons were fugitives. As well, the older Brassell was guilty of aiding and abetting criminals when he hid them, fed them, and rode with them.[25]

Delony's version of events has the ring of truth, for he was nonpartisan. He was a young part-time lawman, and he simply wanted to know exactly what had happened and how many men were involved. His investigation notwithstanding, members of the posse had to face murder charges once the Taylor gang's rumors became public. Reacting to rumors, Ranger Lieutenant Hall and his men arrested Cuero City Marshal Bill Meador, DeWitt County Deputy Sheriff Joe Sitterlee, and posse members Bill Cox, Jake Ryan, Dave Augustine, and Frank Heister. Later Hall arrested Charley Heissig, too.[26]

In the subsequent legal proceedings, Delony offered to testify before the grand jury, but Dist. Atty. A. B. Davidson, an ex-Rebel who believed that the Taylors were champions of the "Lost Cause," refused to allow Delony's request, and trial Judge H. Clay Pleasants accepted Davidson's judgment. Next, a squad of rangers took the defendants from Clinton to Galveston. After a change in venue that moved the trial to San Antonio, Delony attended the trial and again offered to testify, but the authorities turned him down, the result being that a jury gave death sentences to posse members Joe Sitterle, Jake Ryan, and Bill Cox. Then came appeals, the result being that the three lawmen eventually went free. As Delony put it, "they came clear" when jurors realized that they had killed a known felon and a man who aided and abetted that felon. Over the years, others in the posse also "came clear."[27]

Judge Henry Clay
Pleasants complicated
matters for lawmen by
refusing to consider
Delony's testimony about
his findings in the Brazzile
case.
Courtesy Sharon Barnes,
Director, Regional History Center
of the Victoria College/University
of Houston at Victoria Library

In legal proceedings that lasted until 1896, the state only convicted one
other member of the posse, David Augustine. Afterward, he immediately went
to the Texas penitentiary in Huntsville where he picked up the governor's
pardon that awaited him there. He came home a vindicated man. Ultimately,
only one man was punished for the Brassell incident, but it was not at the
hands of the authorities. John Guyens had ridden with the posse that killed
the Brassells. Afterward, when he realized people believed the Taylor version
of the event, he decided to run rather than to risk imprisonment or execution. Just after he rode north, hoping to lose himself in the Indian Nations,
Bolivar Pridgen went after him and tracked him first to Decatur in North
Texas. From there, Pridgen followed him and caught him just north of the
Red River, where the ex-legislator murdered him.[28]

A few other loose ends remained. In April 1877, an officer of the Texas Ranger Frontier Battalion finally captured Bill Taylor in Coleman County where he was engaged in the "cattle business." It is unknown if his business was legitimate or if he was engaged in rustling as in days of yore. Either way, when he came into Coleman town, a local officer recognized and arrested him. The rangers took him to Austin and tossed him in jail. Soon, lawmen took him to Indianola for trial. Judge Pleasants granted a change of venue and sent Taylor to Texanna, the seat of Jackson County.[29]

Taylor was represented by four attorneys: Lackey and Stayton of Victoria, F. M. White of Texanna, and "General" Woodward of Indianola. He came to trial for the murder of Bill Sutton, appearing before Judge William Buckhardt. In a travesty of justice—due in part to the lack of witnesses—a jury found Taylor not guilty. Also to be tried for the murder of Gabriel Slaughter, Taylor learned that the state had asked for a continuance, the prosecutor again citing lack of witnesses. Taylor's lawyer then secured a writ of habeas corpus, and a judge allowed him to go free after four friends posted a $5,000 bail. At least three had been involved with the Taylor crime ring and at least one, ex-senator Pridgen, had himself committed unpunished murders; the other two were John Taylor and Eugene Kelly. Later, the state had to ask again for one continuance and then another. Asking for a third continuance on July 17, 1879, the prosecutor faced a judge who refused to grant it. Thereafter, the state's attorney asked to dismiss the case.[30]

Now a free but unreformed man, Billy Taylor could not stay out of trouble. In January 1880, he was once again in the DeWitt County jail, arrested along with a man named Middleton, both charged with the multiple rape of the young daughter of Cuero's Caesar Brown, whom observers called a "peaceable colored man." To the bitter end, then, the Taylor bunch continued to have their way with freedpeople. Frank Blair, a member of the old Taylor gang, was implicated, but a judge allowed him to give bail of $1,500, after which he disappeared. At first disallowed bail, Taylor and Middleton remained locked up until their judge reconsidered and allowed them to post a bond and released them. Of course, once free, Taylor vanished, only to turn up in Kimble County in 1881 where he generally raised "cain," to hear a ranger captain tell it. After making bond, he disappeared again, this time for good. Some people believed he left Texas altogether and went into the Indian Nations, where he eventually settled down after a Cherokee stockman hired him to do ranch work.[31]

Only one loose end remained—the fate of John Wesley Hardin, the Taylor gang's coleader and hired killer. Using Walker as his alias, Hardin met his family in New Orleans, but soon moved to Cedar Keys, Florida, and from there on to Gainesville where he bought a saloon under the name John H. Swain.

He quickly learned that a man cannot always escape his past. On opening day, Frank Harper and Bill McCullough walked into the saloon and asked for whiskey. They were cowboys who knew Hardin from the Texas years. The three had a happy reunion, of sorts. They had always been friendly, but John Wesley worried that they might expose him. Soon, that worry faded when "Swain" found bigger trouble. He beat one man and shot another. Next, he was in a party of masked men who burned the city jail, thereby cremating a black man named Eli who stood accused, but not convicted, of raping a white woman.[32]

To avoid lawmen, Hardin relocated to Micanopy, Florida, where he bought another saloon, but by July 1875, "Swain" and family moved again, this time to Jacksonville. After he lost money on a business deal involving a cattle sale, John Wesley became a butcher. Gambling winnings added to his income. While the Hardin family appeared to have a decent life, problems beset the breadwinner, one being the large reward that the Texas Legislature offered for his capture. The money was enough to interest the Pinkerton Detective Agency and many individual bounty hunters. That he was being hunted helps explain why he moved so frequently.[33]

When hunters closed in on him in Jacksonville, he sent his family to Eufaula, Alabama. Then, in the company of a former Jacksonville police-man, Gus Kennedy, he moved stealthily, largely because Kennedy told him that two detectives were in Jacksonville looking for him. Near the Georgia line, he and Kennedy had to fight and kill two Pinkerton men. Hardin then settled anew in Pollard, Alabama, and had his family join him there. They lived with Jane's brother Brown Bowen, the killer of Tom Holderman (men-tioned in a previous chapter). When Texas lawmen were finally closing in on him, the murderer Bowen had fled first to Kansas and then to Florida be-fore moving to Alabama. Still living with Bowen, Hardin, with partner Shep Hardy, set up a logging operation on the River Styx, but the enterprise failed due to John's lack of attention. He preferred to gamble and drink his days away. He frequently rode to Mobile with Kennedy to gamble; the two men used marked cards when playing poker, and each took turns being the other's shill. Apparently, John Wesley and his family lived off his winnings, but he was spending more and more time in Mobile and less time with his family. During the political season of 1876, a fight between political partisans in a Mobile saloon entrapped Hardin and Kennedy. They apparently killed two men, but they threw away their weapons before the police arrived. Arrested for malicious mischief, they spent a few days in jail before being released for lack of evidence.[34]

Concurrently, Texas Rangers John Armstrong and Jack Duncan were still working the Hardin case, trying to gain information. As well, David Holder-

The mature John Wesley
Hardin, on the run from
lawmen.
Courtesy Sharon Barnes, Director,
Regional History Center of the
Victoria College/University of
Houston at Victoria Library

man, father of the man Bowen had murdered, kept pressure on Texas political officials until they offered a $500 reward for Bowen. Going "undercover,"
Duncan worked on both cases. Shortly, Duncan went to Gonzales County
and, posing as a merchant who wanted to rent a storehouse, met Neill Bowen, Jane Hardin's father, who owned a store. Using an alias, Duncan frequented the store regularly, buying sundry items. In time, he became a close
acquaintance of the store owner. One day, Duncan accompanied Bowen to
the local post office. The ranger noted that Bowen received a letter from Pollard, Alabama. Later that day, Duncan had dinner at Bowen's house. When
Bowen was temporarily distracted, Duncan managed to grab and read the
letter. Although it was a vague missive, at one point John Wesley referred to
"Jane." That was all that Duncan needed to pick up a trail. He went to the

local postmaster after Bowen had written a reply and learned that it was addressed to J. H. Swain of Pollard.[35]

After Duncan informed Ranger Lieutenant Armstrong of the new information, the chase was on. Armstrong and Duncan took a train to Montgomery, Alabama, arriving there on June 20, 1877. Duncan then went to Pollard and made inquiries about "Swain" and Bowen. He learned that Hardin was in Pensacola gambling. After going to the junction at Whiting, Duncan talked to Will Chipley, manager of the station who had earlier had an altercation with Bowen. Chipley told the rangers that he knew "Swain" and Bowen and that the felons were indeed in Pensacola. The rangers, Chipley, and some Florida officers went there and learned that Hardin was planning to leave on an afternoon train to return to Pollard. The lawmen decided that arresting him on the train was the safest ploy. When the train left, Hardin, in a party of four, rode in the smoking car. Once the iron horse was rolling, two Florida lawmen entered Hardin's car from the rear. They caught him from behind and wrestled him to the floor. Just behind them, Armstrong came forward and clubbed him unconscious with a sixgun. Before Hardin regained his senses, the officers put him in leg irons, tied his hands with a rope, and took his handgun, which he had secreted in one of his pants pockets. Shortly, in a related development—thanks to the help of Chipley—Duncan found and arranged the arrest of Bowen, who was sent to visit the hangman for the murder of Halderman.[36]

Meanwhile, once the lawmen had Hardin in custody, they took him to the Travis County jail in Austin. Soon came officers from Comanche County, who drug him to Comanche town to stand trial for the 1874 murder of Brown County Deputy Sheriff Charlie Webb. Found guilty of second degree murder, he received a sentence of twenty-five years in the penitentiary. In part, elements of the testimony that convicted Hardin appear most confused. James Carnes Jr. offered information that included dubious dialog between Hardin and Webb, which suggested that Webb did not know John Wesley, whereas, in fact, they had met before. As mentioned, while looking for a murder suspect, Webb had encountered Hardin and some of his men when they were accumulating a stolen Brown County cattle herd that they intended to sell. Webb talked to the men but did not investigate because of Hardin's hostility and because he was alone and obviously outnumbered.[37]

After vanishing into the Huntsville lockup, Hardin proved to be a challenge for his guards. His repeated attempts to escape and his all-around misbehavior tormented his keepers. He was sullen and vicious. Despite John Wesley's worrisome nature, in 1891, his attorney, W. S. Fly of Gonzales, began legal proceedings that ultimately freed Hardin after he had served approximately seventeen years of his sentence. Although most indictments for his earlier crimes had been dropped, Hardin's 1873 murder of DeWitt County Deputy Sheriff James Morgan was problematic because county authorities refused to drop the charge. To settle the issue, Fly convinced Hardin to voluntarily return to DeWitt County to answer for Morgan's death. As a result of a plea bargain, the jury found Hardin guilty of manslaughter and gave him a two-year sentence to run concurrently with his original term. Next, Fly and a long-time Hardin friend, the attorney William B. Teagarden, led a petition drive and a political campaign to free John Wesley on condition that he become a model prisoner who deserved consideration. Teagarden blamed the notorious Yankees for launching Hardin upon his life of crime even though said Yankees had nothing to do with his early criminal behavior. Petitions, mostly started by Teagarden, came from most of the counties where Hardin had committed earlier crimes, and Teagarden's influential friends lobbied Gov. James Hogg to forgive John Wesley. He did so. Hardin left the prison on February 17, 1894, and celebrated his freedom.[38]

Hardin settled in Gonzales and opened a law practice but soon ran afoul of local politics. In the 1894 sheriff's race, he opposed the candidacy of ex-sheriff William E. Jones, who had once helped the Taylor gang break him out of the Gonzales jail in return for a hefty bribe. When Jones won in a close race, Hardin understood that his days in Gonzales were finished. After

John Wesley Hardin's grave in El Paso. The rock and iron enclosure is to protect John Wesley Hardin's remains from being stolen.
Courtesy Henry Wolff

leaving the town, he had a few more episodes in central and western Texas, one being a failed marriage to the young teenager Callie Lewis, his first wife Jane having died while he was in prison. After his experience with Callie he moved to El Paso where he opened a law practice but seldom practiced law. Instead, he frequented saloons and continued to drink his life away. He supported himself on his poker winnings. He soon ran afoul of Constable John Selman. After a confrontation, Selman shot and killed Hardin on August 19, 1895, in the Acme Saloon.[39]

According to the traditional accounts of Hardin's death, Constable Selman walked into the Acme Saloon, saw John Wesley standing at the bar, his back facing the entrance. Selman had his opportunity, drew a gun, and shot Hardin in the back of the head. Continuing to fire, Selman put three other bullets in Hardin's body. However, there is controversy, for some sources say that all of Selman's bullets entered the killer from the front. One shot went through his left eye into his brain; another hit the man's little finger on his left hand. One ball went into his right arm, and yet another hit his upper right breast. A correspondent named O'Keeffe took a photo of Hardin's body two days after the desperado died. He then sent a copy to the *San Antonio Express* in August 1895. The photo has been used to illustrate a copious number of books and articles on Hardin. One only needs to look at the photo to see that the entry wounds were all striking his front.[40]

Hardin's death tied up the last of the "loose ends" related to the demise of the Taylor gang, except for Billy and Creed Taylor and Bolivar Pridgen. Billy escaped into the Indian Nations and may have lived a long life. Creed not only survived but also remarried, started a new family, sired more children, and lived on until 1906. Pridgen died of old age in 1903. None of them were ever tried and convicted for their crimes.[41]

AFTERWORD

HERETOFORE, most authors who have written on what has been called the "Sutton-Taylor Feud" presented traditional, pro-Confederate propaganda in which myth, legends, and faulty memories stood equal to truth. No one bothered doing the real research necessary to understand the struggle. Most studies glorified the former Rebels, personified by the Taylors, and condemned DeWitt County Deputy Sheriff William "Bill" Sutton, the only member of his family to become involved with the Taylor ring. Exceptions include Robert Sutton Jr. and Chuck Parsons. In their work on the feud, which I have cited throughout this work, they were more objective than other writers. But they focused on DeWitt County, only one small area of the Taylors' operations. As well, they accepted the conceptual framework of a feud, which, in the case of the Taylors, obscured black and white and turned the colors to gray. Judgments of right and wrong became useless because the very word *feud* suggests that two families or two individuals just had personal animosities and that ideas of right and wrong ultimately did not apply. Such views allowed the Taylors and members of their cabal to escape responsibility for their actions. Thus was Bill Sutton vilified, and that defamation continued after his death. He was murdered in 1874, but writers continued to talk about a "feud" that lasted into the 1880s as if a dead man could return from the grave and continue to fight.

There was no feud. Rather, at least 197 men were at some point members of the Taylors' criminal conspiracy. The men had one thing in common: At some point over a span of twenty-five or so years, they rode with the Taylors and joined them as fellows in crime. However, most also operated independently at times in situations that were always fluid. These men spread chaos and lawlessness into at least forty-five Texas counties. Collectively, they rustled cattle and stole horses. They murdered scores of people, usually targeting white Unionists and their allies, freedpeople, and Yankee soldiers until the occupation of Texas ended. They declared open warfare on lawmen who opposed them and rewarded several who did not. In destabilizing their areas of operations, they helped the Democratic redeemers reassert their power. Joined by outlaw guerrillas in other parts of Texas and by terrorist groups of Klansmen who thrived in at least seventy-seven counties, the Taylor ring spread the turmoil that led to the collapse of the Reconstruction process in the Lone Star State. The Taylors eventually ran afoul of the Democratic Re-deemers because they did not realize that the political shift from Republican to Democrat had changed the nature of Texas politics. Out of power, leading Democrats accepted (some even encouraged) violence because it served their purpose of tarring and weakening the Republicans. But, once in power, those Democrats now wanted "law and order" because such was necessary for the new status quo that the Redeemers intended to maintain.

In the historiography of the larger problems of the Reconstruction era, various scholars have offered revisionist interpretations that should inform anyone's inquiry into the "Sutton-Taylor Feud." Two are Edgar Sneed and Barry A. Crouch. Long ago now, in 1969, Sneed observed that most accounts of Reconstruction had been (and still are) written by descendants of Con-federates and that those writers generally accepted their ancestors' pro-Rebel interpretation without much thought at all (and still do). Sneed held that such writers offered a "traditional history, in which folk myth stands equal to historical analysis." He added that many researchers accepted Rebel accounts of Reconstruction without question and, indeed, without much analysis at all, whereas former Confederates, trying to win the war that was Recon-struction, ignored "reality . . . [as] they vigorously denounced every real and imagined sin they could attribute to their enemies."[1] Crouch updated Sneed's analysis in 1990 and found that, while revisionists had made much headway in the scholarly community and had corrected many of the myths associated with Reconstruction, much of the "reading available to the general public still conveyed the story of military dominance and Radical misrule," facts that never were.[2]

Now, even after all those years when Sneed and Crouch wrote, the con-tinuing saga of the "Sutton-Taylor Feud" (that never was) proves that re-visionists still have work to do. The stakes are high. History needs to be rescued from neo-Confederates who still think that the war is ongoing and that Dixie still has a chance to win if they can only shout loud enough, long enough. The Taylor saga neatly factors into neo-Confederate thought, for the Taylors and their men were and are seen as noble defenders of the South while only occasionally stealing a few horses and cows and killing only a few people who needed killing.

Rather, Reconstruction was merely a continuation of the Civil War in another guise. The South won that second War of Reconstruction, and in their corner of Dixie, the Taylor ring members helped win that war while en-riching themselves in the process. History needs to be reclaimed from myth, legend, and lore. This volume challenges the old worn views and, hopefully, other books to come will do the same.

APPENDIX

Members of the Taylor Criminal Conspiracy (197 men)[1]

Allen (first name unknown)
Ham Anderson
John Anderson
Watt Anderson
Mason Arnold
Alexander Barekman
Thomas Bass
"Wild Bill" Bateman
Jim Bell
Bateman Bell
W. J. A. Bell
Jim Beard
Joe Bennett
Rockwood Birtsell
Frank Blair
James M. Bockius
Brown Bowen
George Brassell
James Brassell
William Brocken
William Brookings
the Broolans (2 brothers)
A. G. Brown
Sol Brown
"Pink" Burns
Colin Campbell
John Carnes
William Casion
Dick Chisholm
Crockett Choate
Henry Choate
John Choate
Bob F. Civas
John Civas
Jeff Clark
Joseph Clarke
Gyp Clements
Jim Clements
Joe Clements
Mannen Clements
Cole (first name unknown)

James Collins
Jack Connor
William Connor
James Cook
Stephen Cowan
John Criswell
Alexander Cudd
Bill Cunningham
Charlie Davis
Edd Davis
John Davis
Alf Day
Charlie Day
L. C. Day
John Denton
Bud Dixon
Tom Dixon
Bill Dodd
James Dodd
Tom Dodd
the Doughtys (2 brothers)
Patrick "Bud" Dowlearn
Fred Duderstadt
John Edwards
J. Elder
King Fisher
Frank Frisbie Jr.
Frank Frisbie Sr.
Fulcrod (first name unknown)
Sam Gibson
Short Gibson
Gilmore (first name unknown)
Charles Glascock
Sheriff Dick Glover
Edward Glover
Jim Glover
John Glover
Jesus Gonzales
The Gormans (2 brothers)
Bill Green

William S. Halsey
Jim Hamilton
John Wesley Hardin
Jo Hardin
Billy Harper
Jess Harper
John Harper
Drew Hassley
Sam Hassley
Jim Henderson
A. R. Hendricks
Ben Hinds
Charlie Hodges
Tom Holderman
Robert Holliday
George Johnson
"Pleas" Johnson
Whit Johnson
John P. Jones
William E. Jones
George Kelleson
Eugene Kelly
Henry Kelly
Wiley Kelly
William Kelly
Killensworth (first name unknown)
Mark King
Chris Kirlicks Jr.
Chris Kirlicks Sr.
George Kirlicks
John Kirlicks
William Kirlicks
William Kirtner
Ben Lane
Asa Langford Jr.
Asa Langford Sr.
"Wild Bill" Longley
James Lunsford
McCormick (first name unknown)
Bud McFadden

S. W. McKee
Middleton (first name unknown)
Jake Miller
Jim Miller
Jim Millican
Moore (first name unknown)
David "Dave" Morris
Sol Nicholson
George Nickles
Lazarus Nickles
G. W. Parkes
James Patterson
Clint Peace
Mat Peace
Fred Pell
Jordan Perkins
the Perrys (2 brothers)
George Pierce
Dobe Poole
James Poole
Bolivar J. Pridgen
Wiley Pridgen
Ben F. Prior
Pruitt (2 brothers)

Reuben Purcell
Purcell (first name unknown)
Alexander Reed
Buck Roland
James Roland
James Rutland
James Sharpe
Short (first name unknown)
Frank Skidmore
Richard Slades
Thomas Slades
David Spencer
R. W. "Ran" Spencer
James Stapp
J. O. Steven
Joe Sunday
Billy Taylor
Buck Taylor
Charles Taylor
Creed Taylor
Doughboy Taylor
Hays Taylor
Jim Taylor
Joe Taylor

Martin Taylor
Pitkin Taylor
Scrap Taylor
George Tennille
Bill Thompson
Henry Thompson
James Thompson (alias Jim Tope)
David Thorp
"Hun" Tuggle
"Kute" Tuggle
Turk Turner
James "Buck" Waldrip
Thomas J. Waldrip
Rufus Weaver
George West
T. C. West
Henry Westfall
Jim White
Frank Wilcox
Isaac Wright
James Wright
John Wright
Riall Wright

Areas of Operations or Scenes of Robberies and Other Atrocities Perpetrated by the Taylor Ring (by county; 45)

Angelina
Atascosa
Bastrop
Bell
Bexar
Brazoria
Brown
Caldwell
Calhoun
Coleman
Colorado
Comanche
Coryell
DeWitt
Fayette

Fort Bend
Gillespie
Goliad
Gonzales
Guadalupe
Hamilton
Hill
Houston
Karnes
Kimble
Lafayette
Lampasas
Lavaca
Liberty
Limestone

McLennan
McMullen
Mason
Milam
Nueces
Panola
Polk
Refugio
San Patricio
San Saba
Trinity
Victoria
Walker
Washington
Wilson

NOTES

Abbreviations used in the notes

AGO Adjutant General's Office, Austin, Texas
AAG Acting Adjutant General
AAAG Assistant Acting Adjutant General
BRFAL Bureau of Refugees, Freedmen, and Abandoned Lands
CAH Center for American History, University of Texas Libraries, Austin, Texas
DT Department of Texas
5MD Fifth Military District
GP Governor's Papers, Texas State Library, Austin
LR Letters Received
LS Letters Sent
MS Unpublished Manuscript
NA National Archives, Washington, D.C.
NHT *New Handbook of Texas*
RG Record Group
SWHQ *Southwestern Historical Quarterly*
TSL Texas State Library
UTL University of Texas at Austin Library
UHV University of Houston at Victoria, Texas
VC Victoria College, Victoria, Texas
VC/UHV VC/UHV Library
VF Vertical File

Introduction

1. Fleming, G. A. Wright, William Barnett, et al. to Gov. Coke, May 28, 1874, GP, RG 301, Archives, TSL, Austin, Texas; *Dallas Weekly Herald,* June 6, 1874; T. R. Havins, *Something about Brown: A History of Brown County, Texas* (Brownwood: Banner Printing Company, 1958), 28; John Wesley Hardin, *The Life of John Wesley Hardin as Written by Himself* (reprint; Norman: University of Oklahoma Press, 1961), 88–89.

2. Mollie Moore Godbold, "Comanche and the Hardin Gang," *SWHQ* 67 (July 1963), Pt. 1: 66–73; *Dallas Weekly Herald,* June 6, 1874; Havins, *Something about Brown,* 28–30; Hardin, *Life,* 90.

3. Havins, *Something about Brown,* 28–30; Godbold, "The Hardin Gang," *SWHQ,* Pt. 1:66–73; *Dallas Weekly Herald,* June 6, 1874.

4. Godbold, "Comanche"; *Dallas Weekly Herald,* June 6, 1874; Havins, *Something about Brown,* 28–30.

5. Grand Jury Indictment, October 1874, Comanche County Courthouse; Havins, *Something About Brown,* 28–30; Godbold, "The Hardin Gang," SWHQ, Pt. 1:66–73; *Dallas Weekly Herald,* June 6, 1874.

6. Grand Jury Indictment, October, 1874, Comanche County Courthouse; petitioners Fleming, Wright, Barnett, et al. to Gov. Coke, May 28, 1874, GP, RG 301, Archives, TSL; Havins, *Something About Brown,* 28–30; Godbold, "The Hardin Gang," *SWHQ,* Pt. 1:66–73.

7. Grand Jury Indictment, October 1874, Comanche County Courthouse; Fleming, Wright, Barnett, et al. Coke, May 28, 1874; *Dallas Weekly Herald,* June 6, 1874; Havins, *Something about Brown,* 28–30.

8. See, for example, Robert Sutton Jr., *The Sutton-Taylor Feud* (Quanah: Nortex Press, 1974); Chuck Parsons, "The DeWitt County Feud," in DeWitt County Historical Commission, *The History of DeWitt County* (2 vols.; Dallas: Curtis Media Company, 1991); Lewis Delony, "40 Years a Peace Officer," *Old West* 7 (Winter 1970). Delony's article is a reprint of a short book he privately published in 1937.

9. For the traditional national overview of Reconstruction, see William A. Dunning, *Reconstruction, Political and Economic, 1865–1877* (New York: Harper Brothers, 1907); Dunning, *Essays on the Civil War and Reconstruction* (New York: Mcmillian, 1904); for state studies that stress the Dunning interpretation, see Walter L. Fleming, *The Civil War and Reconstruction in Alabama* (New York: Columbia University Press, 1905), and Charles Ramsdell, *Reconstruction in Texas* (New York: Columbia University Press, 1910). From the 1950s to the 1980s, some Texas historians still stressed the traditional interpretation. See, for example, W. C. Nunn, *Texas Under the Carpetbaggers* (Austin: University of Texas Press, 1962); Nunn, *Escape from Reconstruction* (Fort Worth: Texas Christian University Press, 1956); Earnest Wallace, *Texas in Turmoil* (Austin: Steck-Vaughn, 1965); Wallace, *The Howling of the Coyotes: The Reconstruction Attempts to Divide Texas* (College Station: Texas A&M Press, 1979).

10. For examples of expositions on how myth, memory, and propaganda have distorted the interpretation of the Civil War and Reconstruction, see David W. Blight, *Race and Reunion: The Civil War in American Memory* (Cambridge: Harvard University Press, 2001); Gary W. Gallagher and Alan T. Nolan, eds., *The Myth of the Lost Cause and Civil War History* (Bloomington: Indiana University Press, 2001); James McPherson, "Southern Comfort," *New York Times Review of Books* 48 (April 12, 2001): 28, 30–31. Leading revisionists on Reconstruction Texas include Barry A. Crouch, Donaly Brice, Randolph B. Campbell, Carl Moneyhon, Dale Baum, James M. Smallwood, and various others. For citations of the many secondary works on Reconstruction in Texas, see Bruce A. Glasrud and Laurie Champion, eds., *Exploring the Afro-Texas Experience: A Bibliography of Secondary Sources about Black Texans* (Alpine: Center for Big Bend Studies, 2000), 32–40. For the latest revisionist synthesis, see Carl Moneyhon, *Texas after the Civil War* (College Station: Texas A&M University Press, 2004).

CHAPTER I

1. William Weisiger, "Sutton-Taylor Feud," notes, VF, William Weisiger Collection, Regional History Center, VC/UHV Library; Tom Stell, "The Taylor-Sutton Feud," *Taylor Family News* [newsletter], 8(1): 3, copy in possession of the author courtesy of Henry Wolff, columnist for the *Victoria Advocate;* Wolff, "Oldtimers Sure Got Around," *Victoria Advocate,* March 25, 1990; Jack Hays Day, *The Sutton-Taylor Feud* (San Antonio: Sid Murray and Son, 1937), 6, 9; A. J. Sowell, "Frontier Days of Texas," *San Antonio Light,* October 27, 1912; Creed Taylor, letter to the editor, *San Antonio Daily Express,* June 28, 1905.

2. Parsons, "DeWitt County Feud," 31–32. For more on Creed Taylor, see Maud

Gilliland, *Wilson County Texas Rangers, 1837–1977* (Privately printed, 1977); John Warren Hunter, "Literary Effort Concerning Activities of Creed Taylor and Others in the Mexican War," ms, Creed Taylor, pay vouchers no. 479 and no. 487, Archives, TSL; R. Sutton, *The Sutton-Taylor Feud,* 10, 12–14; Sowell, "Frontier Days," *San Antonio Light,* October 27, 1912; Dovie Hall, "Creed Taylor," *NHT* (6 vols.; Austin: Texas State Historical Association), 6: 215–16; J. Marvin Hunter, "Capt. Creed Taylor Bet Col. Bales 100 Bales and More," *Houston Post,* December 19, 1937; Sowell, "Creed Taylor Was an Early Texas Ranger," *Frontier Times* 15 (November 1937): 77–81.

3. L. W. Kemp, "Was Creed Taylor at San Jacinto?" *Frontier Times* 13 (April 1936): 335–37.

4. Parsons, "DeWitt County Feud," 31–32; Hunter, "Literary Effort"; Creed Taylor, pay vouchers no. 479 and no. 487, Archives, TSL; R. Sutton, *Taylor-Sutton Feud,* 10, 12–14; Hall, "Creed Taylor"; Sowell, "Creed Taylor Was an Early Texas Ranger." For copious material on Taylor genealogy, see Marjorie Burnett Hyatt, *The Taylors, the Tumlinsons, and the Feud,* 2d ed. (Smiley, Texas: Privately published, 1988); Mike Taylor, "Trouble Ahead: The Start of the Feud," *Taylor Family News* 1 (August 1990): 2, copy in possession of the author.

5. Creed Taylor, "Memoirs," ms, Archives, TSL; R. Sutton, *Sutton-Taylor Feud,* 31–32; see Sutton for a discussion of the cattle business, including "mavericking" and cattle rustling, 4–5, 7.

6. N. Gusset to AG, February 1865, AGO, RG 401, Archives, TSL; R. R. Smith to C. L. Sonnichsen, October 1, 1943, C. L. Sonnichsen Papers, Archives, University of Texas at El Paso; Parsons, "DeWitt County Feud," 36; R. Sutton, *Sutton-Taylor Feud,* 14.

7. J. B. Polley, "The Taylor Boys Made Things Interesting," *Frontier Times* 9 (December 1931): 113; for more on the Cattle Kingdom and the trail, see Wayne Gard, *The Chisholm Trail* (Norman: University of Oklahoma Press, 1954).

8. *San Antonio Light,* June 29, 1913; *Indianola Scrapbook,* comp. and ed. by editors of *Victoria Advocate* (Victoria: Victoria Advocate Publishing Company, 1936), 88; Havins, *Something about Brown,* 26–27; Polley, "The Taylor Boys," 114–15.

9. Polly, "The Taylor Boys," 113–15.

10. Parsons, "DeWitt County Feud," 31–32; Hunter, "Literary Effort"; Archives, TSL; R. Sutton, *Taylor-Sutton Feud,* 10, 12–14; Hall, "Creed Taylor,"; Sowell, "Creed Taylor Was an Early Texas Ranger." 77–81.

11. Capt. Edward Miller to AAAG Lt. S. H. M. Taylor, December 10, 1865, Sub-Assistant Commissioner, Victoria; Lt. Hiram Clark to AAAG, July 5, 1867, Sub-Assistant Commissioner, Clinton, LS, Shreveport, Louisiana, "Record of Complaints," vol. 441, BRFAL, RG 105, NA.

12. Miller to Taylor, December 10, 1865, Sub-Assistant Commissioner, Victoria, LS, Shreveport, Louisiana, "Record of Complaints," vol. 441, BRFAL, RG 105, NA; Henrietta Frey, Nora Gugenheim, et al. to Theo Hertzberg, November 4, 1867, LR, Box 3, DT, 5MD, RG 393, NA; R. Sutton, *Taylor-Sutton Feud,* 14–16; William L. Richter, "Spread Eagle Eccentricities: Military-Civilian Relations in Reconstruction Texas," *Texana* 8 (1970): 313, 315; C. L. Sonnichsen, "Sutton-Taylor Feud," *NHT,* 6: 162–63.

13. Miller to Taylor, December 10, 1865, Sub-Assistant Commissioner, Victoria, LS, Shreveport, Louisiana, "Record of Complaints," vol. 441, BRFAL, RG 105, NA; Frey, Gugenheim, et al. to Herzberg; November 4, 1867, LR, Box 3, DT. 5MD, RG 393, NA; Lt. Col. H. S. Hall, testimony, February 20, 1866, United States Congress, "Report of the Joint Committee on Reconstruction: Part IV: Florida, Louisiana, and Texas," 39th

Cong., 1st sess. (Washington, D.C.: Government Printing Office, 1866), 48; R. Sutton, *Taylor-Sutton Feud,* 14–16; Richter, "Military-Civilian Relations"; Sonnichsen, "Sutton-Taylor Feud." *NHT,* 6: 162–63.

14. Col. George A. Custer to Zachariah Chandler, January 8, 1866, Zachariah Chandler Papers, Manuscript Division, Library of Congress, Washington, D.C.

15. Ibid.

16. Ibid.

17. Ibid.; and see Custer to Chandler, January 14, 1866, ibid.

18. Capt. William Horton to AAG Lt. Col. H. A. Ellis, November 13, 1866, Sub-Assistant Commissioner, Halletsville, LS, BRFAL, RG 105, NA.

19. Custer to Chandler, January 8, 14, 1866, Chandler Papers, Manuscript Division, Library of Congress.

20. Lt. William Hoffman, Post of Greenville, to Capt. Charles J. Whiting, Commander, Post of Greenville, July 27, 1869, LR, Box 16, DT, 5MD, RG 393, NA. Also see James M. Smallwood, Barry A. Crouch, and Larry Peacock, *Murder and Mayhem: The War of Reconstruction in Texas* (College Station: Texas A&M Press, 2003), 115–16.

21. Capt. Miller to AAAG Lt. Taylor, September 10, 1866, Sub-Assistant Commissioner, Victoria, LS, BRFAL, RG 105, NA; Creed Taylor, "Memoirs."

22. Capt. Miller to AAAG Lt. Taylor, April 10, 1866, Sub-Assistant Commissioner, Victoria, LS, Shreveport, Louisiana, "Record of Complaints," vol. 441, BRFAL, RG 105; Frey, Gugenheim, et al. to Hertzberg, November 4, 1867, LR, Box 3, DT, 5MD, RG 393, NA, R. Sutton, *Taylor-Sutton Feud,* 14–16; Creed Taylor, "Memoirs," ms, Archives, TSL.

23. Miller to Taylor, April 10, 1866, Sub-Assistant Commissioner, Victoria, LS, Shreveport, Louisiana, "Record of Complaints," vol. 441, BRFAL, RG 105, Frey, Gugenheim, et al. to Hertzberg, November 4, 1867, LR, Box 3, DT, 5MD, RG 393, NA, R. Sutton, *Sutton-Taylor Feud,* 14–16; Sonnichsen, "Sutton-Taylor Feud," *NHT,* 6: 162–63; De Witt Reddick, "The Taylor-Sutton Feud," *Frontier Times* 2 (June 1925): 16–17; J. B. Polley, "The Taylor Boys," *Frontier Times* 5 (July 1928): 401–402; Creed Taylor, "Memoirs," ms, Archives, TSL.

24. Gov. A. J. Hamilton to Gen. H. G. Wright, September 27, 1865, A. J. Hamilton, GP, RG 301, Archives, TSL; Custer to Chandler, January 8, 14, 1866, Chandler Papers, Manuscript Division, Library of Congress; Claude Elliott, "Constitutional Convention of 1866," *NHT,* 2: 283–84.

25. William Alexander to Judge Salmon P. Chase, July 17, 1866, Salmon Chase Papers, Manuscript Division, Library of Congress.

26. Gen. Charles Griffin to Gen. Philip Sheridan, July 20, 1867, Philip Sheridan Papers, Manuscript Division, Library of Congress.

27. James Thompson, "Statement under Oath of James Thompson alias James Tope of the Murder of Five Discharged Soldiers in June of 1866," enclosed in Gen. John Mason to AAAG Lt. C. E. Morse, April 7, 1868, LR, Box 5, DT, 5MD, RG 393, NA; M. ?? Taylor, "The Start of the Feud," *Taylor Family News,* 1–2.

28. Capt. Miller to AAAG Lt. Taylor, March 10, 1866, Sub-Assistant Commissioner, Victoria, LS, Shreveport, Louisiana, "Record of Complaints," vol. 441, BRFAL, RG 105; Frey, Gugenheim, et al. to Hertzberg, November 4, 1867, LR, Box 3, DT, 5MD, RG 393, NA; R. Sutton, *Taylor-Sutton Feud,* 14–16, 33; Sonnichsen, "Sutton-Taylor Feud"; Parsons, "DeWitt County Feud," 32; Reddick, "The Taylor-Sutton Feud,"

17; Victor Rose, *Texas Vendetta; or, the Sutton-Taylor Feud* (New York: J. J. Little and Company, 1880), 12.

29. Capt. Miller to AAAG Lt. Taylor, March 10, 1866, Sub-Assistant Commissioner, Victoria, LS, Shreveport, Louisiana, "Record of Complaints," vol. 441, BRFAL, RG 105, Frey, Gugenheim, et al. to Hertzberg, November 4, 1867, LR, Box 3, DT, 5MD, RG 393, NA; R. Sutton, *Sutton-Taylor Feud,* 14–16, 33.

30. Capt. Garza Haraszthy to AAAG Capt. George R. Sherman, March 5, 28, April 13, 1866, LR, Box 1, DT, 5MD, RG 393, NA.

31. Gen. Griffin to Gov. James W. Throckmorton, January 21, 1867, Henry Beaumont to Gov. Throckmorton, February 13, 1867, James W. Throckmorton, GP, RG 301, Archives, TSL; Agnes Kane Callum, *Colored Volunteers of Maryland, Civil War, 7th Regiment, U.S. Colored Troops, 1863–1865* (Baltimore: Mullac Publishers, 1990), 35; Col. James Shan Jr. to AAG Col. C. Whittelsey, September 1866, Seventh Infantry Regiment, AGO, RG 94, NA.

32. "Criminal Offences Committed in the State of Texas," September 18, 1866, case nos. 147–151, DT, 5MD, RG 393, NA; M. Taylor, "Trouble Ahead," *Taylor Family News,* 2.

33. Thompson, "Statement under Oath of Thompson alias Tope," enclosed in Gen. Mason to AAAG Lt. Morse, April 7, 1868, LR, Box 5, DT, 5MD, RG 393, NA.

34. Capt. Miller to Taylor AAAG Lt. December 10, 1866, Sub-Assistant Commissioner, Victoria, LS, Shreveport, Louisiana, "Record of Complaints," vol. 441, BRFAL, RG 105, Frey, Gugenheim, et al. to Hertzberg, November 4, 1867, LR, Box 3, DT, 5MD, RG 393, NA; R. Sutton, *Taylor-Sutton Feud;* 14–16, Sonnichsen, "Sutton-Taylor Feud," *NHT,* 6: 162–63. Tom Stell, "The Taylor-Sutton Feud," *Taylor Family Newsletter* 8 (February 1998): 4, copy in possession of the author.

35. Thompson, "Statement of Thompson alias Tope on the robbing of a Mexican and cutting his wife," in Gen. Mason to AAAG Lt. Morse, April 7, 1868, LR, Box 5, DT, 5MD, RG 393, NA.

36. Thompson, "Statement of Thompson alias Tope on the Stealing of four Mules from some wagons this side of Helena" in Gen. Mason to AAAG Lt. Morse, April 7, 1868, LR, Box 5, DT, 5MD, RG 393, Capt. Miller to AAAG Lt. Taylor, Sub-Assistant Commissioner, Victoria, LS, BRFAL, RG 105, NA.

37. Capt. G. H. Heinstand to AAAG. Lt. J. T. Kirkman, March 1, 1867, Sub-Assistant Commissioner, Hallettsville, LS, BRFAL, RG 105, NA.

38. Capt. Heinstand to AAAG Lt. E. M. Harris, March 22, 25, 1867, Sub-Assistant Commissioner, Hallettsville, LS, BRFAL, RG 105, NA.

39. For more on the Reconstruction Acts as applied to Texas, see James Alex Baggett, "Fifth Military District," *NHT,* 2: 996; Carl Moneyhon, "Reconstruction," *NHT,* 6: 474–81.

40. Lt. J. R. Fitch to AAAG Lt. Taylor, February 15, 1867, A. M. Boatright to Gen. J. J. Reynolds, January 10, 1867, LR, Box 1, DT, 5MD, RG 393, NA; Baggett, "Fifth Military District."

41. Lt. Bryon Porter to AAAG Lt. Kirkman, March 4, 1867, Sub-Assistant Commissioner, Bastrop, LS, "Criminal Offences Committed in the State of Texas, February, 1867," case no. 545, BRFAL, RG 105, NA.

42. Capt. Heinstand to AAAG Lt. Kirkman, March 25, 29, 1867, LR, Box 2, DT, 5MD, RG 393, NA.

43. Ibid.

CHAPTER 2

1. Gov. Elisha M. Pease, *Communication from Governor Pease of Texas Relative to the Troubles in That State,* U.S. House of Representatives, 40th Cong., 2d sess., Misc. Doc. No. 127, 16; Capt. Porter to AAAG Lt. Kirkman, April 2, 1867, Sub-Assistant Commissioner, Bastrop, LS, BRFAL, RG 105, NA.

2. DeWitt County Judge James F. Kilgore, H. B. Boston, F. B. Webb, et al. to Gov. Throckmorton, April 17, 1867, I. Haywood, affidavit, April 12, 1867, Throckmorton, GP, RG 301, Archives, TSL; Gov. E. Pease, *Troubles in Texas,* U.S. House, Misc. Doc. No. 127, 7.

3. Kilgore, Boston, Webb, et al. to Gov. Throckmorton, April 17, 1867, I. Haywood, affidavit, April 12, 1867, Throckmorton, GP, RG 301, Archives, TSL; Gov. E. Pease, *Troubles in Texas,* U.S. House, Misc. Doc. No. 127, 7.

4. Thompson, "Statement of the Stealing of McDermott's Mules near Gonzales in April, 1867," in Gen. Mason to AAAG Lt. Morse, April 7, 1868, LR, Box 5, DT, 5MD, RG 393, NA.

5. Hyatt, *The Taylors, the Tumlinsons,* 67; Weisiger, "Sutton-Taylor Feud," notes, 1, 4, 7–9; R. Sutton, *Sutton-Taylor Feud,* 28–31.

6. Hyatt, *The Feud,* 67; Weisiger, "Sutton-Taylor Feud," notes, 1, 4, 7–9, VF, in Weisiger Collection, Regional History Center, VC/UHV; R. Sutton, *Sutton-Taylor Feud,* 28–31; Sonnichsen, "Sutton-Taylor Feud"; Rose, *Texas Vendetta,* 13; Henry Wolff, "Many Versions of the Bill Sutton Story," *Victoria Advocate,* February 22, 1998.

7. Capt. Miller to Gen. J. B. Kiddoo, December, 1866, January 11, 1867, Sub-Assistant Commissioner, Victoria, LS, BRFAL, RG 105, NA; Gen. Charles Griffin to Maj. George A. Forsyth, June 10, 1867, Sheridan Papers, Manuscript Division, Library of Congress; Pease, *Communication from Governor.*

8. "Criminal Offences Committed in the State of Texas, July, 1867," case no. 809, Lt. Hiram Clarke to AAAG Lt. J. Kirkman, August 31, 1867, Sub-Assistant Commissioner, Clinton, LS, BRFAL, RG 105, NA; R. Sutton, *Sutton-Taylor Feud,* 16–17; Pease, *Communication from Governor;* U.S. House, misc. Doc. 127, 7; Polley, "The Taylor Boys." 115.

9. "Criminal Offences Committed in the State of Texas, May 25, 1867," case no. 693, BRFAL, RG 105, Lt. Harris to AAAG Lt. J. Kirkman, June 17, 1867, LR, Box 3, DT, 5MD, RG 393, NA.

10. Jack Helm to Gen. James Oakes, July 15, 1867, LR, Box 2, DT, 5MD, RG 393, NA.

11. Ibid.

12. M. G. Jacobs, M. L. Norton, Charles Coleman, et al. to Gen. Griffin, July, 1867, copy in Barry Crouch Collection, Regional History Center, VC/UHV; D. D. Stubblefield to Col. Evans, July 12, 1867, Capt. James Emerson to Gen. Oakes, July 8, 1867, LR, Box 1, DT, 5MD, RG 393, NA.

13. M. L. Longworth to W. Longworth, June 29, 1867, Creed Taylor to "Sir," June 15, 1867, LR, Box 2, DT, 5MD, RG 393, NA.

14. Maj. George W. Smith to AAAG Lt. Kirkman, July 4, November 23, 1867, Sub-Assistant Commissioner, Seguin, LS, BRFAL, RG 105, NA.

15. Ibid.

16. Creed Taylor, affidavit, July 27, 1867, in Maj. Smith to AAAG Lt. Kirkman, November 23, 1867, Sub-Assistant Commissioner, Seguin, LS, BRFAL, RG 105, NA.

17. Ibid.

18. Gen. Griffin, endorsement, July 16, 1867, in Maj. Smith to AAAG Lt. Krkman, November 23, 1867, Sub-Assistant Commissioner, Seguin, LS, BRFAL, RG 105, NA.

19. "Criminal Offences Committed in the State of Texas, July, 1867," case nos. 823, 824, 1020, BRFAL, RG 105, NA.

20. Lt. Hiram Clark to AAAG Lt. Kirkman, August 31, 1867, Sub-Assistant Commissioner, Clinton, LS, BRFAL, RG 105, NA; R. Sutton, *Sutton-Taylor Feud*, 16–17; Pease, *Communication from Governor;* U.S. House, misc. doc. 127, 17, 20; Polley, "The Taylor Boys." 115.

21. Clark to Kirkman, August 31, 1867, Sub-Assistant Commissioner, Clinton, LS, BRFAL, RG 105, NA; R. Sutton, *Sutton-Taylor Feud;* Pease, *Communication from Governor;* U.S. House, misc. doc. 127, 17, 20; Polley, "The Taylor Boys." 115.

22. Capt. E. J. Conway, Fort Inge, to AAAG, December 5, 1867, LR, Box 3, DT, 5MD, RG 393, NA; Weisiger, "Sutton-Taylor Feud," notes, 10, VF, Weisiger Collection, Regional History Center, VC/UHV.

23. Capt. Conway, Fort Inge, to AAAG, December 5, 1867, LR, Box 3, DT, 5MD, RG 393, NA; Weisiger, "Sutton-Taylor Feud," notes, 10. VF, Weisiger Collection, Regional History Center, VC/UHV.

24. Capt. P. A. Lathrop to AAAG Lt. Taylor, August 28, 1867, LR, Box 2, DT, 5MD, RG 393, NA.

25. Seabury Phillips to Capt. Lathrop, August 28, 1867, LR, Box 2, DT, 5MD, RG 393, NA.

26. Frey, Gugenheim, et al. to Hertzberg, November 4, 1867, LR, Box 3, DT, 5MD, RG 393, NA.

27. Frey, Gugenheim, et al. to Hertzberg, November 4, 1867, LR, Box 3, Charles S. Bell to AAAG Lt. Morse, November 28, 1869, LR, Box 14, DT, 5MD, RG 393, NA; Sonnichsen, "Sutton-Taylor Feud." *NHT,* 6: 162–63.

28. Frey, Gugenheim, et al. to Hertzberg, November 4, 1867, LR, Box 3, DT, 5MD, RG 393, NA.

29. Special Committee, Texas Legislature, *Report on Lawlessness and Violence* (Austin: *Austin Daily Republican,* 1868), 12–13; David M. Jordan, *Winfield Scott Hancock: A Soldier's Life* (Bloomingdale: Indiana University Press, 1988), 203–5.

30. A. M. Boatright to Gen. Griffin, April 21, 1867, copy in Crouch Collection, Regional History Center, VC/UHV; Boatright to Gen. Reynolds, January 11, 1867, LR, Box 1, DT, 5MD, RG 393, NA; M. L. Longworth to Joseph Spence, August 19, 1867, Willis Fawcet to Gov. Pease, August 18, 1867, W. M. Varrnell to Gov. Pease, November 27, 1867, E. Pease, GP, RG 301, Archives, TSL.

31. Lt. Clark to AAAG Lt. Charles Garretson, September 30, 1867, Sub-Assistant Commissioner, Clinton, LS, "Criminal Offences Committed in the State of Texas, October, 1867," case no. 1293, BRFAL, RG 105, NA; Pease, *Communication from Governor;* U.S. House, misc. doc. 127, 22; Weisiger, "Sutton-Taylor Feud" notes, 10, 15–17, VF, Weisiger Collection, Regional History Center, VC/UHV.

32. Gen. Sheridan to Gen. John A. Rawlins, November 21, 1867, Sheridan Papers, Manuscript Division, Library of Congress.

33. R. Sutton, *Sutton-Taylor Feud,* 16–17; Creed Taylor, "Memoirs," ms, Archives, TSL: Polley, "The Taylor Boys"; J. Marvin Hunter Sr., "The Taylor Boys, Outlaws," *Frontier Times* 27 (September 1950): 343–44; *Georgetown Watchman,* quoting the *Austin Daily State Journal,* May 21, 1870.

34. "Criminal Offences Committed in the State of Texas, December, 1867," case nos. 1371–1372, BRFAL, RG 105, NA; Polley, "The Taylor Boys," *Frontier Times,* 115; R. Sutton, *Sutton-Taylor Feud,* 16–17; Creed Taylor, "Memoirs"; Pease, *Communication for Governor;* U.S. House, misc. doc. 127, 22; M. Taylor, "Trouble Ahead," *Taylor Family News,* 3.

35. "Criminal Offences Committed in the State of Texas, December, 1867," case nos. 1371, 1372, BRFAL, RG 105, NA. Several sources provided details on the 1867 murders. See E. B. Dwyer to Huntsville Post Commander, September 5, 1869, C. Bell to AAAG Lt. Morse, October 4, 1869, Conway to AAAG, December 5, 1867, LR, Box 3, C. Bell to AAAG Morse, November 28, 1869, LR, Box 14, DT, 5 MD, RG 393, NA; Parsons, "DeWitt County Feud," 32; Creed Taylor, "Memoirs," ms, Archives, TSL; Polley, "The Taylor Boys"; M. Taylor, "Trouble Ahead." *Taylor Family News,* 3.

36. Lt. Smith to AAAG Lt. Morse, November 16, 1867, Maj. C. S. Bowman to Lt. Smith, November 15, 1867, Special Order No. 180, November 16, 1867, LR, Box 3, "Criminal Offences Committed in the State of Texas," n.d., case no. 52, DT, 5MD, RG 393, NA.

37. Lt. Smith to AAAG Morse, November 23, 1867, Sub-Assistant Commissioner, Seguin, LS, BRFAL, RG 105, NA.

38. Ibid.

39. Lt. Horton to AAAG Lt. Richardson, November 1, 1867, Sub-Assistant Commissioner, Hallettsville, LS, BRFAL, RG 105, NA.

40. "Criminal Offences Committed in the State of Texas, November, 1867," case no. 1349, BRFAL, RG 105, NA; E. Pease, *Communication from Governor.* U.S. House, misc. doc. 127, 22.

41. Capt. Conway to AAAG, December 5, 1867, LR, Box 3, DT, 5MD, RG 393, NA; R. Sutton, *Taylor-Sutton Feud,* 16–17; J. Hunter Sr., "The Taylor Boys, Outlaws." 343–44.

CHAPTER 3

1. Lt. Clark to AAAG Lt. Charles Vernou, July 2, 1868, Sub-Assistant Commissioner, Clinton, LS, BRFAL, RG 105, NA.

2. Lt. J. D. Verney to Capt. George W. Smith, February 1, 1868, LR, Box 5, DT, 5MD, RG 393, NA.

3. Lt. Porter to AAAG, January 4, 1868, Sub-Assistant Commissioner, Bastrop, LS, BRFAL, RG 105, NA; J. Schutze to Gov. E. Pease, March 28, 1868, GP, RG 301, Archives, TSL.

4. Gen. Mason to AAAG Lt. Morse, April 7, 1868, LR, Box 5, DT, 5MD, RG 393, NA; *San Antonio Express,* March 28, 1868.

5. Gov. E. Pease to Gen. Reynolds, May 2, Andieas Kiesnick to Pease, April 20, 1868, LR, Box 6, DT, 5MD, RG 393; Lt. Porter to AAAG, April 1, 1868, Sub-Assistant Commission, Bastrop, LS, BRFAL, RG 105, NA.

6. J. Schutze to Gov. E. Pease, April 4, 1868, Capt. Charles S. Roberts to AAAG Lt. Morse, May 8, 1868, LR, Box 5, DT, 5MD, RG 393, NA.

7. J. K. Williams to AGO, March 20, 1868, AGO, Archives, TSL; Lt. Clark to AAAG Lt. Richardson, March 8, 1868, Sub-Assistant Commissioner, Clinton, LS, BRFAL, RG 105, NA.

8. Lt. Porter to AAAG, March 4, 1867, April 1, 1868, Sub-Assistant Commissioner, Bastrop, LS, BRFAL, RG 105, NA; *Galveston Daily News,* April 7, 1868, May 19, 1875;

Grimes, *300 Years in Victoria County,* 340; *Indianola Scrapbook,* 88; Rose, *Texas Vendetta,* 12–13; and see Parsons, "DeWitt County Feud," 32; Tom Stell, "Tom Stell on the Feud," *Taylor Family Newsletter* 8 (February 1998): 4, copy in possession of the author.

9. Lt. Porter to AAAG, March 4, 1867, April 1, 1868, Sub-Assistant Commissioner, Bastrop, LS, BRFAL, RG 105, NA; *Galveston Daily News,* April 7, 1868, May 19, 1875; Author Reddick, in "Taylor-Sutton Feud," got some of the details wrong, but he agrees that Sutton's posse killed Charles Taylor in Bastrop. Also see Grimes, *300 Year in Victoria County,* 340. Grimes set April 1, 1868, as the date of the shoot-out in Bastrop and believed that the posse may have murdered Sharpe on the trail. Some of the facts in the *Indianola Scrapbook* (p. 88) are dubious, but the editor had the general story correct. See also Rose, *Texas Vendetta,* 12–13; Parsons, "DeWitt County Feud," 32.

10. Porter to AAAG, April 1, 1868, Sub-Assistant Commissioner, Bastrop, LS, BRFAL, RG 105, NA; Schutze to Pease, March 28, 1868; E. Pease, GP, RG 301, Archives, TSL; *Galveston Daily News,* April 7, 1868, May 19, 1875; Grimes, *300 Years in Victoria County,* 340; *Indianola Scrapbook,* 88; Rose, *Texas Vendetta,* 12–13; Parsons, "DeWitt County Feud," 32.

11. Porter to AAAG, April 1, 1868, Sub-Assistant Commissioner, Bastrop, LS, BRFAL, RG 105, NA; Shutze to Pease, March 28, 1868; GP, RG 301, Archives, TSL; *Galveston Daily News,* April 7, 1868, May 19, 1875; Grimes, *300 Years in Victoria County,* 340; *Indianola Scrapbook,* 88; Rose, *Texas Vendetta,* 12–13; Parsons, "DeWitt County Feud," 32.

12. Porter to AAAG, April 1, 1868; Sub-Assistant Commissioner, Bastrop, LS, BRFAL, RG 105, NA; *Galveston Daily News,* April 7, 1868, May 19, 1875; Grimes, *300 Years in Victoria County,* 340; *Indianola Scrapbook,* 88; Rose, *Texas Vendetta,* 12–13; Parsons, "DeWitt County Feud," 32. Some lay historians, not understanding research methodology and the importance of primary sources, have slaughtered the true account of Taylor's death. Some sources have him unjustly arrested for cattle rustling; then, when he did the natural thing and tried to escape, Bill Sutton shot him in the back, that falsehood cited to explain why Buck Taylor confronted Sutton later. Some lay sources even add fake dialog, having Buck Taylor say "Bill Sutton, you damned coward! You plugged Charlie in the back an' never gave him no fair chance." All of this is foolish. Taylor died in Bastrop while shooting a gun and violently resisting arrest. For an example of mythical conversations, see *Indianola Scrapbook,* 86–87. The book has Charlie Taylor killed in 1866, when infact he was not killed until 1868. The volume has military commanders "outlawing all Taylors [between] the Rio Grande and the tall pines of the Sabine," 88–89. The statement is rubbish, but unfortunately, some myths take on lives of their own.

13. Porter to AAAG, April 1, 1868, Sub-Assistant Commissioner, Bastrop, LS, BRFAL, RG 105, NA; Shutze to Pease, March 28, 1868, Pease, GP, RG 301, Archives, TSL.

14. Porter to AAAG, April 1, 1868, Sub-Assistant Commissioner, Bastrop, LS, BRFAL, RG 105, NA.

15. Shutze to Pease, March 28, 1868, Pease, GP, RG 301, Archives TSL.

16. Lt. Porter to AAAG, January 4, April 30, 1868, Sub-Assistant Commissioner, Bastrop, LS, BRFAL, RG 105, NA.

17. James Brady to Gen. Reynolds, April 30, 1868, LR, Box 4, DT, 5MD, RG 393, NA.

18. Gen. Mason to AAAG Lt. Morse, April 7, 1868, LR, Box 5, DT, 5MD, RG 393, NA; *San Antonio Express,* March 28, 1868.

19. Mason to Morse, April 7, 1868, LR, Box 5, DT, 5MD, RG 393, NA; *San Antonio Express,* March 28, 1868.

20. See W. B. Moore to Gen. Mason, April 4, 1868, and Adams Wickes to Col. I. G. C. Lee, April 5, 1868, enclosed in Mason to Morse, April 7, 1868; LR, Box 5, DT, 5MD, RG; 393, NA; *San Antonio Express,* March 28, 1868.

21. *San Antonio Express,* March 28, 1868.

22. Col. Samuel H. Starr to Col. H. Clay Wood, AAG, November 2, 1869, LR, Box 25, DT, 5MD, RG 393, NA.

23. Ibid.; *Indianola Scrapbook,* 88.

24. *Victoria Advocate,* September 23, 1869; "Obituary of Charles S. Bell," *Dayton Ohio Journal,* February 22, 1879; *New York Times,* February 24, 1879; Creed Taylor, "Memoirs," ms, Archives, TSL; R. Sutton, *Sutton-Taylor Feud,* 9; Rose, *Texas Vendetta,* 13–15.

25. *Victoria Advocate,* September 23, 1869, Creed Taylor, "Memoirs," ms, Archives, TSL; and for much detail, see David Pickering and Judy Falls, *Brush Men and Vigilantes: Civil War Dissent in Texas* (College Station: Texas A&M Press, 2000).

26. AAG Townsend to Buchanan, July 9, 1868, LR, AAG Capt. Roberts, "Reward Proclamation," October 31, 1868, LS (copy of), Box 15, DT, 5MD, RG 393, NA; *Victoria Advocate,* September 23, 1869; Creed Taylor, "Memoirs," ms, Archives, TSL.

27. See, for example, the *Victoria Advocate,* September 23, 1869.

28. C. S. Bell to AAAG Lt. Morse, November 28, 1869, LR, Box 14, DT, 5MD, RG 393, NA. Although Bell's report is given in November 1869, he was summarizing many earlier developments.

29. Ibid.

30. Ibid.

31. Ibid.

32. Ibid.

33. Ibid.

34. Ibid.

35. Ibid; Parsons, "DeWitt County Feud," 32.

36. E. J. Davis to Gen. Reynolds, August 3, 1868, "Resolution of the Convention," August 3, 1868, LR, Box 6, DT, 5MD, RG 393, NA; and see Moneyhon, *Texas after the Civil War,* 93–96.

37. Gen. Mason to AAG Capt. Roberts, October 21, 1868, LR, Box 5, DT, 5MD, RG 393, NA, copy in Crouch Collection, Regional History Center, VC/UHV.

38. See "Official Report of Gen'l Reynolds," December 4, 1868, in *Majority Report of the Special Committee on the Condition of the State: Reported in Convention, December 23, 1868,* 7–8, and *Minority Report of the Special Committee on the Condition of the State: Reported in Convention, December 23, 1868,* 14–16 (Austin: *Austin Daily Republican,* 1868).

39. Matilda C. Frisbie to Gov. E. Pease, December 2, 1868, LR, Pease, GP, RG 301, Archives, TSL; Bell to AAAG Lt. Morse, June 9, 1869, LR, Box 27, DT, 5MD, RG 393, NA.

40. Lt. Vernou to AAG Capt. Roberts, October 19, 1868, copy reprinted in *Flake's Daily Bulletin,* January 22, 1869.

41. For the quote, see R. Sutton, *Sutton-Taylor Feud,* 33; Rose, *Texas Vendetta,* 122–23; Grimes, *300 Years in Victoria County,* 343; Lewis S. Delony, "Forty Years a Peace Officer," *Old West* (Winter 1970). Delony was one of the few writers who studied the

Taylor ring who gave a positive interpretation of the actions of Sutton and other authorities as they chased the gang.

42. For the quote, see R. Sutton, *Sutton-Taylor Feud,* 33; Rose, *Texas Vendetta,* 122–23; Grimes, *300 Years in Victoria County,* 343; Weisinger, "Sutton-Taylor Feud," notes, 2–3, VF, Weisinger Collection, Regional History Center, VC/UHV; Delony, "Forty Years a Peace Officer."

CHAPTER 4

1. Judge A. K. Foster, Lavaca County, to AAAG Lt. Louis V. Carsiac, February 6, 1869, Lt. Canfield to AAAG, April 4, 1869, Sheriff W. H. Coleman to AG, February 5, 1869, LR, Box 23, DT, 5MD, RG 393, NA.

2. Foster to Carsiac, February 6, 1869, Lt. Canfield to AAAG, April 4, 1869, Sheriff W. H. Coleman to AG, February 5, 1869, LR, Box 23, DT, 5MD, RG 393, NA.

3. Judge M. Kreible to A. H. Jordan, January 28, 1869, LR, Box 9, DT, 5MD, RG 393, NA.

4. Jack Helm to Gov. E. Pease, February 18, 1869, E. Pease, GP, RG 301, Archives, TSL.

5. Foster to Carsiac, February 6, 1869, LR, Box 23, H. Rosecrans to Post Commander, Indianola, February 20, 1869, LR, Box 10, DT, 5MD, RG 393, NA.

6. Rosecrans to Post Commander, February 20, 1869, Indianola, February 20, 1869, LR, Box 10, Foster to Carsiac, February 6, 1869, Box 11, DT, 5MD, RG 393, NA.

7. Helm to Pease, February 1869, E. Pease, GP, RG 301, Archives, TSL.

8. William Echols, Justice of the Peace, Yorktown, to Maj. Gen. commanding the 5MD, February 5, 1869 (Coroners' inquest of February 3 attached), LR, Box 8, DT, 5MD, RG 393, NA; [?] to "My Dear Friend," February 4, 1869, copy in Crouch Collection, Regional History Center, VC/UHV.

9. Sheriff W. W. Hammed to AAAG, February 12, 1869, LR, Box 16, DT, 5MD, RG 393, NA.

10. See, for example, *Victoria Advocate,* September 23, 1869.

11. Ben F. Gooch et al. to Gen. E. R. S. Canby, January 26, 1869, LR, Box 11, DT, 5MD, RG 393, NA.

12. *Victoria Advocate,* September 23, 1869; Rose, *Texas Vendetta,* 16.

13. William T. Allen to Gen. James Carleton, April 21, 1869, R. Platt to Gen. Carleton, April 23, 1869, Gen. Carleton to AAAG Lt. Morse, April 24, 1869, LR, Box 6, DT, 5MD, RG 393, NA.

14. Bell to AAAG Lt. Morse, May 17, 1869, LR, Box 7, DT, 5MD, RG 393, NA.

15. Ibid.

16. Bell to AAAG Lt. Morse, June 9, 1869, LR, Box 27, DT, 5MD, RG 393, NA; Matilda Frisbie to Gov. E. Pease, December 2, 1868, E. Pease, GP, RG 301, Archives, TSL.

17. Bell to Lt. William A. Thompson, post of Helena, June 8, 1869, LR, Box 27, DT, 5MD, RG 393, NA.

18. Ibid.

19. Bell to Thompson, June 8, 1869, Bell to Morse, June 9, 1869, LR, Box 27, DT, 5MD, RG 393, NA.

20. Bell to Thompson, June 8, 1869, LR, Box 27, DT, 5MD, RG 393, NA.

21. Lt. Thompson to AAAG Lt. Morse, June 22, 1869, LR, Box 7, DT, 5MD, RG 393, NA.

22. Ibid.

23. Ibid.

24. Helm to Gen. Reynolds, July 8, 1869, LR, Box 7, DT, 5MD, RG 393, NA.

25. Ibid.

26. Ibid.

27. Special Officer M. P. Hunnicutt to AAAG Lt. Morse, August 30, 1869, Helm to Gen. Reynolds, endorsement by DeWitt County Sheriff George W. Jacobs, July 8, 1869, LR, Box 7, DT, 5MD, RG 393, NA.

28. Helm to Reynolds, endorsed by Jacobs, July 8, 1869; Hunnicutt to Morse, August 30, 1869, LR, Box 7, DT, 5MD, RG 393, NA.

29. Lt. Thompson to AAAG Lt. Morse, July 7, 1869, Helm to Reynolds, July 8, 1869, Hunnicutt to Morse, August 30, 1869, LR, Box 7, DT, 5MD, RG 393, NA.

30. Thompson to Morse, July 7, 1869, Helm to Gen. Reynolds, July 8, 1869, LR, Box 7, DT, 5MD, RG 393, NA.

31. Thompson to Morse, July 7, 1869, Helm to Reynolds, July 8, 1869, LR, Box 7, DT, 5MD, RG 393, NA; *Victoria Advocate,* September 23, 1869. A secondary account has Stapp luring Jacobs into his home where the brothers were hiding. When the sheriff was distracted, both brothers stepped through a doorway and shot him to death. The result, of course, was the same: Another lawman had fallen to the Taylor gang.

32. *Victoria Advocate,* September 23, 1869; R. Sutton, *Sutton-Taylor Feud,* 20,

33. *Victoria Advocate,* September 23, 1869; R. Sutton, *Sutton-Taylor Feud,* 20.

34. Lt. Thompson to AAAG Lt. Morse, June 21, 1869, LR, Box 7, DT, 5MD, RG 393, NA.

35. *Victoria Advocate,* September 23, 1869; R. Sutton, *Sutton-Taylor Feud,* 19–20; Thompson to Morse, June 21, 1869, LR, Box 7, DT, 5MD, RG 393, NA.

36. Cyrus Marion VanCleave, "Autobiography of Cyrus Marion VanCleave," ms, copy in possession of the author, courtesy of Patsy Hand from Victoria, Texas.

37. Hunnicutt to Gen. Reynolds, August 6, 1869, LR, Box 7, DT, 5MD, RG 393, NA.

38. Bell to AAG Col. Wood, August 26, 1869, LR, Box 7, DT, 5MD, RG 393, NA.

39. Capt. T. M. K. Smith to Maj. C. L. Davis, Post of Corpus Christi, August 8, 1869, Bell to AAAG Lt. Morse, August 16, 1869, LR, Box 7, DT, 5MD, RG 393, NA.

40. Bell to AAAG Lt. Morse, August 8, 16, 1869, Helm to Gen. Reynolds, August 28, 1869, LR, Box 7, DT, 5MD, RG 393, NA; R. Sutton, *Sutton-Taylor Feud,* 20.

41. Bell to Morse, August 8, 16, 1869, Helm to Reynolds, August 28, 1869, Hunnicutt to AAAG Lt. Morse, August 30, 1869, LR, Box 7, DT, 5MD, RG 393, NA; R. Sutton, *Sutton-Taylor Feud,* 20.

42. Bell to Morse, August 8, 16, 1869, LR, Box 7, DT, 5MD, RG 393, NA; R. Sutton, *Sutton-Taylor Feud,* 20.

43. Hunnicutt to Morse, August 30, 1869; Helm to Reynolds, August 28, 1869, LR, Box 7, DT, 5MD, RG 393, NA. The quote comes from author Sutton.

44. Helm to Reynolds, August 28, 1869; Hunnicutt to Morse, August 30, 1869, LR, Box 7, DT, 5MD, RG 393, NA.

45. Maj. George H. Crosman to Maj. James Callahan, September 19, 1869, Maj. Crosman to AAAG, September 20, 1869, "Special Order No. 62," September 19, 1869, LR, Box 27, DT, 5MD, RG 393, NA.

CHAPTER 5

1. Special Order No. 71, August 3, 18, 1869, LR, Box 3; Capt. T. M. K. Smith to Gen. Reynolds, August 8, 1869, LR, Box 7, DT, 5MD, RG 393, NA.

2. Smith to Reynolds, August 8, 1869.

3. Bell to AAAG Lt. Morse, August 8, 16, 1869, LR, Box 7, DT, 5MD, RG 393, NA.

4. Ibid.

5. Citizens' Petition, Lavaca County, 1869, copy in Crouch Collection, Regional History Center, VC/UHV.

6. Bell to Morse, August 8, 16, 1869, LR, Box 7, DT, 5 MD, RG 393, NA.

7. Ibid.

8. Ibid.

9. Capt. Crosman to AAAG, September 9, 1869, LR, Box 27, DT, 5MD, RG 393, NA; Thomas W. Cutrer, "John Littleton," *NHT,* 4: 238–39; Polley, "The Taylor Boys," 116–17; R. Sutton, *Sutton-Taylor Feud,* 18; Creed Taylor, "Memoirs," ms, Archives, TSL.

10. Crosman to AAAG, September 9, 1869; Polley, "The Taylor Boys," 116–17; R. Sutton, *Sutton-Taylor Feud,* 18; Creed Taylor, "Memoirs," ms, Archives, TSL.

11. William A. G. Lewis, "Sworn Statement of William A. G. Lewis in Relation to the Murder of Capt. Littleton and William Stannard," in Crosman to AAAG, September 9, 1869, LR, Box 27, DT, 5MD, RG 393, NA; *Georgetown Watchman,* quoting the *Austin Daily State Journal,* May 21, 1870; Polley, "The Taylor Boys," 116–17; R. Sutton, *Sutton-Taylor Feud,* 18.

12. Lewis, "Sworn Statement"; Capt. Crosman to AAAG, September 9, 1869, LR, Box 27, DT, 5MD, RG 393, NA; Polley, "The Taylor Boys," 116–17; R. Sutton, *Sutton-Taylor Feud,* 18.

13. Polley, "The Taylor Boys," 120; Bell to Morse, August 8, 16, 1869, LR, Box 7, DT, 5MD, RG 393, NA.

14. Bell to AAAG Lt. Morse, August 23, 1869, LR, Box 20; Helm to Gen. Reynolds, August 28, 1869, Hunnicutt to AAAG Lt. Morse, August 30, 1869, LR, Box 7, DT, 5MD, RG 393, NA; Polley, "The Taylor Boys," 120; Creed Taylor, "Memoirs," ms, Archives, TSL.

15. Bell to Morse, August 23, 1869; Helm to Reynolds, August 28, 1869, LR, Box 7, DT, 5MD, RG 393, NA.

16. Helm to Reynolds, August 28, 1869; Hunnicutt to Morse, August 30, 1869, LR, Box 7, DT, 5MD, RG 393, NA; Polley, "The Taylor Boys," 120; Creed Taylor, "Memoirs," ms, Archives, TSL.

17. Bell to Morse, August 23, 1869, LR, Box 20, DT, 5MD, RG 393, NA

18. Bell to Gen. Reynolds, August 23, 1869, LR, Box 20, DT, 5MD, RG 393, NA.

19. Helm to Reynolds, August 28, 1869; Hunnicutt to Morse, August 30, 1869, LR, Box 7, DT, 5MD, RG 393, NA; *Austin* State Gazette, June 20, 1870.

20. Helm to Reynolds, August 28, 1869; Hunnicutt to Morse, August 30, 1869, LR, Box 7, DT, 5MD, RG 393, NA; *Austin State Gazette,* June 20, 1870.

21. Lt. Thompson to AAAG Lt. Morse, September 2, 1869, Capt. Crosman to AAAG Lt. Morse, September 3, 1869, LR, Box 21; Crosman to Morse, September 20, 1869, LR, Thomas H. Stribling to Reynolds, September, September 9, 1869, Box 7, DT, 5MD, RG 393, NA; Creed Taylor, "Memoirs."

22. Thompson to Morse, September 2, 1869; Crosman to Morse, September 3, 1869, LR, Box 21, bond of Creed Taylor, $10,000, September 18, 1869, Circulars, September 19, 1869, Special Order No. 61; Crosman to Morse, September 20, 1869, LR, Box 7, DT, 5MD, RG 393, NA; *Austin State Gazette,* June 20, 1870; Creed Taylor, "Memoirs," ms, Archives, TSL.

23. Thompson to Morse, September 2, 1869; Crosman to Morse, September 3, 1869, LR, Box 21, Crosman to Morse, September 20, 1869; bond of Creed Taylor, $10,000,

September 18, 1869, Circulars, September 19, 1869, Special Order no. 61, Box 7, DT, 5MD, RG 393, NA; *Austin State Gazette,* June 20, 1870; Creed Taylor, "Memoirs," ms, Archives, TSL.

24. Creed Taylor, "Memoirs," ms, Archives, TSL.

25. Houston County Clerk E. B. Dwyer to Huntsville Post Commander, September 5, 1869, LR, Box 15, J. P. Delespine to AAG Col. Wood, September 9, 1869, LR, Box 7, Bell to AAAG Lt. Morse, March 13, 1870, LR, Box 24, DT, 5MD, RG 393, NA.

26. John Dickson and James Bennett to Gen. Reynolds, September 27, 1869, Denton County Judge J. E. Martin, Order of the Court, September, 27, 1869, LR, Box 6; Bell to Gen. Reynolds, October 4, 1869, Texas Secretary of State W. Philips to AAAG Lt. Morse, October 5, 1869, LR, Box 20, DT, 5MD, RG 393, NA.

27. Dickson and Bennett to Reynolds, September 27, 1869, Martin, Order of the Court, September 27, 1869, LR, Box 6, Bell to Reynolds, October 4, 1869; Philips to Morse, October 5, 1869, LR, Box 20, Dickson and Bennett to Gov. E. Pease, September 27, 1869, copy in LR, Box 21, DT, 5MD, RG393, NA.

28. Capt. Charles A. Wikoff, post commander, Columbus, to AAAG Lt. Morse, September 16, 1869, LR, Box 7, DT, 5MD, RG 393, NA.

29. Capt. G. G. Huntt, Post of Helena, to AAAG Lt. Morse, October 29, 1869, LS, Box 17, DT, 5MD, RG393, NA.

30. Lt. Thompson to Huntt, October 18, 1869, LS, Box 17, DT, 5MD, RG393, NA.

31. Bell to AAAG Lt. Morse, October 30, 1869, LR, Box 26, DT, 5MD, RG393, NA.

32. Ibid.

33. Ibid.

34. For Hardin, see letter from [?] to Texas Ranger Maj. John W. Jones, attached to Bell to Morse, October 30, 1869, LR, Box 26, DT, 5MD, RG393, NA.

35. Bell to Morse, October 8, November 12, 1869, LR, Box 14, DT, 5MD, RG 393, NA.

36. Bell to Morse, November 12, 1869, LR, Box 14, DT, 5MD, RG 393, NA.

37. Ibid.

38. Bell to Lt. Morse, November 12, 28, 1869, LR, Box 14, DT, 5MD, RG 393, NA.

39. Bell to Morse, November 28, 1869, LR, Box 14, DT, 5MD, RG 393, NA.

40. Ibid.

41. Capt. L. C. Degress, post commander, Fort Duncan, to Bell, December 7, 1869, LS, Box 23, DT, 5MD, RG 393, NA.

42. Bell to AAAG Lt. Morse, December 29, 1869, LR, Box 23, DT, 5MD, RG 393, NA.

43. Ibid.

44. Ibid.

45. Ibid.

46. Ibid.

CHAPTER 6

1. Bell to AAAG Lt. Morse, January 14, 1870, LR, Box 23, DT, 5MD, RG 393, NA.

2. W. J. Neely to Gov. Davis, January 24, 1870, L. M. Shockley to Gov. Davis, March 8, 1870, Davis, GP, RG 301, Archives, TSL; Davis to Gen. Reynolds, January 29, 1870, LR, Box 32, DT, 5MD, RG 393, NA.

3. B. O. Stout to Gen. Reynolds, February 27, 1870, LR, Box 25, DT, 5MD, RG 393, NA.

4. W. A. Jacobs to Post Commander, Columbus, LR, Box 24, DT, 5MD, RG 393, NA.

5. Bell to AAAG Lt. Morse, March 13, 1870, LR, Box 24, DT, 5MD, RG 393, NA.

6. Ibid.

7. Ibid.

8. Ibid.

9. Ibid.

10. Ibid.

11. Day, *Sutton-Taylor,* 12–13. Day was a partisan propagandist for the Taylor ring. His widowed grandmother remarried to none other than Pitkin Taylor. While some of Day's book seems accurate relative to a few of the facts, on almost every page, Day explodes with vitriolic rage against anyone opposed to the Taylors. He stands history on its head and turns lawmen into villains and the real villains into harmless victims.

12. Bell to AAAG Lt. Morse, May 6, 11, 1870, LR, Box 24, DT, 5MD, RG 393, NA.

13. General Order Nos. 11–12, March 24, "Enrollment, DeWitt County," March 24, "Enrollment, Karnes County," March 24, AAAG Lt. J. Kirkman to Helm, March 24 (copy in Box 27), AAAG Lt. Kirkman to William Elder, March 24, 1870, Capt. Crosman to AAAG Lt. Morse, April 4, 1870, LR, Box 27, DT, 5MD, RG 393, NA.

14. *Georgetown Watchman,* quoted by the *Austin Daily State Journal,* May 21, 1870.

15. Helm to Gen. Reynolds, May 30, 1870, LR, Box 25, DT, 5MD, RG 393, NA.

16. *San Antonio Daily Herald,* June 24, 1870, Helm to Gen. Reynolds, May 30, 1870, LR, Box 25, DT, 5MD, RG 393, NA; Craig H. Roell, "Bolivar Jackson Pridgen," *NHT,* 5: 337.

17. *San Antonio Daily Herald,* June 24, 1870; Helm to Gen. Reynolds, May 30, 1870, LR, Box 25, DT, 5MD, RG 393, NA.

18. James Alex Baggett, "Fifth Military District," *NHT,* 2: 996.

19. *Flake's Dailey Bulletin,* July 1, 1871; and see John G. Johnson, "State Police," *NHT,* 6: 75.

20. *Flake's Daily Bulletin,* July 1, 1871; Johnson, "State Police."

21. H. P. N. Gammel, *Laws of Texas, 1822–1897* (Austin: Gammel, 1898); AG James Davidson, *Report of the Adjutant General of the State of Texas for the Year 1870* (Austin: Tracy, Siemering, and Company, 1870) 11; Ann Patton Baenziger, "The Texas State Police During Reconstruction: A Reexamination," *SWHQ* 72 (March 1968): 460–97; *San Antonio Daily Herald,* November 1, 1871; Roster of Special Police, Gonzales County, 1872, AGO, RG 401, Archives, TSL; Johnson, "State Police," *NHT,* 6: 75; Walter Prescott Webb, *The Texas Rangers: A Century of Frontier Defense* (reprint; Austin: University of Texas Press, 1965), 220–21. Webb was extremely biased toward the State Police. He condemned the force even though it had a record of positive achievements. That said, some policemen undoubtedly exceeded their authority; some were dismissed because of their wrongdoing.

22. Helm to Gov. Davis, June 14, 26, 1870, Davis, GP, RG 301, Archives, TSL; *Dayton Journal* (Ohio), February 22, 1879; *New York Times,* February 24, 1879.

23. For the militia, see Otis Singletary, "The Texas Militia During Reconstruction," *SWHQ* 60 (July 1956).

24. Davidson, *Report of the Adjutant General for the Year 1870,* 11; Baenziger, "The Texas State Police, 471–74; *Austin Daily State Journal,* September 17, 1871; *San Antonio Daily Herald,* November 1, 1871; Roster of Special Police, Gonzales County, 1872, AGO, RG 401, Archives, TSL; Johnson, "State Police," *NHT,* 6: 75; Webb, *The Texas Rangers,* 220–21.

25. Davidson, *Report of the Adjutant General for the Year 1870,* 11; Baenziger, "The Texas State Police During Reconstruction," 471–74; *Austin Daily State Journal,* September 17, 1871; *San Antonio Daily Herald,* November 1, 1871; Roster of Special Police, Gonzales County, 1872, RG 401, AGo, Archives, TSL; Johnson, "State Police," *NHT,* 6: 75; Webb, *The Texas Rangers,* 220–21. For the organization of terrorist groups, also see James M. Smallwood, "When the Klan Rode: White Terror in Reconstruction Texas, *Journal of the West* 25 (October 1986): 4–13; Smallwood, *Time of Hope, Time of Despair: Black Texans during Reconstruction* (New York: Kennikat Press, 1981), 29, 51, 53, 55, 61–62, 83–84, 93–94, 126–27, 132, 141–46, 152, 155–57; Barbara Leah Clayton Barnhill, "Lone Star Conspiracy: Racial Violence and the Ku Klux Klan Terror in Post-War Texas, 1865–1877" (M.A. thesis, Oklahoma State University, 1979), passim.

26. C. E. Garland to George Williams, April 6, 1872, Box 674, Department of Justice, NA; and see Baenziger, "Bold Beginnings."

27. For the most thorough examination of high crimes, see Texas Reconstruction Convention, *Reconstruction Convention Journal, 1868–1869,* 1st sess. (Austin: Tracy, Siemering and Company, 1870), 193–94, 500–505; also see summary by Baenziger, "Bold Beginnings," 10–14; Garland to Williams, April 6, 1872, Box 674, Department of Justice, NA.

28. Texas Reconstruction Convention, *Reconstruction Journal,* 1st sess., 198; *Austin Daily State Journal,* August 31, 1871; Davidson, *Report of the Adjutant General, 1870,* 10; Davidson, *Report of the Adjutant General for 1872* (San Antonio: James P. Newcomb and Company, 1873), 10, 237.

29. Texas Reconstruction Convention, *Reconstruction Journal,* 1st sess., 198; *Austin Daily State Journal,* August 31, 1871; Davidson, *Report of the Adjutant General, 1870,* 10; Davidson, *Report of the Adjutant General, 1872,* 10, 237.

30. Garland to Williams, April 6, 1872; Davidson, *Report of the Adjutant General, 1870; Austin Daily State Journal,* August 31, 1871; Baenziger, "Bold Beginnings," 10–14.

31. "Captain Jack Helm," *Gonzales Index,* reprinted in *San Antonio Daily Herald,* July 27, 1870; *Austin Daily State Journal,* August 6, 1870; *Victoria Advocate* August 8, 1870.

32. Baenziger, "State Police," 473–75; R. Sutton, *Sutton-Taylor Feud,* 26–27.

33. R. Sutton, *Sutton-Taylor Feud,* 27–28.

34. *Houston Telegraph,* quoted by *San Antonio Daily Herald,* July 27, 1870.

35. *Austin Daily State Journal,* August 16, 1870.

36. I. R. Kean to Gov. Davis, July 10, 1870, Davis, GP, RG 301, Archives, TSL.

37. AG Davidson to Helm, August 12, 1870, AGO, RG 401, Archives, TSL; *Flake's Daily Bulletin,* September 22, 1870.

38. AG Davidson to Helm, August 31, 1870, AGO, RG 401, Archives, TSL; *Austin Daily State Journal,* August 16, September 2, 1870; *San Antonio Daily Herald,* September 4, 1870; R. Sutton, *Sutton-Taylor Feud,* 34–35.

39. *Austin Daily State Journal,* August 16, September 2, 1870; *San Antonio Daily Herald,* September 4, 1870; Davidson to Helm, August 31, 1870; R. Sutton, *Sutton-Taylor Feud,* 34–35.

40. AG Davidson to Judge Henry Maney, October 31, 1870, Creed Taylor, "Memoirs"; *Austin Daily State Journal,* October 19, 23, 1870; Day, *Sutton-Taylor,* 14; for a review of Henry Kelly's crimes, see Lt. Horton to AAAG Lt. Harris, March 22, 35, 1867, Lt. Horton to AAAG Lt. Richardson, November 1, 1867, Sub-Assistant Commissioner, Hallettsville, LS, BRFAL, RG 105, NA.

41. *Austin Daily State Journal,* October 19, 23, 1870; R. Sutton, *Sutton-Taylor Feud,* 35–36; Creed Taylor, "Memoirs"; AG Davidson to Judge Henry Maney, October 31, 1870, AGO, RG 401, Archives, TSL.

42. *Austin Daily State Journal,* October 19, 23, 1870; R. Sutton, *Sutton-Taylor Feud,* 35–36; Creed Taylor, "Memoirs"; Davidson to Maney, October 31, 1870; Day, *Sutton-Taylor,* 14.

43. Day, *Sutton-Taylor,* 14; R. Sutton, *Sutton-Taylor Feud,* 35–36.

44. *San Antonio Daily Herald,* November 22, 1870; *Austin Daily State Journal,* August 14, October 13, 1870.

45. *Weekly Austin Republican,* November 9, 1870.

46. *Austin Daily State Journal,* August 14, October 13, 1870.

47. *Austin Daily State Journal,* August 14, October 13, November 1, 1870, December 8, 1871; B. J. Pridgen to AG Davidson, September 27, 1870, Gov. Davis to Pridgen, October 7, 31, 1870, Pridgen to Gov. Davis, November 4, 1870, RG 307 (Secretary of State), Archives, TSL; *Austin Daily State Journal,* October 19, 22, 1870; R. Sutton, *Sutton-Taylor Feud,* 34–36.

48. *Austin Daily Republican,* November 1, 1870, December 8, 1871; Pridgen to Davidson, September 27, 1870; Davis to Pridgen, October 7, 31, 1870; Pridgen to Davis, November 4, 1870; *Austin Daily State Journal,* October 19, 22, 1870; Parsons, "DeWitt County Feud," 34–35; R. Sutton, *Sutton-Taylor Feud,* 34–36.

49. *Austin Daily Republican,* November 1, 1870, December 8, 1871; Pridgen to Davidson, September 27, 1870; Davis to Pridgen, October 7, 31, 1870; Pridgen to Davis, November 4, 1870; *Austin Daily State Journal,* October 19, 22, 1870; Parsons, "DeWitt County Feud," 34–35; R. Sutton, *Sutton-Taylor Feud,* 34–36.

50. F. E. Grothaus to Editor, *Austin Daily State Journal,* November 13, 1870.

51. *Austin Daily State Journal,* September 4, 1870.

52. Camillus Jones to editor, *Houston Daily Union,* December 17, 1870. Two other letters to the editor published on December 17 discussed the case, offering various details.

53. *Austin Daily State Journal,* April 11, 1871.

54. *Austin Daily State Journal,* June 7, 871.

55. W. E. Horne to AG Davidson, February 24, 1871, AGO, RG 401, Archives, TSL.

56. Capt. John Sansom to AG Davidson, February 17, 1871, AGO, RG 401, Archives, TSL.

57. Capt. A. McCluny to Gov. Davis, June 17, 1871, Gov. Davis to McCluny, July 17, 1871, Davis, GP, RG 301, Archives, TSL; *Austin Daily State Journal,* April 25, 1871; *San Antonio Daily Herald,* April 21, May 3, 1871.

58. McCluny to Davis, June 17, 1871; Davis to McCluny, July 17, 1871; *Austin Daily State Journal,* April 25, 1871; *San Antonio Daily Herald,* April 21, May 3, 1871.

59. *Austin Daily State Journal,* April 25, 1871; *San Antonio Daily Herald,* April 21, May 3, 1871; McCluny to Davis, June 17, 1871; Davis to McCluny, July 17, 1871; Sonnichsen, *I'll Die Before I'll Run,* 31.

Chapter 7

1. Midwife, quoted in John Warren Hunter, "Inside Story of Life of John Wesley Hardin," *Frontier Times* 1 (April 1924): 8–10; Anonymous, *Over a Century of Faith* (Whitewright, Texas: First United Methodist Church, n.d); 2–5, copy in Crouch Collection, Regional History Center, VC/UHV; Metz, *Dark Angel,* 1–4.

2. Robert Wooster, "Moscow, Texas," *NHT,* 4: 852–53; and see Polk County Bicentennial Commission, *Pictorial History of Polk County, Texas, 1846–1910,* rev. ed. (Livingston: Polk County Bicentennial Commission, 1978); Patricia B. Hensley, "Sumter, Texas," *NHT,* 6: 150; see also Ed E. Bartholomew, *800 Texas Ghost Towns* (Fort Davis: Frontier Press, 1971); John Leffler and Christopher Long, "Trinity County, Texas," *NHT,* 6: 565–67; Patricia B. and Joseph W. Hensley, eds. *Trinity County Beginnings* (Dallas: Curtis Media Corporation, 1985); U.S. Census, Trinity County, 1860, for population statistics.

3. Richard B. McCaslin, "Polk County," *NHT,* 5: 157–59; and see Polk County Bicentennial Commission, *Polk County, 1846–1910;* U.S. Census, Polk County, 1860, for population statistics.

4. Metz, *Dark Angel,* 6.

5. Smallwood, *Time of Hope,* 126, 149; Web Mattox, *The Black Sheep* (Quanah: Nortex Press, 1975), 50–52.

6. For the classic volume on the coming of the Civil War, see David M. Potter, *The Impending Crisis, 1846–1861* (New York: Harper and Row, 1976). Also see Potter's *Divisions and Stresses of Reunion, 1845–1876* (Glenview: Scott, Foresman, 1973).

7. Hardin, *Life,* 5–6; and see Maddox, *Black Sheep,* 51; Potter, *Impending Crisis* and *Divisions and Stresses.*

8. Hardin, *Life,* 5–6; Maddox, *Black Sheep,* 51.

9. Lt. Charles Schmidt to Lt. Vernou, April 30, May 31, December 30, 1868, Sub-Assistant Commissioner, Sumter, LS, BRFAL, RG 105, NA.

10. H. S. Johnson to George Allen, August 31, 1867, Lt. Schmidt to Lt. Vernou, April 30, May 31, December 30 1868, Sub-Assistant Commissioner, Sumpter, LS, BRFAL, RG 105, NA; Gov. E. Pease to Gen. Reynolds, October 8, 1868, anonymous to Gov. E. Pease, November 12, 1868, E. Pease, GP, RG 301, Archives, TSL; Paul R. Scott, "Reconstruction," in *Trinity County Beginnings,* unnumbered pages.

11. Lt. Schmidt to Lt. Vernou, October 4, 1868, Sub-Assistant Commissioner, Moscow, LS, BRFAL, RG 105, NA.

12. Lt. James P. Butler to AAAG Lt. Richardson, November 30, 1867, Sub-Assistant Commissioner, Huntsville, LS, Schmidt to Vernou, October 4, 1868, Sub-Assistant Commissioner, Moscow, LS, BRFAL, RG 105, J. C. DeLossas to Gen. J. A. Hoover, September 29, 1865, AAAG Maj. T. J. Hayden to Col. E. [?], March 10, 1870, LR, Box 1, DT, RG 393, NA; A. J. Harrison to Morgan C. Hamilton, March 14, 1870, Davis, GP, RG 301, Archives, TSL.

13. Vincent P. Rennert, *Western Outlaws* (New York: Crowell-Collier Press, 1968), 6; Metz, *Dark Angel,* 6–7; A. J. Wright, "A Gunfighter's Southern Vacation," *Quarterly of the National Association and Center for Outlaw and Lawman History,* n.d., 12, copy in Crouch Collection, Regional History Center, VC/UHV; Maddox, *The Black Sheep,* 53.

14. Scott, "Reconstruction" Norman B. Wiltsey, "40 Times a Killer!" *Frontier Times* (December/January 1964): 6; Aline Rothe, "Where Hardin Started Running," *Frontier Times* (June/July 1977): 36–38; Rennert, *Western Outlaws,* 7; Metz, *Dark Angel,* 11–14.

15. Scott, "Reconstruction"; Wiltsey, "40 Times a Killer!" 6; Rothe, "Where Hardin Started Running," *Frontier Times,* 36–38; Rennert, *Western Outlaws,* 7; Metz, *Dark Angel,* 11–14.

16. Scott, "Reconstruction"; Wiltsey, "40 Times a Killer!" 6; Rothe, "Where Hardin Started Running"; Rennert, *Western Outlaws,* 7; Metz, *Dark Angel,* 11–14.

17. Hunter, "Inside Story of Hardin," *Frontier Times,* 8–10.

18. Lt. Schmidt to AAAG, November 29, 1868, Sub-Assistant Commissioner, Livingston, Texas, LS, BRFAL, RG 105, NA.

19. Ibid.

20. Metz, *Dark Angel,* 15–16; Maddox, *The Black Sheep,* 55.

21. Wiltsey, "40 Times a Killer!" 6–7; Maddox, *The Black Sheep,* 54–55; Metz, *Dark Angel,* 16.

22. For accounts of Reconstruction violence that ex-Confederate Democrats aimed at white Unionists and freedpeople, see James M. Smallwood, "When the Klan Rode: White Terror in Reconstruction Texas," *Journal of the West* 25 (October 1986): 4–13; Barbara Clayton Barnhill, "The Lone Star Conspiracy: Racial Violence and the Ku Klux Klan in Post-Civil War Texas, 1865–1877" (M.A. thesis, Oklahoma State University, 1979); Rebecca Kosary, "Regression to Barbarism in Reconstruction Texas: White Violence against African-Americans from the Texas Freedmen's Bureau Records, 1865–1868" (M.A. thesis, Sam Houston State University, 2002). Also see Smallwood, Crouch, and Peacock, *Murder and Mayhem.*

23. See "Monthly Rosters of Bureau Agents in Texas," BRFAL, RG 105, NA.

24. Wyvonne Putman, *Navarro County History* (Quanah: Nortex Press, 1975), 97, 113–15; and see *Dallas News,* July 2, 1861; *Dallas Times Herald,* August 15, 1962; Metz, *Dark Angel,* 16–17; Rennert, *Western Outlaws,* 8.

25. Putman, *Navarro County History,* 97; Wiltsey, "40 Times a Killer!" 7–8; Metz, *Dark Angel,* 17–18; Rennert, *Western Outlaws,* 8–10.

26. Hardin, *Life,* 19–21; Putman, *Navarro County History,* 97; Wiltsey, "40 Times a Killer!" 7–8; Metz, *Dark Angel,* 17–18; Rennert, *Western Outlaws,* 8–10; for more on Simp Dixon's nefarious career of crime, see Smallwood, Crouch, and Peacock, *Murder and Mayhem.*

27. *Austin Daily Democratic Statesman,* August 30, 1877; *El Paso Daily Herald,* September 4, 1895; Chuck Parsons, "Tell Wes to be a Good Man: Examining an Early Hardin Killing," *National Outlaw and Lawman Association Quarterly* 6 (April 1981): 3–8.

28. Hardin, *Life,* 23–24; Metz, *Dark Angel,* 22–23; Rennert, *Western Outlaws,* 9–10; Charles Askins, *Gunfighters* (Washington, D.C.: National Rifle Association, 1981), 119.

29. Hardin, *Life,* 23–24; Metz, *Dark Angel,* 22–23; Rennert, *Western Outlaws,* 9–10; Askins, *Gunfighters,* 119.

30. Wiltsey, "40 Times a Killer!" *Frontier Times,* 10; Rennert, *Western Outlaws,* 10–12; Owen P. White, *Triggerfingers* (New York: G. P. Putnam's Sons, 1926), 269–70, 276–77; Capt. John Whitney to AAAG Lt. Morse, February 15, 1870, LR, Box 14, DT, 5MD, RG 393, NA.

31. Whitney to Morse; Wiltsey, "40 Times a Killer!" 10; Rennert, *Western Outlaws,* 10–12; White, *Triggerfingers* 269–70, 276–77.

32. Wiltsey, "40 Times a Killer!" 10; William Waters, *A Gallery of Western Badmen* (Covington: Americana Publications, 1954), 5–6.

33. Judge C. C. Wood to Gov. Davis, November 10, 1870, Davis, GP, RG 301, Archives, TSL; Metz, *Dark Angel,* 28, 313.

34. *Flake's Daily Bulletin,* February 4, 1871; *Denison Daily Herald,* August 26, 1877; Metz, *Dark Angel,* 28–33; Wiltsey, "40 Times a Killer!" 10–11.

35. *Flake's Daily Bulletin,* February 4, 1871; *Denison Daily Herald,* August 26, 1877; Metz, *Dark Angel,* 28–33; Wiltsey, "40 Times a Killer!" 10–11.

36. *Denison Daily Herald,* August 26, 1877; Wiltsey, "40 Times a Killer!" 11.

37. *Galveston Daily News,* March 8, 1876; Manning C. Clements to Shirley J. Norris, July 20, 1983, copy in Crouch Collection, Regional History Center, VC/UHV; Hardin, *Life,* 33; Metz, *Dark Angel,* 33–34.

38. *Galveston Daily News,* March 8, 1876; Metz, *Dark Angel,* 33–34; Hardin, *Life,* 33.

39. Metz, *Dark Angel,* 34–72; Metz, *The Shooters* (El Paso: Mangan Books, 1976), 256–57; K. S. White, "Genealogy of Frederick Duderstadt and Henrietta Tennille Duderstadt," ms, copy in Crouch Collection, Regional History Center, UV/UHV.

40. Beauregard Moye, "Babe Moye, Biographical notes," n.d., copies in possession of Wayne A. Sirmon and in possession of the author; Metz, *Dark Angel,* 34–72; Metz, *The Shooters,* 245–57.

41. Waldo E. Koop, "Enter John Wesley Hardin: A Dim Trail to Abilene," *The Prairie Scout* 2 (1974): 1–29, copy in Crouch Collection, Regional History Center, VC/UHV.

42. Ibid., 29.

43. For the charge against Hardin in Missouri, see AG Davidson, *Report of the Adjutant General of the State of Texas for the Year 1871* (San Antonio: James P. Newcomb and Company, 1872); for Johnson's crimes, see Smallwood, Crouch, and Peacock, *Murder and Mayhem.*

44. *Galveston Daily News,* March 8, 1876; Metz, *Dark Angel,* 34–74; Hardin, *Life,* 33–61.

CHAPTER 8

1. *San Antonio Daily Herald,* October 31, November 9, 1871; Metz, *Dark Angel,* 73–75; John "Red" Dunn, *Perilous Trails of Texas* (Dallas: Southwest Press, 1932), 10–11; Hardin, *Life,* 62–63; and see AG Steele to Gov. Coke, July 10, 1874, Coke, GP, RG 301, Archives, TSL.

2. Hardin, *Life,* 25.

3. *Austin Daily State Journal,* April 11, June 7, September 9, 1871; as noted in another chapter, for Helm's troubles in Hopkins County, see Pickering and Falls, *Brush Men and Vigilantes.*

4. *Flake's Semi-Weekly Bulletin,* November 8, 1871; *San Antonio Daily Herald,* October 31, November 9, 1871; James H. Thompson, "A Nineteenth Century History of Cameron County, Texas" (M.A. thesis, University of Texas, 1965), 99; Metz, *Dark Angel,* 73–75; Dunn, *Perilous Trails,* 10–11; Hardin, *Life,* 62–63; Henry Maney to Gov. Davis, October 29, 1871, Davis, GP, RG 301, Archives, TSL.

5. Maney to Davis, October 29, 1871; Gov. Davis, "Proclamation of Reward," November 5, 1871, Davis, GP, RG 301, Roster of Special Police, Gonzales County, AGO, RG 401, Archives, TSL; Hardin, *Life,* 62; Wesley G. Hardin [John Wesley Hardin], indictment for murder, Grand Jury, Gonzales County, October 24, 1871, No. 1005, copy in possession of the author, copy in Crouch Collection, Regional History Center, VC/UHV; Metz, *Dark Angel,* 73–75; *Flake's Semi-Weekly Bulletin,* November 8, 1871; *San Antonio Daily Herald,* October 31, November 9, 1871.

6. Wesley G. Hardin indictment for murder; *Flake's Semi-Weekly Bulletin,* November 8, 1871; *San Antonio Daily Herald,* October 31, November 9, 1871; Maney to Davis, October 29, 1871; Davis, "Proclamation of Reward"; November 5, 1871, Davis, GP, RG 301, Archives, TSL; Hardin, *Life,* 63; Dunn, *Perilous Trails,* 10–11; Roster of Special Police, Gonzales County, AGO, RG 401, Archives, TSL; Metz, *Dark Angel,* 73–75.

7. *Flake's Daily Bulletin,* January 31, 1872.

8. Metz, *Dark Angel,* 77; Hardin, *Life,* 63–64.

9. W. Harden [sic] and Jane Bowen, marriage license no. 1576, February 27, 1872, Gonzales County, copy in possession of the author, copy in Crouch Collection, Regional History Center, VC/UHV; Wolff, "Gunslinger Called Smily Home," *Victoria Advocate,* May 16, 1990.

10. Norman Barnett, "Coon Hollow," *Nixon News,* April 24, 1986, copy in possession of the author, copy in Crouch Collection, Regional History Center, VC/UHV; Wolff, "Gunslinger," *Victoria Advocate,* May 16, 1990. For more information on Jane Hardin, see Nelson Allen, "Gonzales County Bears Marks of Texas Gunfighter," *San Antonio Express-News,* August 19, 1989. For more on Fred Duderstadt, see Francis Duderstadt Hartmann, *The Duderstadts* (La Vernia, Texas: privately printed, 1967).

11. Charley Eckhardt, "New Biography Explores Life of Hardin," *Seguin Gazrette-Enterprise,* n.d., clipping in Crouch Collection, Regional History Center, VC/UHV; and see Hardin, *Life,* passim; Metz, *Dark Angel,* 77–79, 206–7.

12. *State of Texas vs. John Wesley Hardin,* no. 1060–1336, *State of Texas vs. John Wesley Hardin,* no. 1003, District Court, Gonzales County, Gonzales County Courthouse, copy in Crouch Collection, Regional History Center, VC/UHV; Wolff, "Gunslinger," *Victoria Advocate,* May 16, 1990.

13. Hardin, *Life,* 66–67; Metz, *Dark Angel,* 80–81.

14. Hardin, *Life,* 66–67; Metz, *Dark Angel,* 80–81.

15. Harrell Odom, "Hardin Wounded in Trinity," unidentified newspaper clipping, July 20, 1990, in Crouch Collection, Regional History Center, VC/UHV; Hardin, *Life,* 68–69; John Wesley Hardin, Murder indictment, August 29, 1874, Grand Jury, Trinity County, copy in Archives, TSL.

16. Odom, "Hardin Wounded in Trinity"; Hardin, *Life,* 68–69; Hardin, murder indictment, August 29, 1874, Grand Jury, Trinity County, copy in Archives, TSL.

17. Odom, "Hardin Wounded in Trinity"; Hardin, Murder indictment, August 29, 1874.

18. Odom, "Hardin Wounded in Trinity"; Hardin *Life,* 68–76; Metz, *Dark Angel,* 85–87.

19. Odom, "Hardin Wounded in Trinity"; Hardin, *Life,* 68–76; Metz, *Dark Angel,* 85–87.

20. Odom, "Hardin Wounded in Trinity"; *Austin Daily Democratic Statesman,* August 10, 30, 1877; *San Antonio Daily Herald,* March 25, 1873; Hardin, *Life,* 76–77; Metz, *Dark Angel,* 86–87.

21. *Austin Daily Democratic Statesman,* August 10, 30, 1877; *San Antonio Daily Herald,* March 25, 1873; Odom, "Hardin Wounded in Trinity"; Hardin, *Life,* 76–77; Metz, *Dark Angel,* 86–87.

22. *Austin Daily State Journal,* August 20, 24, 1872.

23. AG Steele to Gov. Coke, July 10, 1874, AGO, RG 401, Archives, TSL; R. Sutton, *Sutton-Taylor Feud,* 36–37; Hyatt, *The Feud,* 67. A tall tale about Pitkin's death has survived into the contemporary era. Supposedly, Bill Sutton and others had taken a cow bell, entered Taylor's cornfield, and rang the bell, knowing that Pitkin would come outside and run the cow out of the field. However, that same tall tale was used by other Taylors to explain other shootings. One Bill Sutton descendant even held that it was the Taylors who actually rang a cow bell on one occasion when they were trying to get Sutton out of his house to kill him. Given the complete lack of evidence, such a tale should probably be forgotten.

24. John R. Shook, telegram, to Gov. Davis, May 31, 1873, William [?] to Gov. Davis, April 25, 1873, Davis, GP, RG 301, Archives, TSL; Parsons, "Postscript to the Death of Brown Bowen," *Real West* (September 1979): 36–39, 61–62; Gonzales County Historical Commission, *The History of Gonzales County, Texas* (Dallas: Curtis Media Corporation, 1986), 222; Metz, *Dark Angel,* 88–91.

25. Tom Holderman, inquest, copy in Crouch Collection, Regional History Center, VC/UHV; Shook, telegram, to Davis, May 31, 1873, [?] to Davis, April 25, 1873; Parsons, "Death of Brown Bowen"; Gonzales County Historical Commission, *History of Gonzales County,* 222; Metz, *Dark Angel,* 88–91.

26. William Steele, *Report of the Adjutant General of the State of Texas for the Year 1873* (Austin: np., 1874), 122.

27. Ibid.

28. AG Britton to Gov. Davis, "Report on Crime," April 18, 1873, [?] to Davis, April 25, 1873, Davis, GP, RG 301, Archives, TSL; Parsons, "Death of Brown Bowen" *Gonzales Inquirer,* April 13, 1878; Gonzales County Historical Commission, *History of Gonzales County,* 222; Metz, *Dark Angel,* 88–91; Parsons, *Bowen and Hardin,* 45–46.

29. AG Britton to Gov. Davis, "Report on Crime," April 18, 1873, Davis, GP, RG 301, Archives, TSL; Holderman, inquest, copy in Crouch Collection, Regional History Center, VC/UHV; Parsons, "Death of Brown Bowen," *Real West:* 36–39, 61–62; *Gonzales Inquirer,* April 13, 1878; Gonzales County Historical Commission, *History of Gonzales County,* 222; Metz, *Dark Angel,* 88–91; Parsons, *Bowen and Hardin,* 45–46.

30. AG Britton to Gov. Davis, "Report on Crime," April 18, 1873, Davis, GP, RG 301, Archives, TSL.

31. I.B. Lyman, W. M. Bryce, et al. to Gov. Davis, May 1, 1873, AG Britton to Gov. Davis, "Report on Crime," April 18, 1873, Davis, GP, RG 301, Archives, TSL.

32. B. Lyman, W. M. Bryce, et al. to Gov. Davis, May 1, 1873, AG Britton to Gov. Davis, "Report on Crime," April 18, 1873, Davis, GP, RG 301, Archives, TSL.

33. AG Britton to Gov. Davis, "Report on Crime," April 18, 1873, Davis, GP, RG 301, Archives, TSL; Hardin, *Life,* 79–80; Sutton, *Sutton-Taylor Feud,* 41; Odom, "Hardin Wounded in Trinity," unidentified newspaper clipping, July 20, 1990, in Crouch Collection, Regional History Center, VC/UHV.

34. AG Britton to Gov. Davis, "Report on Crime," April 18, 1873, Davis, GP, RG 301, J. R. Raby, Sheriff of Coryell County, to AG, April 4, 1873, AGO, RG 401, Archives, TSL; Parsons, "DeWitt County Feud," 36.

35. AG Britton to Gov. Davis, "Report on Crime," April 18, 1873, Davis, GP, RG 301, Archives, TSL.

36. Ibid.

37. *San Antonio Herald,* R. June 20, 1873; Sutton, *Sutton-Taylor Feud,* 40, 45; Metz, *Dark Angel,* 101; Parsons, "DeWitt County Feud," 36; Raby to AG Steele, April 4, 1873, Parsons, "Treaties of Peace, Acts of War," *Real West Yearbook,* 50–52.

38. Johnson, "State Police," 75.

39. Metz, *Dark Angel,* 107–8.

40. J. Redmon to AG Britton, May 1, 1873, AGO Papers, RG 401, Archives, TSL.

41. Ibid.

42. Ibid.

43. L. B. Wright to Gov. Davis, August 16, 1873, Davis, GP, RG 301, Archives, TSL; *Houston Telegraph,* July 27, 1873; Parsons, "DeWitt County Feud," 36; White, *Trigger-*

fingers, 124; Hardin, *Life,* 82; Metz, *Dark Angel,* 108–9; Parsons, "Treaties of Peace," 50–52.

44. *LaGrange Fayette County New Era,* August 8, 1873; Parsons, "DeWitt County Feud," 36; *San Antonio Daily Express,* July 25, 1873; *Houston Telegraph,* July 30, 1873; *Austin Daily Democratic Statesman,* November 8, 1874.

45. *LaGrange Fayette County New Era,* August 8, 1873; Parsons, "DeWitt County Feud," 36. Various state newspapers reported the death of Helm, but most gave inaccurate details. See *San Antonio Daily Express,* July 25, 1873; *Houston Telegraph,* July 30, 1873; *Austin Daily Democratic Statesman,* November 8, 1874; *Dallas Times Herald,* August 2, 1873. Although some writers have observed that most likely Helm did not have the intellect of an inventor, indeed he was one. See Helm patent, no. 139,062, May 20, 1873, copy in Roy Slyvan Dunn Papers, CAH, UTL.

46. John W. Hardin, Arrest Warrant, August 9, 1873, District Court, DeWitt County Courthouse, copy in Crouch Collection, Regional History Center, VC/UHV; Britton to Davis, "Report on Crime."

47. Wright to Gov. Davis, August 16, 1873, Davis, GP, RG 301, Archives, TSL; *San Antonio Daily Express,* August 17, 1873; *Houston Telegraph,* August 20, 1873; *Gonzales Inquirer,* quoted by *Austin Daily State Journal,* August 20, 1873; Parsons, "DeWitt County Feud," 37; Hardin, *Life,* 84–85.

48. Wright to Davis, August 16, 1873, Davis, GP, RG 301, Archives, TSL; Metz, *Dark Angel,* 115–16; Sutton, *Sutton-Taylor Feud,* 46.

49. Wright to Davis, August 16, 1873; *San Antonio Daily Express,* August 17, 1873; *Houston Telegraph,* August 20, 1873; *Gonzales Inquirer,* quoted by *Austin Daily State Journal,* August 20, 1873; Parsons, "DeWitt County Feud," 37; Hardin, *Life,* 84–85; Metz, *Dark Angel,* 116.

50. Wright to Davis, August 16, 1873; *Gonzales Inquirer,* quoted by *Austin Daily State Journal,* August 20, 1873; *Houston Telegraph,* August 20, 1873; Parsons, "DeWitt County Feud," 37–38; Parsons, "Treaties of Peace," 50–51.

51. Wright to Davis, August 16, 1873; *Gonzales Inquirer,* quoted by *Austin Daily State Journal,* August 20, 1873; *Houston Telegraph,* August 20, 1873; Parsons, "DeWitt County Feud," 37–38; Parsons, "Treaties of Peace," 50–51.

52. *Cuero Star,* December 31, 1873; Wiesiger, "Sutton-Taylor Feud," notes, 10; Wolff, "Taylor-Sutton Feud," notes; Parsons, "DeWitt County Feud," 38. And see U.S. House, Misc. Doc., no. 127, passim; Day, *Sutton-Taylor,* 19–20, 40; R. Sutton, *Sutton-Taylor Feud,* 50.

53. *Cuero Star,* December 31, 1873, January 9, 1874; Parsons, "DeWitt County Feud," 38; Metz, *Dark Angel,* 117–18; Day, *Sutton-Taylor,* 20–21; Parsons, "Treaties of Peace," 52.

54. *Cuero Star,* December 31, 1873, January 9, 1874; Parsons, "DeWitt County Feud," 38; Metz, *Dark Angel,* 117–18; Day, *Sutton-Taylor,* 20–21; Parsons, "Treaties of Peace," 52.

55. Maj. Jones to AG Steele, July 15, 1874, AGO, RG 401, Archives, TSL.

CHAPTER 9

1. Havins, *Something about Brown,* 28; Eckhardt, "New Biography Explores Life of Hardin," *Seguin Gazette-Enterprise,* n.d., newspaper clipping in Crouch Collection, Regional History Center, VC/UHV; Metz, *Dark Angel,* 119–24.

2. "Historical Memoranda of Comanche," *Comanche Chief,* June 6, 1924.

3. Criminal Docket no. 310, District Court, Comanche County, February 10, 1874, copy in Crouch Collection, Regional History Center, VC/UHV; *Comanche Chief,* June 6, 1924; Metz, *Dark Angel,* 125.

4. Havins, *Something about Brown,* 28; W. M. Green, "Breaking up the Lawless Element in Texas," *Frontier Times* (May 1924): 3.

5. Weisiger, "Sutton-Taylor Feud," notes, 9, 13–14, VF; Hardin, *Life,* 86.

6. *Victoria Advocate,* May 21, 1874; Parsons, "DeWitt County Feud," 40; R. Sutton, *Sutton-Taylor Feud,* 52–53; *Clarksville Standard,* June 7, 1873; Metz, *Dark Angel,* 127–30; Hardin, *Life,* 86–87; Walter Clay Dixson, "The Barekman-Anderson Prelude to Comanche," *Quarterly of the National Association for Outlaw and Lawman History* 18 (April–June 1994): 11–13; Craig H. Roell, "Bolivar Jackson Pridgen," *NHT,* 5: 337; Day, *Sutton-Taylor Feud,* 23; Weisiger, "Sutton-Taylor Feud," notes, 10–11.

7. *Victoria Advocate,* May 21, 1874; Parsons, "DeWitt County Feud," 40; R. Sutton, *Sutton-Taylor Feud,* 37, 52–53; Metz, *Dark Angel,* 127–30; Day, *Sutton-Taylor,* 23–24.

8. Weisiger, "Taylor-Sutton Feud," notes, 11–12; *Victoria Advocate,* May 21, 1874; Parsons, "DeWitt County Feud," 40; R. Sutton, *Sutton-Taylor Feud,* 37, 52–53; Metz, *Dark Angel,* 127–30; Day, *Sutton-Taylor,* 23–24.

9. *Victoria Advocate,* May 21, 1874; Parsons, "DeWitt County Feud," 40; R. Sutton, *Sutton-Taylor Feud,* 37, 52–53; Metz, *Dark Angel,* 127–30; Day, *Sutton-Taylor,* 23–24; Weisinger, "Taylor-Sutton Feud," notes, 11–12, Wolff, "DeWitt Feud Was Longest, Deadliest in Texas History," *Victoria Advocate,* December 5, 2003; Cynthia Salm to Wolff, e-mail, December 7, 2003, copy in Wolff, "Sutton-Taylor Feud," VF, copy in possession of the author.

10. *Victoria Advocate,* May 21, 1874; Parsons, "DeWitt County Feud," 40; R. Sutton, *Sutton-Taylor Feud,* 52–53; Metz, *Dark Angel,* 127–30; Wolff, "DeWitt County Feud," *Victoria Advocate,* December 5, 2003.

11. Green, "Breaking up the Lawless Element in Texas," *Frontier Times,* 3; Havins, *Something about Brown,* 28.

12. Green, "Breaking up the Lawless Element in Texas," *Frontier Times,* 3; Havins, *Something about Brown,* 28.

13. *Cuero Star,* January 23, April 8, 15, June 11, 1874; *San Antonio Daily Express,* June 14, 1874; *Galveston Daily News,* November 19–23, 1875; *Austin Daily Democratic Statesman,* January 6, 1876.

14. *Cuero Star,* January 23, April 8, 15, June 11, 1874; *San Antonio Daily Express,* June 14, 1874; *Galveston Daily News,* November 19–23, 1875; *Austin Daily Democratic Statesman,* January 6, 1876; Parsons, "Rube Brown and the Atmosphere of Violence," *The Brand Book* 24 (Winter 1986): 13–20; Parsons, "DeWitt County Feud," 40; Webb, *The Texas Rangers,* 233.

15. *Cuero Star,* January 23, April 8, 15, June 11, 1874; *San Antonio Daily Express,* June 14, 1874; *Galveston Daily News,* November 19–23, 1875; *Austin Daily Democratic Statesman,* January 6, 1876; Parsons, "Rube Brown," in *The Brand Book,* 13–20; Parsons, "DeWitt County Feud," 40; Webb, *The Texas Rangers,* 233.

16. Hardin, *Life,* 88–89; Dixson, "Barekman-Anderson Prelude," 13.

17. Capt. John R. Waller to Coke, June 6, 1874, AGO, RG 401, Petitioners J. R. Fleming, G. A. Wright, William Barnet, et al. to Coke, May 28, 1874, Coke, GP, RG 301, Archives, TSL; Havins, *Something about Brown,* 28–29; *Dallas Weekly Herald,* June 6, 1874; Hardin, *Life,* 88–89.

18. Waller to Coke, June 6, 1874; Fleming, Wright, Barnes, et al. to Coke, May 28, 1874; Coke, GP, RG 301, Archives, TSL; Green, "Breaking up the Lawless Element," *Frontier Times,* 3–6; Havins, *Something about Brown,* 29–30; Hardin, *Life,* 93–94; Dixson, "Barekman-Anderson Prelude," 19; Metz, *Dark Angel,* 139.

19. Fleming, Wright, Barnes, et al. to Coke, May 28, 1874; Green, "Breaking up the Lawless Element," 3–6; Havins, *Something about Brown,* 29–30; Hardin, *Life,* 93–94; Dixson, "Barekman-Anderson Prelude," 13; Metz, *Dark Angel,* 139.

20. Fleming, Wright, Barnes, et al. to Coke, May 28, 1874; Green, "Breaking up the Lawless Elements," 3–6; Havins, *Something about Brown,* 29–30.

21. Fleming, Wright, Barnes, et al. to Coke, May 28, 1874; Green, "Breaking up the Lawless Element," 3–6; Havins, *Something about Brown,* 29–30.

22. Maj. John Jones, General Order No. 6, June 3, 1874, Waller to Jones, May 30, 1874, Coke, GP, RG 301, Archives, TSL; Molly Godbold, "Comanche and the Hardin Gang," *SWHQ* 67 (July 1963), Pt. 1: 73–77, *SWHQ* 68 (October 1963), Pt. 2: 247; Green, "Breaking the Lawless Element," 3–6; Havins, *Something about Brown,* 29–30; Metz, *Dark Angel,* 142.

23. *Austin Democratic Statesman,* June 17, 1874; Waller to Jones, May 30, 1874, Metz, *Dark Angel,* 142–43.

24. Jones, General Order No. 6; Waller to Jones, May 30, 1874; Godbold, "Comanche and the Hardin Gang" Pt. 1: 73–77, Pt. 2: 247; Green, "Breaking up the Lawless Element," 3–6; Havins, *Something about Brown.* 29–30; Metz, *Dark Angel,* 142.

25. Godbold, "Comanche and the Hardin Gang" SWHQ, Pt. 1: 73–77, Pt. 2, 248–49; Green, "Breaking up the Lawless Element," *Frontier Times,* 3–6; Havins, *Something about Brown,* 29; Hardin, *Life,* 95–96.

26. *Austin Daily Democratic Statesman,* June 17, 1874; Godbold, "Comanche and the Hardin Gang," Pt. 2: 250–52; Hardin, *Life,* 99–100.

27. *Corsicana Observer,* June 17, 1874; *Denison News,* quoted by *Austin Daily Democratic Statesmen,* June 17, 1874; Godbold, "Comanche and the Hardin Gang," Pt. 2: 250–52; Dixson, "Barekman-Anderson Prelude," 15.

28. *Corsicana* Observer, June 17, 1874; *Denison News,* quoted by *Austin Daily Democratic Statesman,* June 17, 1874; Godbold, "Comanche and the Hardin Gang," Pt. 2, 250–52; Dixson, "Barekman-Anderson Prelude," 15.

29. Waller to Coke, June 6, 1874; Jones to Steele, July 1, 1874 AGO, RG 401, Archives, TSL; *Corsicana Observer,* June 17, 1874; Godbold, "Comanche and the Hardin Gang," Pt. 2, 252–53.

30. *Comanche Chief,* quoted by *Austin Daily Democratic Statesman,* n.d., copy in Crouch Collection, Texas History Center, VC/UHV; Green, "Breaking up the Lawless Element," *Frontier Times,* 3–6; Havins, *Something about Brown,* 29–30; "Historical Memoranda of Comanche," *Comanche Chief,* June 6, 1924; Godbold, "Comanche and the Hardin Gang," Pt. 2: 253, 256–57; Waller, "Exhibit D: Log of Company A," AGO, Record Group 401, Archives, TSL.

31. *Comanche Chief,* quoted by *Austin Daily Democratic Statesman,* n.d., copy in Crouch Collection, Texas History Center, VC/UHV; Green, "Breaking up the Lawless Element," *Frontier Times,* 3–6; Havins, *Something about Brown,* 29–30; "Historical Memoranda of Comanche," *Comanche Chief,* June 6, 1924; Goldbold, "Comanche and the Hardin Gang," Pt. 2, 253, 256–57. After Jo Hardin's death, a legend grew that he was *not really hanged.* Bill Hoge, a barber in Oologah, Oklahoma, spread the tale, claiming that he knew Jo Hardin and knew the spot where he was eventually buried

in an unmarked grave in the Oologah Cemetery. The tale is silly at best, ridiculous at worst. See Arthus Shoemaker, "Mysterious Joe Hardin," *True West* 35 (February 1988): 56–57.

32. *Cuero Star,* January 23, April 8, 15, June 11, 1874; *San Antonio Daily Express,* June 14, 1874; *Galveston Daily News,* November 19–23, 1875; *Austin Daily Democratic Statesman,* January 6, 1876; Parsons, "Rube Brown," 13–20; Parsons, "DeWitt County Feud," 40.

33. Jones, General Order No. 2, July 15. 1874, AGO, RG 401, Archives, TSL.

34. Capt. W. J. Maltby to Jones, June 7, 1874, Jones to Steele, July 1, 1874, AGO, RG 401, Archives, TSL; Godbold, "Comanche and the Hardin Gang, Pt. 2: 253; Day, *Sutton-Taylor Feud,* 24–25; Sutton, *Sutton-Taylor Feud,* 61.

35. *San Antonio Daily Express,* May 26, 1874; *New Orleans Daily Picayune,* June 5, 1874; Parsons, "DeWitt County Feud," 40; Day, *Sutton-Taylor,* 29–30.

36. Sgt. J. V. Atkinson to Jones, June 24, 1874, AGO, RG 401, Archives, TSL; *Cuero Star,* quoted by *San Antonio Daily Herald,* June 30, July 1, 1874; Green, "Breaking up the Lawless Element," *Frontier Times,* 3–6; Godbold, "Comanche and the Hardin Gang," Pt. 2: 253–54; Hardin, *Life,* 101; Parsons, "DeWitt County Feud," 40.

37. J. D. Stephens to Gov. Coke, June 10, 1874, Coke, GP, RG 301, Archives, TSL.

38. Atkinson to Jones, June 24, 1874; *Cuero Star,* quoted by *San Antonio Daily Herald,* June 30, July 1, 1874; Green, "Breaking up the Lawless Element," 3–6; Godbold, "Comanche and the Hardin Gang," Pt. 2: 253–54; Hardin, *Life,* 101–2; Parsons, "DeWitt County Feud," 40; Day, *Sutton-Taylor Feud,* 28–29; Henry Wolff, "Taylor-Sutton Feud," *Victoria Advocate,* July 12, 1988.

39. A. Steele to Gov. Coke, July 14, 1874, AGO, RG 401, Archives, TSL.

CHAPTER 10

1. Green, "Breaking up the Lawless Element," *Frontier Times,* 3–6.

2. Ibid.

3. Ibid.

4. Capt. Maltby to Maj. Jones, June 7, 13, 1874, AGO, RG 401, Archives, TSL.

5. Maj. Jones to AG Steele, July 1, 1874, AGO, RG 401, Archives, TSL.

6. VanCleave, "autobiography" Parsons, "DeWitt County Feud," 41; Parsons, "Forgotten Feudist: George Tennille," *Frontier Times* 50 (December–January 1976): 28–29, 44–45; Sutton, *Sutton-Taylor Feud,* 62.

7. VanCleave, "Autobiography"; Parsons, "DeWitt County Feud," 41; Parsons, "George Tennille," *Frontier Times,* 28, 29, 44–45; R. Sutton, *Sutton-Taylor Feud,* 62.

8. Capt. McNelly to AG Steele, August 31, 1874, AGO, RG 401, Archives, TSL.

9. Ibid.

10. Parsons, "DeWitt County Feud," 41; McNelly to Steele, August 31, 1874.

11. AG Steele to Gov. Coke, July 10, 1874, Capt. McNelly to AG Steele, August 8, 9, 31, September 30, October 18, December 10, 1874, Duall Beall to Maj. Jones, September 4, 1874, AGO, RG 401, Archives, TSL; *Galveston Daily News,* September 24, 1874; Webb, *Texas Rangers,* 236; and see Robert M. Utley, *Lone Star Justice: The First Century of the Texas Rangers* (New York: Oxford University Press, 2002).

12. Capt. McNelly to AG Steele, August 7, 31, 1874, AGO, RG 401, Archives, TSL; Parsons, "DeWitt County Feud," 41–42.

13. McNelly to Steele, August 31, October 18, December 10, 1874; Steel to Coke, July 10, 1874. For the reported fate of Abraham, see Day, *Sutton-Taylor,* 22.

14. Steele to Coke, August 31, 1874; Utley, *Lone Star Justice,* 149–50.

15. See, for example, John Wesley Hardin, indictment for assault, battery, and attempted murder, Grand Jury, Trinity County, August 28, 1874, and J. T. Evans to A. W. Deberry, August 28, 1874, copies in Crouch Collection, Regional History Center, VC/UHV; Maj. Jones to headquarters, September 13, 1874, General Order No. 3, September 13, 1874, AGO, RG 401, Archives, TSL.

16. John Wesley Hardin, indictment for murder, September 1874, District Court, Gonzales County Courthouse, copy in Crouch Collection, Regional History Center, VC/UHV; Utley, *Lone Star Justice,* 172–73; Godbold, "Comanche and the Hardin Gang," Pt. 2: 259.

17. Hardin, *Life,* 104–10.

18. Ibid.; Utley, *Lone Star Justice,* 172–73.

19. Parsons, "DeWitt County Feud," 43.

20. Steele to Coke, August 31, 1874; Fourteenth Texas Legislature, 2d sess., "General Laws," Joint Resolution No. 1 (Houston: A. C. Gray, 1875), 189.

21. William M. York to Gov. Coke, February 6, 1875, Coke, GP, RG 301, Archives, TSL.

22. B. J. Pridgen to U.S. Attorney General George Williams, February 5, 1875, Department of Justice, Box 674, NA.

23. Pridgen to Williams, February 5, 1875; Bruce H. Ramsay, "Blacks, Whites, and Justice in the Eastern District of Texas, 1871–1883," 11–12, copies in Crouch Collection, Regional History Center, VC/UHV.

24. Deputy Frederick M. Reinhardt to Marshal L. D. Evans, February 8, 1875, copy in Crouch Collection, Regional History Center, VC/UHV.

25. W. R. French to Gov. Coke, March 23, 1875, Secretary of State Papers, RG 307, Archives, TSL.

26. A. C. Hill to President U. S. Grant, April 6, 1875, U. S. Grant Papers, Manuscript Division, Library of Congress.

27. Ibid.

28. Pridgen to Williams, April 26, 1875, Department of Justice, Box 674, NA.

29. Ramsay, "Blacks, Whites, and Justice," 12–14; Parsons, "DeWitt County Feud," 43.

30. Delony, "40 Years a Peace Officer," 75.

31. Ibid.

32. Ibid.

33. Day, *Sutton-Taylor,* 32; Delony, "40 Years a Peace Officer," 75.

34. Parsons, "DeWitt County Feud," 43–44; Parsons, "Bill Sutton Avenged," in Hyatt, *The Feud,* 105; Day, *Sutton-Taylor,* 31–32; Parsons, "Mason Arnold," *Quarterly of the National Association for Outlaw and Lawman History,* 34–35.

35. New York Times, November 19, 1875. Parsons, "DeWitt County Feud," 43–44; Parsons, "Bill Sutton Avenged," 105; Day, *Sutton-Taylor,* 31–32; Parsons, "Mason Arnold," *Quarterly of the National Association for Outlaw and Lawman History,* 34–35.

36. *Corpus Christi Daily Gazette,* January 6, 1876; *San Antonio Daily Express,* January 3, 1876; Delony, "40 Years a Peace Officer," 76; Sutton, *Sutton-Taylor Feud,* 66–67; Parsons, "DeWitt County Feud," 44; Parsons, "Bill Sutton Avenged," 103–4.

CHAPTER 11

1. *Corpus Christi Daily Gazette,* January 6, 1876; *San Antonio Daily Express,* January 3, 1876; Sutton, R. *Sutton-Taylor Feud.* 66–67; Parsons, "DeWitt County Feud," 44;

Weisiger, "Sutton-Taylor Feud," 12–13; Parsons, "Bill Sutton Avenged," 103–4; Delony, "40 Years a Peace Officer," 76. Delony gives the wrong dates for the convening of court, but his other details are accurate.

2. *Corpus Christi Daily Gazette,* January 6, 1876; *San Antonio Daily Express,* January 3, 1876; R. Sutton, *Sutton-Taylor Feud,* 66–67; Parsons, "DeWitt County Feud," 44; Parsons, "Bill Sutton Avenged," 103–4; Delony, "40 Years a Peace Officer," 76.

3. *Corpus Christi Daily Gazette,* January 6, 1876; *San Antonio Daily Express,* January 3, 1876; Delony, "40 Years a Peace Officer," 76; Parsons, "DeWitt County Feud," 44; Parsons, "Bill Sutton Avenged," 44.

4. *Corpus Christi Daily Gazette,* January 6, 1876; *San Antonio Daily Express,* January 3, 1876; Parsons, "DeWitt County Feud," 44; Parsons, "Bill Sutton Avenged," 104; Delony, "40 Years a Peace Officer," 76; Parsons, "Mason Arnold," 35–36.

5. *Corpus Christi Daily Gazette,* January 6, 1876; Parsons, "DeWitt County Feud," 44; Parsons, "Bill Sutton Avenged," 104; Delony, "40 Years a Peace Officer," 76.

6. *Corpus Christi Daily Gazette,* January 6, 1876; *San Antonio Daily Express,* January 3, 1876; Parsons, "DeWitt County Feud," 44; Weisiger, "Sutton-Taylor Feud," notes, 11–13; Parsons, "Bill Sutton Avenged," 106; Delony, "40 Years a Peace Officer," 76.

7. *Corpus Christi Daily Gazette,* January 6, 1876; *San Antonio Daily Express,* January 3, 1876; Parsons, "DeWitt County Feud," 44; Weisiger, "Sutton-Taylor Feud," notes, 11–13; Parsons, "Bill Sutton Avenged," 106; Delony, "40 Years a Peace Officer," 76.

8. *Corpus Christi Daily Gazette,* January 6, 1876; Parsons, "DeWitt County Feud," 44; Parsons, "Bill Sutton Avenged," 106; *Austin Daily Democratic Statesman,* January 6, 1876; Weisiger, "Sutton-Taylor Feud," notes, 13–14.

9. *Corpus Christi Daily Gazette,* January 6, 1876; Parsons, "DeWitt County Feud," 44; Parsons, "Bill Sutton Avenged," 106; *Austin Daily Democratic Statesman,* January 6, 1876; Weisiger, "Sutton-Taylor Feud," notes, 13–14.

10. Capt. McNelly to AG Steele, March 8, 1876, AGO, RG 401, Archives, TSL; Webb, *Texas Rangers,* 283.

11. Delony, "40 Years a Peace Officer," 79; L. B. Wright to AG Steele, October 18, 1876, AGO, RG 401, Archives, TSL; *Corpus Christi Daily Gazette,* January 6, 1876; *Galveston Daily News,* January 6, 1876; Parsons, "DeWitt County Feud," 44.

12. Delony, "40 Years a Peace Officer," 79; Wright to AG Steele, October 6, 1876, AGO, RG 401, Archives, TSL; *Corpus Christi Daily Gazette,* January 6, 1876; *Galveston Daily News,* January 6, 1876; Parsons, "DeWitt County Feud," 44.

13. Delony, "40 Years a Peace Officer," 79; Wright to Steele, October 6, 1876; *Corpus Christi Daily Gazette,* January 6, 1876; *Galveston Daily News,* January 6, 1876; Parsons, "DeWitt County Feud," 44.

14. Delony, "40 Years a Peace Officer," 79; Wright to Steele, October 6, 1876; *Corpus Christi Daily Gazette,* January 6, 1876; *Galveston Daily News,* January 6, 1876; Parsons, "DeWitt County Feud," 44.

15. Wright to Steele, October 6, 1876, Capt. Lee Hall to AG Steele, December 10, 16, 1876, January 4, 1877, AGO, RG 401, Archives, TSL; *Corpus Christi Daily Gazette,* January 6, 1876; *Galveston Daily News,* January 6, 1876; Parsons, "DeWitt County Feud," 44; Delony, "40 Years a Peace Officer," 77–79; Webb, *The Texas Rangers,* 290; R. Sutton, *Sutton-Taylor Feud,* 71–79; Dora Neill Raymond, *Captain Lee Hall of Texas* (Norman: University of Texas Press, 1940), 57, 63; George Durham, *Taming the Nueces Strip* (Austin: University of Texas Press, 1962), 165–68.

16. Capt. McNelly to AG Steele, March 8, 19, 1876, AGO, RG 401, Archives, TSL.

17. Lt. Hall to AG Steele, October 4, 1876, AGO, RG 401, Archives, TSL; Raymond, *Lee Hall,* 51–56.

18. Delony, "40 Years a Peace Officer," 78; Weisiger, "Sutton-Taylor Feud," notes, 6, 11; Day, *Sutton-Taylor,* 34–35; although most of Day's account of the killing of the two Brassells is myth, he does divulge one of the reasons for the hard feelings between Augustine and Doctor Brassell.

19. Delony, "40 Years a Peace Officer," 78.

20. Delony, "40 Years a Peace Officer," 78; and see Mary Ainsworth, "Reflections of Mary Ainsworth," ms, in Wolff, "Taylor-Sutton Feud," VF, copy in possession of Wolff, copy in possession of the author.

21. Delony, "40 Years a Peace Officer," 78; and see Ainsworth, "Reflections of Mary Ainsworth." Although Ainsworth repeated myths about the fight, she established that there was a major battle with at least one hundred rounds fired, a fact proving that the Brassells were not murdered as Taylor partisans claimed, for the witness would have heard only a few shots, just enough to execute them. Instead, the many shots verified that, indeed, a battle took place.

22. Delony, "40 Years a Peace Officer," 78; Weisiger, "Sutton-Taylor Feud," notes, 6, 11.

23. Posse member, quoted in R. Sutton, *Sutton-Taylor Feud,* 73.

24. Delony, "40 Years a Peace Officer," 78

25. For an example of the myths about the killing of the Brassells, see Day, *Sutton-Taylor,* 34–36; Lt. Hall to AG Steele, December 10, 1876, AGO, RG 401, Archives, TSL; Delony, "40 Years a Peace Officer," 78.

26. Delony, "40 Years a Peace Officer," 78; Lt. Hall to Capt. McNelly, December 22, 1876, AGO, RG 401, Archives, TSL; R. Sutton, *Sutton-Taylor Feud,* 71–79; Raymond, *Lee Hall,* 57, 63; Day, *Sutton-Taylor,* 39; Webb, *The Texas Rangers,* 290; Utley, *Lone Star Justice,* 171.

27. Delony, "40 Years a Peace Officer," 78; Lt. Hall to AG Steele, December 10, 16, 1876, January 4, 1877, Lt. Hall to Capt. McNelly, December 22, 1876, AGO, RG 401, Archives, TSL; R. Sutton, *Sutton-Taylor Feud,* 71–79; *Galveston Daily News,* January 6, 1877; Durham, *Taming the Nueces Strip,* 165–68; Day, *Sutton-Taylor,* 39.

28. Delony, "40 Years a Peace Officer," 78; Hall to Steele, December 10, 16, 1876, January 4, 1877; Hall to McNelly, December 22, 1876, AGO, RG 401, Archives, TSL; R. Sutton, *Sutton-Taylor Feud,* 71–79; Utley, *Lone Star Justice,* 171; Webb, *The Texas Rangers,* 290; Raymond, *Lee Hall,* 57, 63; *Galveston Daily News,* January 6, 1877; Durham, *Taming the Nueces Strip,* 165–68; Day, *Sutton-Taylor,* 39.

29. *Victoria Advocate,* April 28, 1877, June 9, 1878; Vol. C, minutes, District Court Jackson County, Texas, copy in Crouch Collections, Regional History Center, VC/UHV; R. Sutton, *Sutton-Taylor Feud,* 70; Parsons, "DeWitt County Feud," 44–45; Grimes, *300 Years in Victoria County,* 346–47.

30. *Victoria Advocate,* April 28, 1877, June 9, 1878; Vol. C, minutes, District Court Jackson County, Texas, copy in Crouch Collection, Regional History Center, VC/UHV; Sutton; *Sutton-Taylor Feud,* 70; Parsons, "DeWitt County Feud," 44–45; Grimes, *300 Years in Victoria County,* 346–47; Henry Wolff to James Smallwood, e-mail, July 12, 2004, copy in possession of the author.

31. *Victoria Advocate,* April 28, 1877, January 17, 1880; Vol. C, minutes, District

Court, Jackson County; R. Sutton, *Sutton-Taylor Feud,* 70; Parsons, "DeWitt County Feud," 44–45; Grimes, *300 Years in Victoria County,* 347; Wolff to Smallwood, e-mail, July 12, 2004.

32. Wiltsey, "40 Times a Killer!" 68; Metz, *Dark Angel,* 158–59.

33. Wiltsey, "40 Times a Killer!" 68; Metz, *Dark Angel,* 160–62.

34. Metz, *Dark Angel,* 162–64.

35. Wiltsey, "40 Times a Killer!" 69; Metz, *Dark Angel,* 165–66; Utley, *Lone Star Justice,* 173.

36. Metz, *Dark Angel,* 167–69; Parsons, "John Wesley Hardin and the Texas Rangers," *Newsletter of the National Association and Center for Outlaw and Lawman History* 2 (Spring 1976): 9–11; Utley, *Lone Star Justice,* 173–74.

37. For Hardin's trial, his appeal, and a bit of spurious testimony, see Metz, *Dark Angel,* 178–84, 192–93; Utley, *Lone Star Justice,* 174.

38. *San Antonio Daily Express,* January 30, 1892, February 18, 1894; *Gonzales Inquirer,* February 11, 1892; Utley, *Lone Star Justice,* 174–75; Metz, *Dark Angel,* 207–208.

39. For Hardin's El Paso days, see Metz, *Dark Angel,* 209–77.

40. "Identification of John Wesley Hardin's Photograph Collection," copy in Crouch Collection, Regional History Center, VC/UHV; also see *El Paso Times,* March 2, 3, 1933; Utley, *Lone Star Justice,* 174–75.

41. Hall, "Creed Taylor," *NHT,* 6: 215–216; Roell, "B. J. Pridgen," *NHT,* 5: 337.

Afterword

1. Edgar P. Sneed, "A Historiography of Reconstruction in Texas: Some Myths and Problems," *SWHQ* 72 (April 1969): 436–37.

2. Barry A. Crouch, "Unmanacling Texas Reconstruction: A Twenty-Year Perspective," *SWHQ* 93 (January 1990): 302.

Appendix

1. The sources for the names of members of the Taylor ring and the counties where they operated include the Freedmen's Bureau records (RG 105) and the Fifth Military records (RG 393) in the National Archives; the author also drew upon secondary sources, the most valuable being the short book by Robert Sutton Jr. and lengthy articles by Chuck Parsons. All the information is cited in "Note on Sources."

NOTE ON SOURCES

The most valuable sources used in this study include three major record groups in the National Archives in Washington, D.C. Most important are the Records of the United States Army Continental Commands, 1821–1900, and the Army Post Records in RG 393. They are most voluminous, and not all have been microfilmed. Having made many trips to the National Archives, I have used the original documents whenever possible. Also most important are the Records of the Bureau of Refugees, Freedmen, and Abandoned Lands, commonly called the Freedmen's Bureau (RG 105). The Bureau papers have much information that is not available in any other depository. Also worthwhile are the files of the Adjutant General's Office (RG 94).

Some material in the Manuscript Division of the Library of Congress proved important for this study, including the papers of Philip Sheridan, Zachariah Chandler, U. S. Grant, and Salmon Chase.

A number of printed government documents, generated either by Congress or by the Texas Legislature, informed this study. The records of the Congressional Committee of Fifteen that investigated white Southern abuses in the early phase of Reconstruction were among the most important.

Other indispensable sources are found in the Texas State Library in Austin. The Governors' Papers (RG 301) of Hamilton, Throckmorton, Pease, Davis, and Coke contain valuable material, as does the Adjutant General's Office (RG 401). The latter collection is perhaps most valuable because Adjutant Generals Davidson, Britton, Steele, and their staffs kept copious records on criminal activity in Texas.

Various period newspapers are good sources of information if one is aware of the Confederate bias of some of them. The pro-Democrat papers were much less valuable because, basically, the editors often made up their own news. For example, some of the pro-Confederate papers repeatedly denied that terrorist Klan-like groups existed in Texas, whereas, in fact, such groups flourished in at least seventy-seven Texas counties. As well, they claimed that little violence occurred, whereas the records of the Adjutant General's Office proves otherwise. Typically, Unionist newspapers were more reliable and a bit more objective. Two that were most valuable were the *San Antonio Express* and the *Austin Daily State Journal.*

Any serious researcher of the Taylor ring must consult several sources at the Regional History Center at VC/UHV. Sidney Weisiger, a descendant of William Weisiger who had a crucial role in destroying the Taylor ring, left William's papers to the Regional History Center. They are most informative. As well, the new Barry A. Crouch Collection at the center is extremely useful for the collection contains photocopies of (or Crouch's notes on) copious reports made by the local agents of the Freedmen's Bureau and reports made by local military commanders. The Crouch Papers cannot cancel a researcher's need to go to the National Archives, but Crouch's material is a good place to start. In addition, the Regional History Center at VC/UHV is home to many article-length secondary works on the Taylor ring that are difficult to find in other libraries.

Of individual efforts to sort out the facts of what previously has been called the "Sutton-Taylor Feud," the works of Lewis Delony, Chuck Parsons, and Robert Sutton Jr. must be consulted. A lawman for forty years, Delony was a contemporary of the "feud" although he seldom used that word to refer to the Taylor problem. He was sometimes an eyewitness and at other times, a participant. Parsons has been a toiler in the Texas history vineyards for at least forty years. He has penned numerous articles on the Taylor problem wherein he used the "feud" conceptual framework. All of Parsons's work proved informative and objective. Robert Sutton, descendent of William "Bill" Sutton, produced a short book on the "feud." Although one might expect bias from Sutton, who wrote about an ancestor, such is not the case. He, too, used the "feud" paradigm, but his work is balanced. He considers his ancestor's point of view but adds that of the Taylors. Delony, Parsons, and Sutton all focused on DeWitt County as the epicenter of the feud and seldom looked at the havoc the Taylor ring caused in other places. In other words, they missed much of the action. As well, they did not consult the records found in the National Archives and the Manuscript Division of Library of Congress. Such records paint a much different picture of the so-called feud than is found in the secondary literature. However, the contributions of Delony, Parsons, and Sutton were valuable, and the reader can scan the endnotes to gauge the huge debt I owe to their works.

A number of other secondary works on the "feud" are problematical. For example, Jack Hays Day contributed a short book that is almost wholly unreliable because he explodes in vitriolic rage page after page, the rage aimed at anyone who opposed the Taylor clan. A descendent of several of the "feudists," Day became the principal propagandist for his ancestors and simply made up much of what is in his work, twisting the facts to such a degree that they cease to be facts. He created and wrote about a reality that never was while substituting mythical folk tales that favored the Taylor ring.

A number of others penned articles that have appeared in such magazines as *Frontier Times.* Lay historians for the most part, these authors committed all kinds of shenanigans. They made up dialog that sounded good to them but failed to attribute any sources for the dialog and/or their other direct quotes; they apparently believed that facts should not be allowed to interfere with a good story. Such articles had only limited value in informing my work. One can consult my endnotes to see how I used these sources.

A number of unpublished manuscripts, book-length and article-length, were useful. For example, the late Barry A. Crouch and Donaly Brice have almost completed their study of the Texas State Police. They graciously allowed me to read the most recent draft of the manuscript. Additionally, a number of M.A. theses were valuable sources. As well, a number of individuals supplied material that was most valuable. The raconteur extraordinaire Henry Wolff Jr., long-time columnist for the *Victoria Advocate,* shared his files on the Taylor clan, as did his wife, Linda. Chuck and Pat Spurlin shared primary material they gleaned from the Center for American History at the University of Texas at Austin.

About my research in general: I tried when possible to use more than one source when presenting information. In other words, I tried to have different sources corroborate each other, especially on controversial points. For formal citations of all my sources, please see the endnotes.

INDEX